Löwendahl's
BOOK COLLECTION

羅氏藏書

吴建明　黄显功　王仁芳　主编

上海古籍出版社

本书系国家社科基金重大项目
"徐家汇藏书楼珍稀文献整理与研究"（18ZDA179）阶段性成果之一

上海文化发展基金会图书出版专项基金资助项目

黄显功

　　在中西文化交流史上，西学的传入以明末清初的传教士来华为标志，其中图书是主要的文化交流载体之一。从利玛窦跨洋万里来到中国开始，天主教传教士们随身携带的"方物"中，图书是不可或缺的必需品。他们历经艰难，绵延不断地向中国输入了相当数量的西文图书。这些以宗教、自然科学、哲学为主要内容的早期西学文献，是传教的重要工具，既是教堂或个人的藏书，也是传教士与中国官员、知识界人士交往的礼物，同时，这些西文图书也成为汉语西学文献翻译的基础。到 18 世纪 20-30 年代因"礼仪之争"传教被禁之前，规模最大的一次西文图书入华是金尼阁受龙华民之命，返回欧洲为中国募集西方文献"七千部"，此举成为中西图书交流史上的重要标志，深受中国学术界的关注与高度评价。之后来华的新教传教士们，不仅携带图书，还引进了印刷技术与设备，发展了中国的出版事业，以图书、报刊的形式为载体传播西学，对中国文化的发展与知识的传播产生了重要的影响，有力地促进了中西文化的交流。中国历史上的西学文献主要有两个部分，一是从域外直接或间接传入中国，二是产生在中国的译作及中外人士的各种著述。其中来自域外的文献作为西学原始资料，具有重要的文献价值、艺术价值和文物价值，20 世纪前出版的入华西学文献，尤其受到学术界的重视，是研究明清时期中西文化接触、传播与影响的对象。所以，西学文献来华，从随行携带到赠送、交换、购买，不同的形式和途径，均蕴含了中外图书交流的特定背景与意义。在当代中西文化交流的图书引进史上，令人瞩目的重大事例并不多，而上海图书馆历时近十年的"罗氏藏书"的入藏，可谓是影响力与价值俱大的成功案例之一，具有独特的文献史研究意义。

　　"罗氏藏书"是指瑞典藏书家、汉学家兼书商罗闻达先生（1941-2013）所藏的汉学文献，共有 1551 种，其中手稿 4 种，另有舆图、版画、徽章等 8 种，是罗闻达先生积二十余年之功，在世界各地广泛收集的 1477 年至 1877 年间出版的有关中国的西文印本。这批图书涉及文字有拉丁文、法文、英文、德文、西班牙文、葡萄牙文、意大利文、瑞典文、俄文等十多个语种，内容包括中国的历史、宗教、风俗、地理、经济、教育、科学技术、语言文字、服饰、工艺等多个方面，著作形式有游记、日记、书信、专著、官书、译作等。这些图书除欧洲出版物外，也包括一些在美国出版的著作，以及 18 世纪末、19 世纪初在印度、东南亚及澳门、香港、上海等中国沿海城市出版的西文印刷品，可以说是当代世界上数量最多的一批西方早期汉学文献的个人专藏。罗闻达先生作为一名汉学家，这批藏书因他编辑出版了《从西文印本书籍（1477—1877）看中西关系、中国观、文化影响和汉学发展》而备受瞩目；罗闻达先生作为一名书商，这批图书的跨国转让也成为他一生中成功的贸易成果，同样深受社会关注。"罗氏藏书"是上海图书馆在引进本批图书后确定的文献专藏名称，还包括后续的罗闻达先生遗赠图书。

上海图书馆自 2008 年起，对于"罗氏藏书"的采购，积极争取，多方联络，在上海市委宣传部的支持下，历经曲折，于 2010 年 11 月成功引进了首批"罗氏藏书"，成为中国图书馆界令人瞩目的文献资源建设的盛事，彰显了作为国际大都市上海的文化软实力和上海开放、包容、创新的城市品格，进一步丰富了上海图书馆中西文化交流研究资料的收藏。罗闻达先生在《从西文印本书籍（1477—1877）看中西关系、中国观、文化影响和汉学发展》书目的基础上，编撰了续编，并承诺将存于泰国住所的四千余种西方书目、书史等方面的参考书与工具书赠送上海图书馆。2013 年，罗闻达先生去世后，其家人遵照遗嘱，确认了图书捐赠事宜，在泰国的藏书于 2016、2017 年分批运抵上海。至 2017 年初，历时近十年，"罗氏藏书"共分三批入藏上海图书馆徐家汇藏书楼。从 2018 年起，"罗氏藏书"成为国家社科基金重大课题《上海图书馆徐家汇藏书楼珍稀文献整理与研究》的主要研究对象。

当首批"罗氏藏书"到馆后，我们在上海图书馆目录大厅举行了一个展览，当时业务处吴建明处长建议出版一本专题图录，以作图书馆藏书史的重要纪念。于是，我组织徐家汇藏书楼的同事，在 2011 年开始了本图录的选编，前期工作由王仁芳负责落实。因拟购的《从西文印本书籍（1477—1877）看中西关系、中国观、文化影响和汉学发展》续编图书正在洽商之中，原计划成功之后，再增补相关文献充实图录，所以，书稿在出版社存放多年而未付梓。当书目续编的图书未能如愿引进后，我们对罗闻达先生的捐赠图书进行了整理，在筹备 2020 年上海图书馆年度精品文献展时，对 10 年前的图录初稿略作调整，由徐锦华等人补充了十种捐赠图书，藉此可管中窥豹，了解"罗氏藏书"的概貌。需要说明的是，其中部分藏书在《文明互鉴：上海图书馆徐家汇藏书楼藏珍稀文献图录》中亦有收录，但本书对"罗氏藏书"的版本及内容介绍更为详细。

在"罗氏藏书"的引进过程中，北京中国科学院韩琦研究员自始至终给予我们很大帮助，上海学术界的熊月之、周振鹤、李天纲、徐文堪、陈克艰诸位学者，以及中国图书进出口上海公司的许建刚、刘志华、陈峰、刘怡茜、吴轶男等均以各种形式为引进"罗氏藏书"给予了推荐、论证、沟通、谈判、进口等工作，对于他们的关怀与贡献，我们深表感谢。

在此，谨以本书向罗闻达先生致敬，表达上海图书馆同仁的深切缅怀，并纪念"罗氏藏书"入藏十周年。

2020 年 12 月

一、本图录从馆藏罗氏藏书中精选其中最为珍贵的手稿 1 种、印本 60 种，以及罗闻达先生遗赠本馆的 5 000 多册图书中选择显示罗闻达先生读书、藏书趣味的图书 10 种，供读者鉴赏和参考。

二、本图录主要根据中国图书馆学会 2003 年修订的《西文文献著录条例》要求著录，以期反映文献内容和形式特征。

三、本图录条目按文献类型和问世年代排序。条目下的著录项目，按照中国读者的阅读习惯，依次为馆藏罗氏藏书编号，中译题名加原文题名，编、译、著等责任说明、出版发行、载体形态、装订形式、文献来源、版本沿革、内容提要等。编著者生卒年及出版时间有存疑者，则以［］标示。

四、本图录条目提供的中译题名仅供参考。本目录款目内容提要阐述的观点和使用的史实以及引文部分借鉴了瑞典藏书家罗闻达的研究成果。如有不当之处，敬请指正。

五、本图录因篇幅有限，仅为每种文献配置了书影等图片若干张，以期读者加深对鉴赏文献的直观印象。

六、本图录因涉及文种众多、编制时间和编者能力所限，不免存在未能及时改正的错误，敬请指正和谅解。

目录

前言 ·· 黄显功　001

编纂说明 ··· 004

傅圣泽神父乘"孔蒂王子"号船携回之中文书籍目录 ················ 001

世界论 ·· 004

曼德维尔游记 ·· 007

马可·波罗游记 ·· 010

亚洲地理及蒙古可汗史 ·· 013

中华大帝国史 ·· 016

1582-1584 年耶稣会士在日本和中国传教信札 ························ 018

关于中国基督教之意见书 ·· 021

中国传教报告书 ·· 023

利玛窦中国札记 ·· 025

东方史 ·· 028

大中国志 ·· 031

鞑靼战纪 ·· 033

中国植物志 ·· 036

荷兰东印度公司使团初访中国记 ·· 038

耶稣会中国传教史 ·· 041

中国图说 ·· 043

中国脉理医论 ·· 046

1581-1669 年间在华活动概述 ·· 049

1659 年至 1666 年中华帝国政治及传教状况记 ·················· 051

中国贤哲孔子 …………………………………… 053

欧洲天文学 ……………………………………… 056

中国新史 ………………………………………… 059

中国近事报道 …………………………………… 063

东方游记合集 …………………………………… 066

中国近事 ………………………………………… 070

数学概要 ………………………………………… 072

数学研究 ………………………………………… 075

中华帝国全志 …………………………………… 078

北狄通史 ………………………………………… 084

中国民用及装饰建筑、中国建筑 ……………… 087

好逑传 …………………………………………… 090

乾隆御制盛京赋 ………………………………… 094

北京来信 ………………………………………… 097

中国通史 ………………………………………… 100

中国概述、中国坤舆总图 ……………………… 103

孔子生平事迹简介 ……………………………… 107

英使谒见乾隆纪实 ……………………………… 110

中国服饰 ………………………………………… 115

中国酷刑 ………………………………………… 119

论语 ……………………………………………… 122

汉法拉字典 ……………………………………… 126

华英字典 ………………………………………… 129

玉娇梨 …………………………………………… 133

诗经 ……………………………………………… 137

汉语札记 ………………………………………… 140

易经 ……………………………………………… 143

中国人：中华帝国及其居民概述 ……………… 147

中国帆船"耆英"号大观 ……………………………… 152

中国人及其革命 …………………………………………… 155

额尔金出使中国日本记 …………………………………… 158

旅华十二年 …………………………………………………… 163

中国经典卷二：孟子 ……………………………………… 166

认字新法　常字双千 ……………………………………… 170

太平天国亲历记 …………………………………………… 173

中国文献纪略 ……………………………………………… 176

最古老与最新奇的帝国：中国和美国 ………………… 179

中药的贡献与中国自然史 ………………………………… 183

英华萃林韵府 ……………………………………………… 186

香港殖民地法令集 ………………………………………… 189

清代图书馆发展史 ………………………………………… 192

国际象棋习题的乐趣 ……………………………………… 195

十八世纪印本书籍爱好者指南 ………………………… 197

羽管键琴与击弦古钢琴 …………………………………… 200

佛国记 ……………………………………………………… 202

普朗克、爱因斯坦、玻尔和索末菲的量子理论 ……… 204

奥洛夫·鲁德贝克《鸟书》 ……………………………… 206

古琴 ………………………………………………………… 208

多国家与文化书籍选目 …………………………………… 210

中国历史新手册 …………………………………………… 212

附录

书香犹在忆故人——与瑞典著名藏书家罗闻达先生交往的点滴回忆

………………………………………………………… 韩　琦 215

"罗氏藏书"入藏记 …………………………………… 黄显功 221

罗氏编号手稿 2

《傅圣泽神父乘"孔蒂王子"号船携回之中文书籍目录》

（*Liste des livres chinois apportés sur le vaisseau nommé Le Prince de Conty par le P. Fouquet*）

编　　者：［法］傅圣泽（Jean-Francois Foucquet，字方济，1663–1740）
编　　写：广州或澳门，［1721］年
载体形态：手稿 8 叶 15 页（欧纸）＋ 20 折叶（汉纸），末叶空白，24.5×14 厘米

内　　容：

　　傅圣泽系法国耶稣会士，在中国 22 年（1699–1721），可谓博览群籍，儒、道、诸子、古代经典、近人注疏，都有涉猎。"傅圣泽西还时携有书籍，选择之善，卷帙之多，前此西士无能及之者。"

　　本目录收录条目涉及傅圣泽乘"孔蒂王子"号自中国携带回欧洲的 340 种近 4 000 册图书，由傅圣泽用法文亲笔书写，并插入中文书目 15 页，每页地脚有注释（可能由傅圣泽的文书助手广州教民胡若翰誊写），每个条目前有傅圣泽手书的序号。首页上题有"傅圣泽神父乘'孔蒂王子'号船携回之中文书籍目录（Liste des livres chinois apportés sur le vaisseau nommé Le Prince de Conty par le P. Fouquet）"。

　　本目录条目排列无特殊次序，所列书籍涉及五经、四书、史书、老子、音韵字书、经书注疏、吏治、科学、教育、礼仪、佛教及传教士中文著述等。后人高度评价这批藏品的价值，费赖之（Louis Pfister，字福民，1833–1891）称："观此中国书籍之目录，尤足证明搜集此种书籍者之学识与鉴赏。"雷慕沙（Jean-Pierre Abel Rémusat, 1788–1832）则称赞傅圣泽的收藏是那个时代"一个欧洲人完成的最大宗、最上乘的收藏"。

　　1720 年 10 月 28 日，傅圣泽收到罗马耶稣会总会长坦布里尼（Tamburini）要求他尽快返回的决定书。11 月 5 日，傅圣泽携带 16 头骡子的骡队离开北京前往广州，打算由广州乘船去法国。他的骡队行囊只能携带部分书籍，另有 1 200 多册书籍只能滞后。傅圣泽于次年 2 月 20 日抵达广州，但是并没有见到预期的法国东印度公司的船只，他等了几乎一年，才于 1722 年 1 月 5 日乘上"孔蒂王子"号商船驶离广州。他收藏的图书（包括他从欧洲邮购的一些书籍）显然收录在本目录中。另有购自南京书肆专为巴黎王家图书馆搜集的 7 箱 1 764 册书籍，比"孔蒂王子"号早两个月先期抵达法国路易港。傅圣泽聘广州教民胡若翰为誊写助手，目录的中文部分很有可能在傅圣泽离开广州前就已由胡若翰誊写完毕。

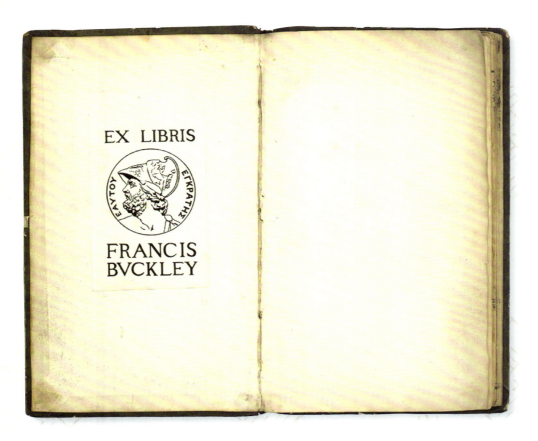

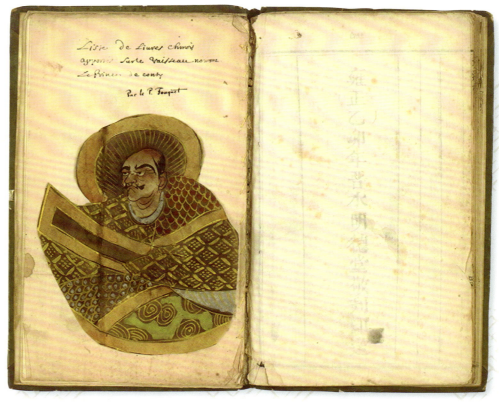

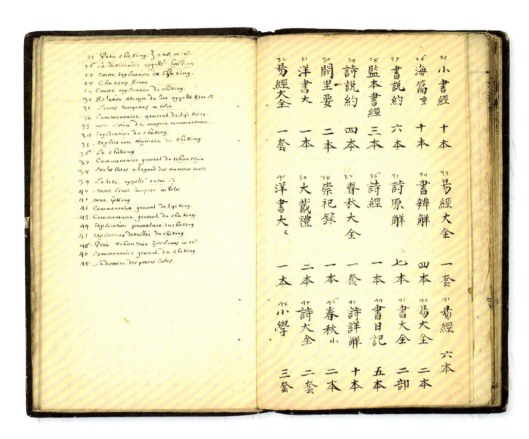

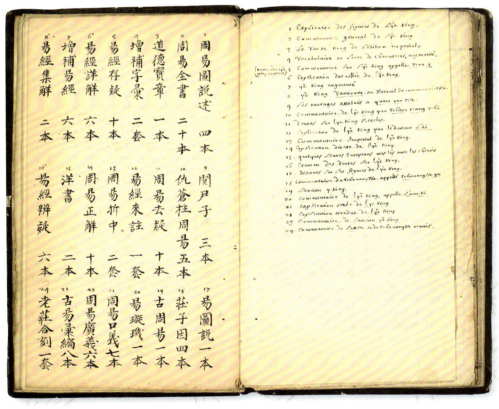

罗氏编号 1

《世界论》
（**De situ orbis**）

作　　者：［希］狄奥尼修斯（Dionysius Periegetes）

出　　版：威尼斯，拉特多尔特（Erhard Ratdolt）、马莱尔（Bernhard Maler）和洛斯莱茵（Peter Loeslein），
1477 年

载体形态：4 开，42 叶，24 行，罗马字体，黑白木刻首字母，a1 叶正面印有黑色木刻边框，页边印有注释

装　　订：18 世纪英国产红色摩洛哥山羊皮面烫金，书脊肋线烫金，书皮边框烫金

来　　源：德文郡（Devonshire）公爵查茨沃斯（Chatsworth）藏书票；沃丁顿（Wardington）勋爵

版　　本：拉丁文初版。

内　　容：

本书首次引用了意大利威尼斯商人和探险家孔蒂（Nicolò de' Conti, 1385–1469 年）关于印度和契丹（中国）描述的段落。该拉丁文版印刷过数次，由希腊文转译而来。其译者维罗纳的安东尼奥·达·贝卡里亚（Antonio Beccaria of Verona）一度是英国人文作家的资助人汉弗莱公爵（Duke Humphrey of Gloucester）的秘书。本书表述了主要是希腊科学作家、天文学家、诗人、已知测量过地球周长的第一人、亚历山大图书馆馆长厄拉多塞（Eratosthenes，约公元前 275–前 194 年）之后的已知世界。

该书的最后两叶罗列了欧洲、非洲和亚洲的国家和岛屿。其亚洲部分涉及了"卡尔曼尼亚沙漠、阿拉伯半岛……印度、中国（Sine）和锡兰"。

直到 13 世纪，印度之外的亚洲对欧洲而言实际还是个未知世界；仅有古希腊和古罗马文献中模糊涉及的"Serica"或"Sinica"才使得有关中国存在的粗浅知识得以鲜活起来。公元 1 世纪罗马无名氏作家笔下的"秦国"（Thin 时而写作 This），以及"中国"（Sin、Chin 或者 China）出现在约公元 50 年的"印度洋航线"（The Periplus of the Erythrean Sea）一文中。这段文字是现存欧洲文献中有关中国的最早记叙。作者在文中写道："过了克利斯（Chryse，今缅甸和马来西亚）之后，大海延伸的尽头止于秦国（Thin），在这个国家的腹地有座大城名称长安（Thinae）。该城出产生丝、丝线和丝织品，由陆路经大夏（Bactria）到巴利加萨（Barygaza），又可由水道取恒河至李密利斯（Limyrice）。然而要顺利抵达这秦国很是不易，所以鲜有人自秦国来。"

早期西方涉及中国的文献还有罗马老普林尼（Pliny the Elder）所著《自然史》、希腊斯特拉伯（Strabo）的《地理志》、罗马梅拉（Pomponius Mela）的《世界地图》和希腊托勒密（Ptolemy）的《世界地图》。

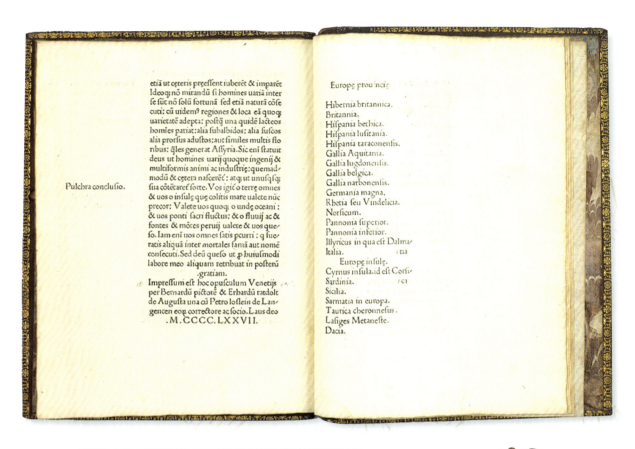

Pulchra conclusio.

etiã ut cęteris pręeſſent iuberēt & imparēt
Ideoq̃ nõ mirandũ ſi homines uariã inter
ſe ſũt nõ ſolũ fortunã ſed etiã naturã cõſe
cuti: cũ uidem⁹ regiones & loca eã quoq̃
uarietatē adepta: poſtq̃ una quidē lacteos
homies patiat: alia ſubalbidos: alia fuſcos
alia protſus aduſtos; aut ſimiles multis flo
ribus: q̃les generat Aſſyria. Sic eñi ſtatuit
deus ut homines uarij quoque ingenij &
multiformis animi ac induſtrię: quemad
modũ & cętera naſceret̃: atq̃ ut unuſq̃ſq̃
ſua cõtētaret ſorte. Vos igit̃ o terrę omnes
& uos o inſulę quę colitis mare ualete nũc
precor: Valete uos quoq̃ o undę oceani :
& uos ponti ſacri fluctus: & o fluuij ac &
fontes & mõtes peruij ualete & uos quę
ſo. Iam eñi uos omnes ſatis pcurri : q̃ fue
ratis aliquã inter mortales famã aut nomē
conſecuti. Sed deũ queſo ut p̃ huiuſmodi
labore meo aliquam retribuat in poſterũ
gratiam.
Impreſſum eſt hoc opuſculum Venetijs
per Bernardũ pictorē & Erhardũ ratdolt
de Auguſta una cũ Petro loſlein de Lan
gencen eoℜ correctore ac ſocio. Laus deo
.M. CCCC. LXXVII.

Europę prouĩcię

Hibernia britannica.
Britannia.
Hiſpania bethica.
Hiſpania luſitania.
Hiſpania taraconenſis.
Gallia Aquitania.
Gallia lugdonenſis.
Gallia belgica.
Gallia narbonenſis.
Germania magna.
Rhetia ſeu Vindelicia.
Norſicum.
Pannonia ſuperior.
Pannonia inferior.
Illyricus in qua eſt Dalma
Italia.   tia
Europę inſulę
Cyrnus inſula.id eſt Corſi
Sardinia.   ca
Sicilia.
Sarmatia in europa.
Taurica cheronneſus.
Laſiges Metaneſte.
Dacia.

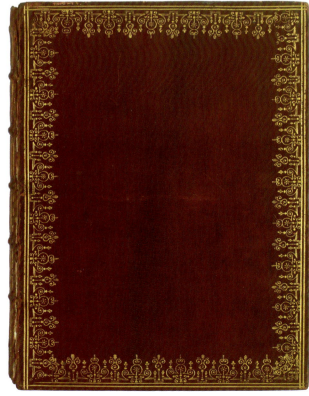

罗氏编号 2

《曼德维尔游记》
(Tractato de le piu maravegliose cosse)

作　　者：［英］曼德维尔（Sir John Mandeville）
出　　版：米兰，科尔内诺彼得鲁斯（Petrus de Corneno），1480 年 7 月 31 日
载体形态：4 开、II+114 叶
装　　订：绯红的摩洛哥山羊皮面烫金；首叶和末十叶为影印叶；原首叶显然是空白叶，缺失。经过清洗处理
版　　本：意大利文初版（已知该版发现的第 13 本）。

内　　容：

　　《曼德维尔游记》署名曼德维尔著，实由佚名作者用法文写作，作者可能是法国北部的圣本笃会修道士。该书最初为欧洲大陆本，存世手稿有 32 部，其中最早的是 1371 年。至晚在 1365 年，该书的一部手稿被带至英国，引发了抄书时尚，形成了英伦岛抄本，所用语言为英文和法文，据 Seymour 2002 年统计，存世抄本 33 部。还有一种欧洲大陆本的校订本即里昂本（时间是 1373 年），存世手稿 7 部。

　　直到 20 世纪末，《曼德维尔游记》已经被翻译成法语、英语、德语、荷兰语、丹麦语等各种欧洲语言，至今约有 300 部手稿存世，当然许多抄本已经遗失。从该书被译语文和存世手稿的数量审视，《曼德维尔游记》比《马可·波罗游记》流传更广，而且是 15 世纪和 16 世纪人们朝圣时必备指南。诸多印本（在摇篮本时期出过至少 35 版）说明了该游记的重要性和其时的商业需求。

　　《曼德维尔游记》声称完成于 1356 年，记述了作者 1322 年从英国出发，周游世界包括中国的见闻。一般认为该书中涉及的中国形象是根据作者所处时代近东和远东的半真实半虚幻的相关资料塑造的。

　　该书的第二部分声称描述了穿越土耳其、亚美尼亚，穿越鞑靼、波斯、叙利亚、阿拉伯半岛、埃及，穿越利比亚、迦勒底及埃塞俄比亚大部，穿越亚马逊、东印度群岛，穿越"蛮子"（中国南方）和契丹等地的旅途见闻。k3 叶之后的文字叙述了"蛮子"和契丹的知识。

　　今天我们所知道的事实是，该书作者本人并没有到过中国。《曼德维尔游记》所树立的半真实半想象的程式化中国形象，在文艺复兴时期的西欧广为流传。他的这一中国形象既是西方社会对中国总体想象的产物，也是作者个人根据书本阅读的体验而塑造的异域形象。这种中国形象受制于欧洲社会文化语境和读者期待视野，也显示了这一时期欧洲作家认为异域中国的现实优越于本土文化而对异域文化的狂热向往，从而呈现出乌托邦式的文化幻象。这一中国形象在中西交流史和世界文明史上具有重要的意义。

Tractato de le piu marauegliose cosse e piu notabile che se trouano in le parte del modo redute t collecte soto breuita in el presente copedio dal strenuissimo caualeri specodoro Jobanne de Mandauilla anglico nato ne la Cita de sancto albano el quale secodo dio prficialmente a uisitato quasi tute le parte habitabel de el modo cossi fidelmte a notato tute quelle piu degne cosse che la trouato e veduto in esse parte t chi bene discorre qsto libeo aueria p secta cognicione de tuti li reami prince natione e populi gente costumi leze bystorie t degne antiquitate co breuitade le quale pte da altri non sono tractate t parte piu cofusamete dalchui gran valente homini son state tocate t amagiore sede el sfato auctore in psona e stato nel 1322 in yerusalem In Asia menore chiamata Turchia i Armenia grande e in la picola. In Sythia zoe in Tartaria in persia In Syria o uero suria In Arabia in egipto alto t in lo inseriore in libia in la parte grande de ethiopia in Caldea in amazonia in india mazore in la meza t in la menore in diuise sette de latini greci iudei e barbari christiani t insideli t molte altre prouincie como appare nel tractato de sotto

QUACHO sia cossa cho la terra ultramaria zoe la terra santa de pmissoe fra tute le altre terre sia la piu excelete cha piu degna e bona sopra tute le altre terre, e sia benedeta e sactificata e psecrata del priososo corpo e sangue del nostro signore iesu xpo. Jui gli piaque obobriarse nella vergie matia e piliare caine humana e nutritura. Cla dita fra calcate e circodare con li soi benediti pedi. Jai volse fare molti miracoli predicare e signare la sede de la lege a nui cristiani como a soi sioli. El questa terra singularmete volse portare calesij destrazi e soffrire per nay molti ipropenij. Cl questa fra singularmente se uolse fare chiamare re del cielo cde la terra e de laire e de laqua e vnyisialmete de tute le cosse che si steneno i quelle e luy medesimo se chiamo re per specialitade di quella terra dicendo rex iadcorui per che questa terra era in qual tempo propria de iudei e questa terra santa e si alta fra tute le altre terre como la meguore cla piu virtuosa ela piu degna de questo mondo. Imperzo chi li sono sate queste cosse t in el mizo loco de tuta la terra del mondo si como dice el philosopho la uertade dele cosse sta nel mezo i quel la dignissima terra uolse el re celestiale usare la uita sua t essere deriso e uituperato da li crudeli iudei e uolse soffrire passione e morte per lo amor nostro e per rescoderne e liberarne dale pene de lo iserno e dela oribile e perpetua morte per lo peccato del nostro primo padre Adam et eua nostra madre. Pero che de uerso luy no baueua ponto meritate malle alchuno impero che lay maie non disse malle nel fece ne peso. Cl bene uolse el re de gloria in que lo locho piu che altroue sostenire passione e morte po chebi uole publicar alchua cossa accio che ciascaduno lo sa

罗氏编号 3

《马可·波罗游记》
（ De consuetudinibus et conditionibus orientalium regionum ）

作　　者：［意］马可·波罗（Marco Polo, 1254–1324）

出　　版：［豪达，莱韦（Gerard Leeu），1483 至 1484 年 6 月 11 日之前］；东京，国立国会图书馆，1949 年影印版；限量影印 800 本中的第 68 号

载体形态：4 开，74 叶

装　　订：板面

版　　本：马可·波罗的《世界见闻录》初现于 1477 年纽伦堡版德文印本中；1481 年奥古斯堡重印。拉丁文初版首现于 1483 至 1484 年 6 月 11 日之前。该拉丁文初版的蓝本是 1302 年和 1314 年间由多明我会的皮皮诺（Francesco Pipino）根据威尼斯文抄本翻译的。1496 年威尼斯意大利文初版问世；1502 年里斯本葡萄牙文版问世；1503 年塞维利亚西班牙文版问世，并于 1518 年和 1529 年重印；法文版于 1556 年现世。

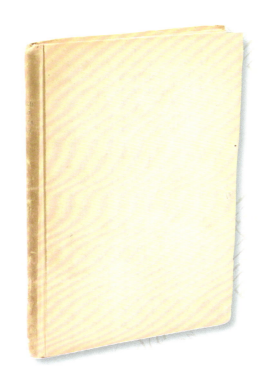

内　　容：

　　我们不知道马可·波罗口述付诸文字时使用了哪种文字，最有可能的是威尼斯或伦巴第方言，随后被翻译成其他意大利方言和拉丁语。

　　马可·波罗据说是在 1275 年到达中国的。他是否亲自来过中国受到了今人伍德（Frances Wood）和史景迁（Jonathan O. Spence）的质疑。他们找出了游记中的错误和省略的部分，辨别了马可·波罗可能用来口述的文献出处，认为马可·波罗笔下的中国影像与鄂多立克（Odoric of Pordenone）和曼德维尔（Mandeville）塑造的真实和想象参半的中国形象趋于一致，没有任何改变。直到 16 世纪初，西方航海旅行家们才得以再次来到中国，亲身体验和目睹中国。

Of the MARCO POLO
ITINERARIUM
Antverpiae, 1485.
Eight hundred copies only have been
reproduced in phototype from the original
edition in possession of THE TOYO BUNKO
(Oriental Library), by the National Diet
Library, Tokyo, Japan.
Collotype work by the Otsuka Kogeisha
Ltd., Tokyo. November, MCMXLIX.

№ 68

Shinobu Iwamura
Jinbunkagaku Kenkyusho
Kyoto University
Kyoto, Japan
Dec. 20, 1950

Dr. N. M. Penzer
18 Manor Court
Pinehurst
Cambridge, England.

Dear Sir,

I am in receipt of your letter of Dec. 5, 1950,
and sending you under a separate cover a copy of the reproduction of Pipino's edition of MARCO POLO. And I take
this opportunity of expressing my admiration for your excellent introduction to the reproduction of the Frampton
version.

The following may be of some interest for you.
A number of Japanese Buddhist priests visited China under
the Mongol domination. Some of them followed Marco Polo's
trails between Kinsay and Taidu, leaving detailed itineraries,
which are still preserved in some old temples in Kyoto.
They may throw a new light to the great traveller's itineraries
in the coastal region of China. I may add that such records
are not extant in China itself.

Would you be kind enough to let me know if there
has appeared any book of importance on MARCO POLO in Europe
since 1939? I am especially anxious to know if vols. iii
and iv of the Moule-Pelliot edition have been published.
If so, is it not possible to have a copy in exchange for
Japanese books?

I beg to remain,

Yours truly,

Shinobu Iwamura

罗氏编号 5

《亚洲地理及蒙古可汗史》
（ Les fleurs des hystoires de la terre d'Orient ［ ... ］divisées en V p［ ar ］ties ）

作　　者：［法］海顿（Prince Hayton，约 1235－1314）著

出　　版：巴黎，出版者不详，约 1520 年

载体形态：4 开，74 叶，题名红黑双色，装饰性木刻大首字，正文双栏编排，哥特体小字，附 13 幅木刻版画（2 幅全页版画）

装　　订：深褐色小牛皮面，装饰图案无色压印，皮覆软板，图案花边包括首字母 F，皮质系带（缺损），书脊首尾有精良修复，边缘处有刮痕，书角磨损，下衬页被切割并已简洁修复

版　　本：法文本。该书文字的形成是在 1307 年。随后 Faulcon 将该文字翻译成拉丁文献给克雷芒五世（1260－1314）教皇。最初的印本约在 1510 年问世，而拉丁文初版于 1529 年出版。法文原始手稿也于 1877 年由 Louis de Backer 影印出版。

内　　容：

　　本书为作者海顿有关西亚和中亚旅行的叙述，是最早和最全面描述蒙古地理与人种的资料，其中包括对于佛教教义、中国人的习俗以及戈壁滩的野蛮部落和野兽等的观察。

¶ Sésuyt la premiere partie qui parle des royaulmes Dasie.

¶ Le premier chapitre parle du royaulme de Cathay.

LE royaulme de Cathay est tenu pour le plus noble ꝗ le plus riche qui soit au monde et est sur le riuaige de la mer occeane. Il y a tant dystes de mer quon ne peut pas bien scauoir le nõbre. Les gẽs qui habitẽt audit royaulme sont appelles cathais et ya plusieurs beaulx hõmes ꝗ plusieurs belles fẽmes selon leur nation/ Mais ilz ont tous les yeulx moult petis/ et ont peu de barbe. Lesses gens ont lettres q̃ de beaulte ressemblent aux lettres satines/ et parlent vne langue ꝗ est moult diuerse des aul-tres langues du monde. La creãce dicelle gent est moult diuerse/ car aucune croyent au soleil/ les autres a la lune/ les autres aux estoilles/ les autres aux natures/ les autres au feu/ les aultres a leaue/ les autres aux arbres/ les autres aux beufz/ pour ce que lesditz beufz labourẽt la terre dont ilz viuent. Et aucũs deulx nont point de loy ne de creance/ mais viuent cõme bestes. Icelles gens qui tant sont sĩples en leur creance et aux choses spirituelles sont plus soubtilz que toutes autres gẽs aux oeu-ures corporelles/ et disent quilz sont ceulx qui voyent de deulx yeulx/ et les latins voyent dug

B j

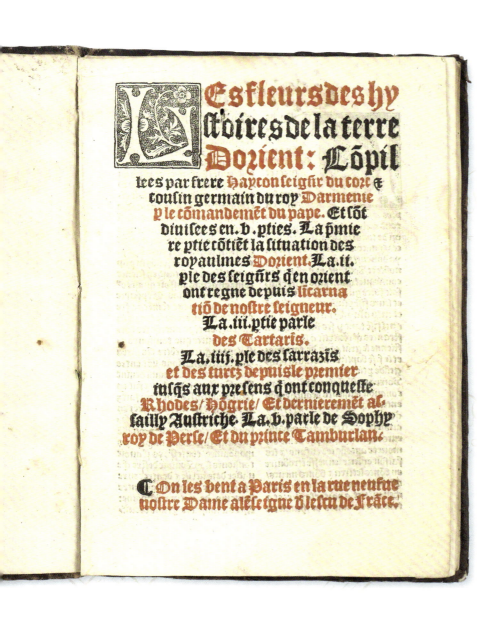

罗氏编号 **13**

《中华大帝国史》

（ Historia de las cosas mas notables, ritos y costumbres, del Gran Reyno dela China ［ ... ］.
Con un itinerario del Nuevo mundo ）

作　　者：［西］门多萨（Juan Gonzalez de Mendoza）著

出　　版：罗马，阿科尔蒂（Vincentio Accolti），1585 年

载体形态：8 开，XXXII 页（末叶空白）+ 440 页，题名上有木刻小纹章，104–105 页上有三个汉字

装　　订：犊皮软面，题名页有短撕口，若干书叶有轻微水渍，原书系带缺失

版　　本：西班牙文初版，16 世纪极其畅销。至 16 世纪末，已经出版了西、意、法、英、德、拉丁和荷兰文
等欧洲语言的版本。该书一直保持着欧洲有关中国论述的权威地位，直到 1615 年奥古斯堡版金尼阁
编《利玛窦中国札记》（罗氏编号 54）和 1654 年安特卫普版卫匡国著《鞑靼战记》（罗氏编号 107）
出版问世，该书的热度才有所下降。

内　　容：

　　也许可以毫不夸张地说，17 世纪初欧洲大多数有教养的人都看过门多萨的书。但门多萨本人从未到过中
国，其著作的价值在于使用了他人所亲眼目睹和亲身体验的参考资料，其中最为重要的是葡萄牙多明我会修
士克鲁兹（Gaspar da Cruz）的《中国纪事》（Tractado em que se contam
muito par estenso as causas da China）和奥古斯丁会修士拉达（Martin de
Rada）的《中国札记》（Ralacion de las cosas de China que propriamente
se llama Taybin）中有关 1575 年访问福建的见闻。拉达的《中国札记》
完全是自己的亲历亲见，但是克鲁兹的《中国纪事》基于 1549–1552
年华南囚犯佩雷拉（Galeote Pereira）的口述。门多萨还参考了埃斯卡
兰特（Bernardino de Escalante）《葡萄牙远航至东方各国及省份及有关
中华帝国的消息》（Discurso de la navegacion que los Portugueses hazen
à los reinos y provincias del Oriente, y de la noticia que se tiene de las
grandezas del reino de la China）1577 年塞维利亚版。埃斯卡兰特显然没
有到过中国，他对中国的描述主要来自克鲁兹和巴罗斯（Barros）的著
作，以及他在葡萄牙和西班牙遇见的到过中国的人们的口信。门多萨的
著作是在教皇的支持下问世的，这一点无疑提升了该书在当时的权威性。

HISTORIA
DELAS COSAS
MAS NOTABLES,
RITOS Y COSTVMBRES,

Del gran Reyno dela China, sabidas assi por los libros
delos mesmos Chinas, como por relacion de Religio-
sos y otras personas que an estado en el dicho Reyno.

HECHA Y ORDENADA POR EL MVY R. P. MAESTRO
Fr. Ioan Gonzalez de Mendoça dela Orden de S. Agustin, y peniten-
ciario Appostolico a quien la Magestad Catholica embio con su real
carta y otras cosas para el Rey de aquel Reyno el año. 1580.

AL ILLVSTRISSIMO S. FERNANDO
de Vega y Fonseca delconsejo de su Magestad y su
presidente en el Real delas Indias.

Con vn Itinerario del nueuo Mundo.

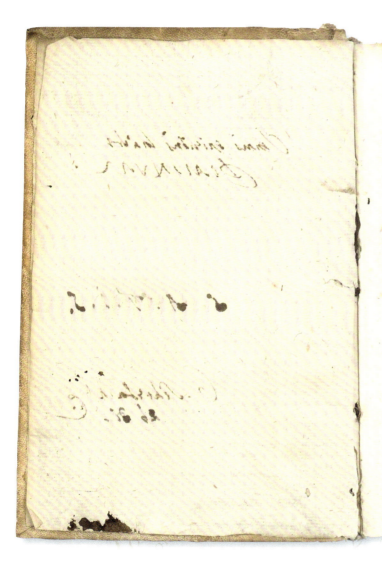

Con Priuilegio y Licencia de su Sanctidad.

En Roma, a costa de Bartholome Grassi. 1585.
en la Stampa de Vincentio Accolti.

罗氏编号 16

《1582－1584 年耶稣会士在日本和中国传教信札》

（*Avvisi del Giapone de gli anni M.D.LXXXII., LXXXIII, et LXXXIV. Con alcuni altri della Cina dell' LXXXIII. et LXXXIV. Cavati dale lettere della Compagnia di Giesù. Ricevute il mese di dicembre M.D.LXXXV*）

作　　者： ［意］罗明坚（Michel Ruggieri，字复初，1543－1607）等著

出　　版： 罗马，泽内蒂（Francesco Zanetti），1586 年

载体形态： 8 开，192 页，末 M8 叶附刊误表，M7 叶空白

装　　订： 犊皮软面。题名上方页边有书主题签和 Osc. Munsterberg 藏书票，前 100 页页边外侧有虫蛀小洞，影响到前后若干通书信；无勘误叶。

版　　本： 意大利文初版。

内　　容：

　　《来自中国的书信》（Avvisi della Cina）刊载于该书 169－188 页，收录了罗明坚 1583 年 2 月 7 日写于肇庆的书信、1584 年 1 月 25 日写于澳门的书信、5 月 30 日写于肇庆的书信、10 月 21 日写于澳门的书信和利玛窦 1584 年 11 月 30 日写于肇庆的书信等等。

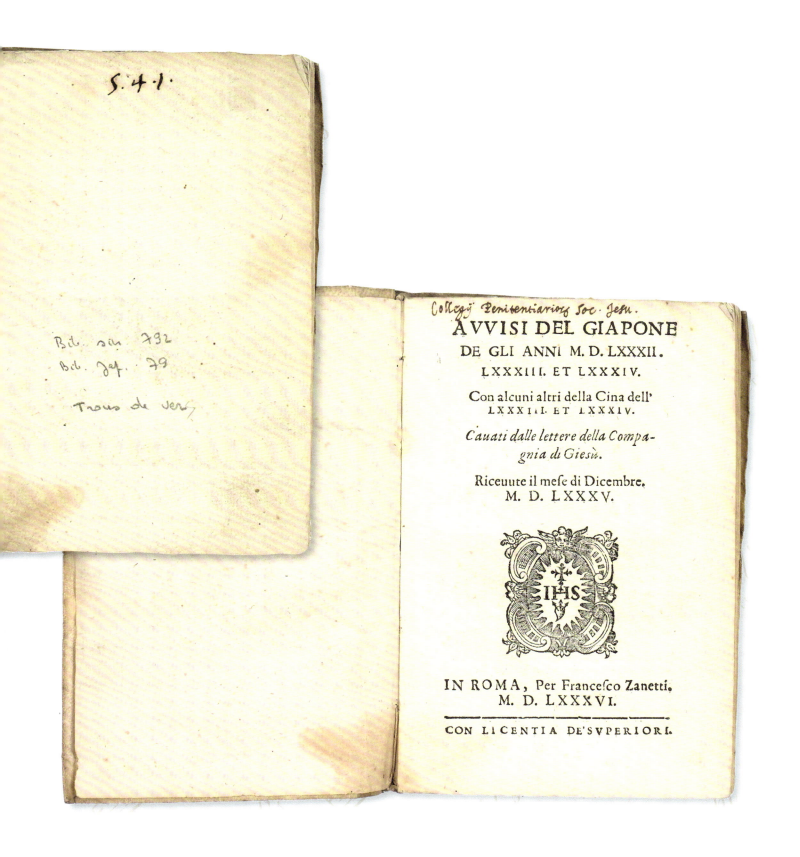

Collegij Penitentiariorg Soc. Jesu.

AVVISI DEL GIAPONE

DE GLI ANNI M. D. LXXXII.
LXXXIII. ET LXXXIV.

Con alcuni altri della Cina dell'
LXXXIII. ET LXXXIV.

Cauati dalle lettere della Compa-
gnia di Giesù.

Riceuute il mese di Dicembre.
M. D. LXXXV.

IHS

IN ROMA, Per Francesco Zanetti.
M. D. LXXXVI.

CON LICENTIA DE'SVPERIORI.

scretione; anzi ha mandato a chiamare, fabri, &
soldati di mare, accioche mettano insieme bar-
coni armati, & s'accostino per acqua sino a dar
l'assalto alle mura : Et era già partito a quella
volta Agostino con la sua gente, & có molto ap-
parecchio di guerra, confessatosi prima, & dispo-
sto per tutto ciò che gli possa auuenire. Questo
è quel che al presente si offerisce di queste parti
del Giapone. Di quello che nell'auuenire accade-
rà, nó lasciaremo di scriuere di mano in mano.
Fra tanto Idio nostro Signore sia in guardia di
V. Paternità, & le dia ad intendere il gran biso-
gno che habbiamo d'aiuto.
Di Nagazachi, alli 3. di Settembre. 1584.

Di Vostra Paternita.

Seruo indegno in Christo
Luigi Froes.

AVVISI
DELLA CINA
DELL'OTTANTATRE,
ET DELL'OTTANTA-
QVATTRO.

Come alcuni della Compagnia sono en-
trati dentro a terra ferma : & di
alcune primitie del Christianesimo:
& della speranza che v'è di pro-
gresso.

Di vna del P. Michele Ruggiero Napoli-
tano de li 7. di Febraro. 1583.
dalla Città di Sciau-
chino.

OPO l'hauere io alcuni anni
atteso nel porto di Amacano
(doue negotiano i mercanti Por
tughesi) ad imparare quella sor
te di lingua, che chiamano man
darina, vsata da questi Magistra-
ti, & Cortigiani (& per vna quasi infinita quáti-
tà di charatteri, tanto difficile, che gl'istessi Ci-
nesi vi spendono gli anni) andai alcune volte có
li

罗氏编号 46

《关于中国基督教之意见书》

(Histori［sche］und eigentliche Beschreibung, erstlich was gestalt［...］der Ehrwürdigen Vätter der Societet Jesu［...］numehr und vor gar wenig Jahren hero, das Evangelium und Lehr Christi in dem grossen und gewaltigen Königreich China eingefuhrt, gepflantzt und geprediget wirdt. Am andern, wie sie alle andere politische und weltliche Sachen unnd Gelegenheiten aldort beschafften, befunden)

作　　者：〔西〕庞迪我（Diego de Pantoja，字顺阳，1571—1618）著

出　　版：慕尼黑，贝尔格（Adam Berg），1608 年

载体形态：4 开，168 页，题名红黑两色套印

装　　订：全犊皮面，部分水渍与污迹，大都位于页边处

版　　本：庞迪我 1602 年 3 月 9 日作于北京的长篇书信的德文初版，译自 1607 年罗马意大利文版，意大利文版译自 Colaco 的 1604 年巴利阿多里德西班牙文简缩版，最后收入《耶稣会士海外传教书简》5 卷本马德里 1614 年版（罗氏编号 52）首卷中。之前有 1603 年埃武拉葡萄牙文摘要版、1607 年拉丁文版问世。

　　　　　庞迪我书信作为单行本首次出版是 1605 年塞维利亚版。

内　　容：

　　该书信提供了 17 世纪前 50 年欧洲关于中国的最为有趣而准确的一些资料。

Histori

Vnd eigentliche beschreibung/ erstlich was gestalt/ vermittelst sonderbarer Hülff vnd Schickung deß Allmächtigen/ dann auch der Ehrwürdigen Vätter der Societet IESV gebrauchten Fleiß/ vnd außgestandener Mühe/ Arbeit vnd Gefahr/ nunmehr vnd vor gar wenig Jahren hero/ das Euangelium vnd Lehr Christi in dem grossen vnd gewaltigen Königreich China eingeführt/ gepflanzt vnd geprediget wirdt.

Am andern/ wie sie alle andere Politische vnd Weltliche Sachen vnnd Gelegenheiten aldort beschaffen/ befunden. Alles lustig vnd nutzlich zulesen.

Durch Egidium Albertinum, auß einem Italienischen/ vnd auß besagtem Königreich China herauß geschicktem Tractät verteutscht.

Gedruckt zu München/ bey Adam Berg.

ANNO M. DC. VIII.

Mit Röm: Keys: May. Freyheit nit nachzudrucken.

Cum Licentia Superiorum.

罗氏编号 47

《中国传教报告书》
（Annua della Cina del M. DC.VI e M. DC.VII）

作　　者：［意］利玛窦（Matteo Ricci，字西泰，1552−1610）著

出　　版：罗马，曾内特（Bartolomeo Zennette），1610 年

载体形态：8 开，48 页

装　　订：新加装饰纸板面

版　　本：意大利文初版，意大利文再版于同年在米兰问世。

内　　容：

　　本书是利玛窦于 1606 年至 1607 年给耶稣会总会长所写的书信、报告的汇编，主要内容为耶稣会士在中国的活动情况、利玛窦的经验自述与在中国的见闻记录等。

　　利玛窦是中西交流的重要人物，也是西方"传教士汉学"的奠基人之一，其践行的"文化适应政策"，不仅扩大了耶稣会士在华活动的局面，更推动了中西之间的天文、地理、数学、思想文化等诸多方面的交流。本书是现存最早的利玛窦书信汇编，内容均由其亲自撰写，保留了信件的原始面貌。在研究利玛窦的资料中，该书的原始性与直接性，是其他同类著作无可比拟的。此外，作为耶稣会士在中国的报告信件，本书在研究耶稣会在华活动史、晚明史、中西文化交流史等方面具有重要史料价值。

罗氏编号 **54**

《利玛窦中国札记》

（ **De Christiana expedition apud sinas suscepta ab Societate Jesu〔...〕libri V〔...〕in quibus sinensis regni mores leges atq instituta & novae illius Ecclesiae difficillima primordial accurate & summa fide describuntur** ）

编 译 者： ［意］金尼阁（Nicolas Trigault，字四表，1577-1628）

出 版： 奥古斯堡，曼朱姆（Christoph Mangium），1615 年

载体形态： 4 开，XII+112 页 +111-646 页 +X 页 +1 幅包含了本书题名、利氏中国地图，及分立地图两旁的圣方济各和利玛窦的全身肖像的版画 +1 幅折叠平面图版画。木刻花饰与首字母

装 订： 木板猪皮面，有铜质书扣。书末若干页页边上部有轻微水渍。包含题名的版画页底部缺损，版画图版有微小撕裂，经修补后完好无损。题名版画页背面贴有米兰加尔默罗会书室的藏书票，末页有书主题签

版 本： 拉丁文初版。1613 年本书的编译者金尼阁携带了利玛窦关于耶稣会和基督教在华传教纪实的手稿从澳门回到了欧洲。根据 Jacques Gernet 的观点，金尼阁将利氏手稿翻译成拉丁文时，对原稿文字进行了随意歪曲、删节和添加。随后金尼阁又在在华传教的龙华民（Nicolas Longobardi，1559-1654）、高一志（Alphonse Vagnoni，1566-1640）和郭居静（Lazare Cattaneo，1560-1640）的葡萄牙文报告，以及熊三拔（Sabbathin de Ursis，1575-1620）1610 和 1611 年的书信的基础上，最后完成了这部书稿的编辑。此后本书的不同版本接二连三地出版，印证了其对 17 世纪初欧洲中国观的巨大影响。其拉丁文初版曾在 1616、1617、1623 年重印过 3 次。法文版于 1616 年在里昂问世，并于 1617 年和 1618 年重印。德文版于 1617 在奥古斯堡问世。西班牙文版 1621 年出版于塞维利亚和利马（罗氏编号 63）。意大利文版 1622 年出版于那不勒斯（罗氏编号 64）。简明英文版于 1625 年在帕切斯问世。英文全译本由 Louis Gallagher 翻译，于 1942 年出版，1953 年重印。利玛窦原始手稿意大利文注释本，由 Pasquale d'Elia 编辑成 3 卷，于 1942-1949 年在罗马问世。

内 容：

该书分为 5 卷，包括中国总论概要和 1582 年以来耶稣会士在华传教初创的详细历史。第一卷的第二章首次把先前认为是两个不同的地方的马可·波罗笔下的"契丹"和"中国"联系了起来。而第三章介绍了对欧洲来说还很陌生的中国茶饮。第四章描述了中国令人羡慕的雕版印刷。第四和第五卷中几乎有 4 章的内容来自在华传教的报告。

IV. *Quid superioribus annis in Sede Nanciani gestum fuerit.* 497

V. *Quid in Xauceano domicilio hoc ipso tempore age-retur.* 503

VI. *Res Christiana Nanchinensis belle procedit, & amicus noster Chiutaisò Christo aggre-gatur.* 509

VII. *Pechinensis Domicilij res gestæ. domus co-empta. Euclides Sinicè editus.* 514

VIII. *P. Alexander Valignanus Visitator, & primus expeditionis huius fundator moritur Amacai.* 522

IX. *In Cantoniensi Metropoli graui tumultu in Nostros excitato Frater noster Franciscus Martinez occiditur.* 525

X. *Cantoniensi tumultu sedato P. Cataneus cũ altero Socio ad stationem suam intra regnũ rediijt.* 535

XI. *Ex India Cataium lustraturus mittitur è nostra Societate Benedictus Goësius Lusita-nus.* 544

XII. *Reliquum itineris Cataium vsque. quod Sinarũ regnum esse compertũ est.* 551

XIII. *Fratris nostri Benedicti mors intra Sinẽ-se regnum postquam ad eũ excipiendum è Nostris vnus Pechino missus aduenisset.* 561

XIV. *Nanciani grauissimus in Nostros tumul-tus exoritur.* 569

XV. *Nanciani exantlato labore gesta.* 579

XVI. *Geographicam orbis descriptionem à P. Matthæo editam Rex ipse intra Palatiũ re-cudi iubet. Et Pechinensis Ecclesia nouis in-crementis augetur.* 583

XVII. *Rei Christianæ apud Nanchinenses pro-gressus.* 590

XVIII. *In Patria Doctoris Pauli vrbe Scian-hai nomine vtiliter biennii spacio P. Cata-neus laborat.* 597

XIX. *In Sede Xauceana res eo tempore gestæ narrantur.* 603

XX. *De felici P. Matthæi obitu.* 610

XXI. *P. Matthæo Ricio ab Rege sepulturâ, Nostris ædes sacræ & Profana designatur.* 616

FINIS CAPITVM.

DE

DE CHRISTIANA

EXPEDITIONE APVD SINAS AB SOCIETATE IESV SVSCEPTA.

Liber primus.

Scriptionis huius causę & modus.
CAPVT PRIMVM.

NON rarò euênit, vt ingentium expe-ditionum, rerumq́; magnarum, quæ labentibus seculis assurrexere, primordia posteri penitùs ig-norârint. Eius rei causam non semel mecum ipse inuestigans, vix aliam deprẹhendi, quàm rerum omnium initia [etiam earum quæ in immensam deinde magnitudi-nem excrescunt] in ortu suo, ita exigua esse & exilia, nihil vt minùs quàm secuturam deinde molem promittere videan-tur; qua ex causa qui res illas ex infantilibus, vt ita dicam, cu-nis educunt, nihil admodum laborant, res memoria tum quidem vt videtur indignas, memoriæ commendare. Nisi fortè magis placet, eiusmodi negotiorum prima rudimen-ta, tot tantísq́; difficultatibus impediri; vt eorum auctores in agendo distentos, à scribendo non temporis minùs quàm virium penuria deterreri fateamur.

Quam ob rem, vt societatis nostræ ingressum in occlusos tot seculis vastissimi huius regni fines, & rei Christianæ pri-mitias, apud illustrem hanc gentem, ab hoc obliuionis in-teritu vindicarem, aggressus sum ea, quæ à P. Matthæo Ric-cio suis commentarijs ad posteritatis memoriam quotidia-nis, post obitum relicta, historica narratione complecti.

Initia rerum magnarũ cur sæpe ignoren-tur.

Causę huius scriptionis.

A

Id

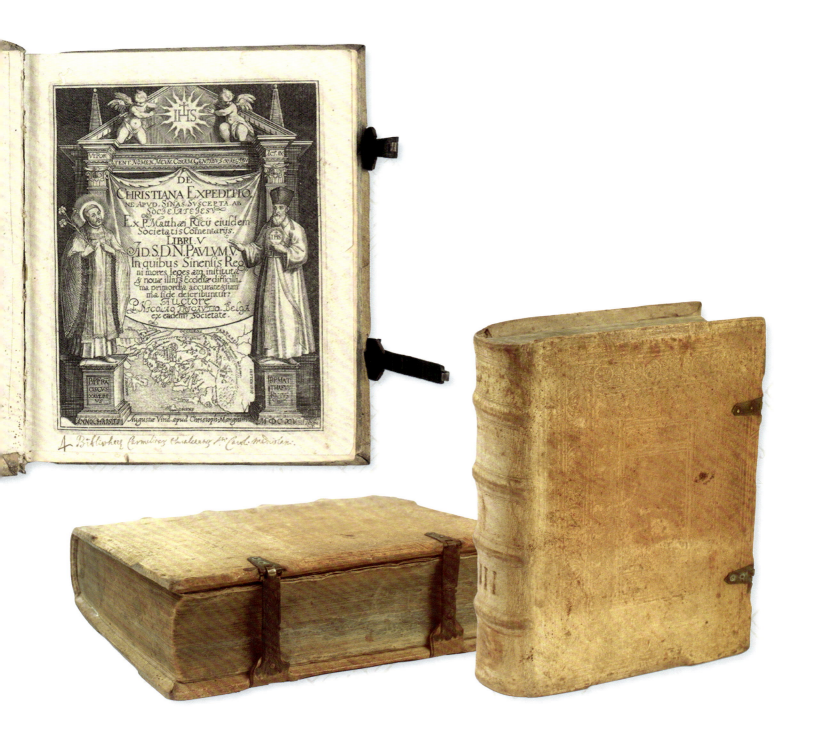

罗氏编号 71

《东方史》，又名《远游记》
（Historia oriental de las peregrinaciones）

作　　者：［葡］品托（Fernao Mendes Pinto,［1510］–1583）

出　　版：马德里，弗拉门戈（Diego Flamenco），1627 年

载体形态：对开，XXXVI+482 页

装　　订：全小牛皮面，书脊烫金但有磨损。诸多书页的天头和地脚已裁切，题名叶和末叶有衬纸，题名叶下角因撕裂造成非重要文字缺失，I4 叶页边被撕去影响到几个字母缺失，书页有水渍而且略微发黄，首末叶页边有批注和涂写的印迹。环衬上有 Dorothy Straight 和 Williard Straight 藏书票

版　　本：西班牙文（加泰罗尼亚语）再版。由 Francisco de Herrera Maldonado 根据 1614 年里斯本葡萄牙文版翻译过来的西班牙文初版于 1626 年问世时有两个印次，分别献给 Flechilla 侯爵 Don Duarte 和 Manuel Severim de Faria。Herrera 的西班牙文译文以后又在 1627 年（再版）、1628 年、1645 年、1664 年和 1666 年重印。除了其绪言篇幅过长外，根据 Rebecca Catz 的观点，其译文也不够准确并且过于在意叙事"风格"。

　　仅在 17 世纪，该书前后出版过总计 19 个版本，涉及 6 种文字。其中葡萄牙文 2 版，西班牙文 7 版，法文 3 或 4 版，荷兰文（缩写）2 版，德文（缩写）2 版，英文（缩写）3 版，还不包括 Purchas 删节版。

　　品托创作《远游记》的时间大约在 1569 年和 1578 年之间。其葡萄牙文初版是皇家编年史家 Francisco de Andrade 根据品托原始手稿（现已遗失）编辑的，略有修改。

内　　容：

　　品托的《远游记》因对东方旅行和探险的出色描述而从同类有关亚洲著述中脱颖而出，对 17 世纪欧洲文学更是产生了巨大的影响。同时，关于这本著作细节的可靠性及其作为历史文献的价值也引发了巨大的争议。

　　有的研究者认为品托本人只到过广东外海的岛屿，而没有踏上过中国大陆，因此本书中关于中国的记载有不少与事实不符之处。有的研究者则认为关于中国内地的描述来源于前人著作以及到过广州和中国内陆城市的葡萄牙商人或者囚犯的口述，虽然有夸张变形，但依旧不失为一份可靠的关于中国的欧洲人观察记录。

　　但无论如何，本书在文学性上的成就是不能抹杀的，即使它有想象的成分在内，也成功激发了欧洲人对于中国的更大渴望与想象，而这些最终化成了欧洲人进一步开拓、建立与中国长期稳定联系的动力。同时，通过对本书的研究，可以看到关于中国的描述是如何镶嵌入欧洲的文学传统之中的。

HISTORIA

ORIENTAL

DE LAS PEREGRINACIONES

DE FERNAN MENDEZ PINTO
PORTVGVES, ADONDE SE ESCRIVEN
muchas, y muy estrañas cosas que vio, y oyò en los Reynos de la China,
Tartaria, Sornao, que vulgarmente se llama Siam, Calaminam, Peguu,
Martauan, y otros muchos de aquellas partes Orientales, de que
en estas nuestras de Occidente ay muy poca, o
ninguna noticia.

CASOS FAMOSOS, ACONTECIMIENTOS ADMIRABLES,
leyes, gouierno, trages, Religion, y costumbres de aquellos
Gentiles de Asia.

*TRADVZIDO DE PORTVGVES EN CASTELLANO POR
el Licenciado Francisco de Herrera Maldonado, Canonigo de la
santa Yglesia Real de Arbas.*

AL EXCELENTISSIMO SEÑOR DON DVARTE, MARQVES
de Flechilla, y Villarramiel, Marques de Malagon, señor de las villas de Paracuellos,
la Porçuna, y Hernancauallero, Alferez mayor de la Orden y Cauallería
de Alcantara, y Comendador de Castilnouo.

CON PRIVILEGIO.
En Madrid, Por Diego Flamenco, Año de 1627.

Impressa a costa de Iuan del Casar, à Mercader de Libros. Vende se
frontero de san Basilio, y en Palacio.

ministro del demonio quiso responder-
le, el padre Francisco le quietò, diziédo
que se quedasse aquel particular para
otro dia, quando el Bonço tuuiesse me-
nos colera, que el siempre le responde-
ria sin ella. Sossegosse el Rey con esto,
aunque quedò pesaroso de auer dexa-
do hablar tanto al Bonço, y assi buelto
para el, le mādò que fuesse a hazer peni-
tencia de aquel pecado que auia come-
tido, por auerle justificado con Dios,
hablando de su grandeza. Colerico se
fue el Bonço, diziendo a vozes al de-
xar la sala, y Rey que tal dezia, le abra-
sasse Dios con fuego: y con esto passò
por todos, sin hazer cortesia al Rey,
que aunque enfadado dissimulò riédo-
se de verle tan descompuesto y necio
y los Caualleros glossaron con algunas
agudezas el termino del religioso tan
tan termino. Llegò el de la hora del comer, y truxeron al Rey la comida, para
la qual combidò al padre Francisco:es-
cusasse desta honra el Varon santo:pe-
ro pudo mas la importuna volútad del
Rey, que sus humildades : porque con
afectos le instaua aquella Alteza, dizien
do:Bien sè yo, padre y amigo mio, que
no tendras necessidad desta comida.
Pero tambien sabras, que para mi co-
nosotros, que dar su mesa los Reyes,
es la mayor muestra de amistad, y el
amor que puede verse entre nosotros,
y assi yo a ti, que te tengo por tan grande amigo mio, pienso que gano mas au-
toridad en combidarte, y ganò mas la
honra, aunque se tiene acà por tāta,en aceptar
el combite. Llegose el padre a besar la
cimitarra que el Rey traia (cortesia de
agradecimiento entre aquellas gentes)
y el con risa le dio los braços, y hazien-
dole llegar mas cerca de si, le puso vn
plato de arroz, que para comer le auian
traydo, y el padre humamente humilde
le dixo, que Dios, por quien entonces
le hazia aquel fauor y gracia, le comu-
nicasse la santa suya desde el cielo, para
que mereciesse professar la ley diuina,
como verdadero siervo suyo, para que
despues de aquesta vida, fuesse a go-
zar la eterna. A lo que el Rey le respon-
dio, con el agrado primero, que quisies-
se su diuina Magestad conceder al padre la merced que en su nombre le su-
plicaua:que esse auia de ser con condi-
cion, que el y el padre auian de estar en el
cielo siempre juntos y sin apartarse,pa-

ra hablar de aquellas cosas que auian
passado ambos. Comieron los dos, po-
niendose los Caualleros de rodillas, sin
leuantarse hasta acabar la comida, y nosotros los Portugueses hizimos lo mis-
mo, y muy alegres por la honra que el
Rey hazia a nuestro padre : de que los
Bonços quedaron llenos de embidia,
viendo tan mal luzidas sus murmura-
ciones y mentiras.

Capitulo CCXI. Quiere el Padre Francisco Xauier passar a la China, y las dis-putas que tiene con los Bon-ços de Fucheo, le detienen en aquella ciudad algu-nos dias.

AVia quarenta y seys dias que el
padre Francisco estaua en la ciudad de Fucheo, Metropoli (como he dicho) del Reyno de Bungo,
en aquella Isla del Iapon, tiépo gastado
de tal manera en la conuersion de aquellos infieles, que no se ocupaua, en vna
cosa de milagro le gozauamos los Portugueses,sino en las noches,que yuan ocu-
cando de las predicaciones y disputas,
nos animaua con alguna platica espiri-
tual, y alguna mañana nos confessaua.
Estrañamosle esta priessa, y los q sin cu-
ua de verle tā desapegado de su regalo,
de vino:porque el verdadero gusto suyo estaua en redimir aquellas almas del
cautiuerio del demonio. Con esta eficacia acudia el sieruo de Dios al aumento
de nuestra Fè Catolica, conuirtiendo
inumerables de aquellas gentes. Famo-
so fue la conuersion de Sacay Eerā, Bonço principal de Canasuma, doctissimo
en su instituto, que despues de auerle cō-
uencido el padre con aparentes verda-
des,

des, conclusiones euidentes y ciertas,
conociendo el infiel, quanto lo auia sido hasta entonces, puesto de rodillas
en la plaça principal de la ciudad de Fucheo, donde auia sido la disputa, y ro-
deado de inumerable pueblo, que espe-
raua el sucesso de las conclusiones : le-
uantando las manos al cielo, y los ojos
llenos de lagrimas, dixo estas palabras
publicamente. A ti Eterno Iesu Christo
Hijo de Dios, seriende mi alma, y te con-
fiesso con la boca,y con el coraçon por
Dios eterno y poderoso, y requiero a
todos quantos me oyen, que me perdo-
nen las vezes que les prediqué por ver-
dad,lo que aora veo y conozco, que es
falsedad y mentira. Esta confession de
este nueuo Christiano, fue causa que lo
fuessen muchos porque como le tenian
todos en opinió de docto, y de Letrado,
creian que lo que el auia escogido era
lo mas seguro, y mas acertado. Dezia-
nos el Padre Francisco, que cō su exēplo
aquel dia, si el Padre quisiera, pudiera
baptizar quinientas personas, mas que
conuenia tratar aquel particular, con
mucha prudencia, y tener gran conoci-
miēto de los afectos y repeticion de a-
ctos,en la persona que desseaua ser Neo-
fito.Porque la mucha facilidad era siē-
pre muy dañosa, y alli lo era mucho:
porque los Bonços aconsejauan a los
infieles, que ya que se querian apartar
de la religiō y patria,y hazerse Christia-
nos, ō pidiessen al Padre mucho dinero
en precio de serlo:porque como el no
podia darlo por ser tan pobre, tragaua
aquello el demonio por medio de a-
quellos sus ministros, para que el Santo Francisco perdiesse el credito con a-
quellas gentes, que tan mal sienten de
la pobreza: y con esso su dotrina, ni
sus persuasiones, no tuuiessen la eficacia
que ellos confessauan:pero Dios con su
diuina misericordia atajò las astucias
del enemigo de su Cruz sagrada, que
para su Magestad bendita no ay cosa
impossible. El Rey todo este tiempo
trataua muy particularmente a nuestro
Santo, siēdole tā acepto, y tan bien visto, que en aquellos dias ninguno de los
Bonços tuuo entrada, luziendole siempre mucho a aquella Alteza,las persuasiones ordinarias, que la conuersion se
hazia en la detestacion de sus vicios, y emiē-
da de sus costumbres:tanto, que auer-
gonçado con la confusion de sus torpe-

zas y pecados grauissimos, en que con
capa de virtud se auian instruydo aquellos ministros infernales; dexò los vicios en que viuia, y lo primero hizo e-
char de su Camara vn mancebo grā pri-
uado suyo, y cōplice de sus deshonesti-
dades y brutezas, y siendo antes nota-
blemente auariento para con los po-
bres(precepto principal de su falso insti
tuto)fue desde entonces con ellos grā-
demente liberal, y limosnero. Mādo tā-
bien debaxo de grandes penas, que ninguna muger pudiesse matar los hijos
que pariesse, que lo hazian entonces
la mayor parte de las de aquel pais,
por precepto particular de su secta, por
auerles vendido aquella crueldad sus
predicadores,por obra muy meritoria.
Otras leyes se promulgaron justissimas
anulando (a persuasion del Padre) muchas crueldades, y pecados de sus ritos
diabolicos, teniendo el Padre Francisco al Rey tan conocido y pesaroso de
las culpas y demasias passadas, que con-
fessò muchas vezes publicamente, que
el venerable y honesto rostro del Padre
Xauier, le seruia de espejo crista-
lino, en que vergonçoso se confundia,
viendo en tanta pureza las maldades
que hasta alli auia hecho. Quien no es-
perara de tan felices principios la conuersion de aquel Reyno, y el amparo
de aquel Rey? Todos la tuuimos por
cierta, y la duracion del Rey en aquellos propositos, por mas segura que to-
do:quien la dudara de aquellos a efe-
tos exteriores? Y verdaderamente se
podia prometer grande felicidad, en la
facilidad y desseo, con que se auia entre-
gado a la voluntad y disposiciō del Padre. Pero al fin no fueron tan durables
aquellos intētos,como se pensaua, por
que el Rey los mudò dentro de pocos
dias,quedandose en la ceguedad prime-
ra, luziosē del Altissimo, ō no es justo
to, que presuma dar alcāce la cortedad
humana. Llegò el tiempo de embarcar-
nos, y para hazerlo nos fuymos a despe-
dir del Rey, el Padre, el Capitan, y los
demas Portugueses, por besarle la mano por el buen acogimiento que nos
auia hecho en su tierra. Recibionos a todos con agrado notable, encareciēdo
quan embidioso quedaua de cada vno,
por ir en compañia del Padre Francisco,
sin quien se auia de hallar tan huer-
fano, y tan solo:porque le parecia, que

罗氏编号 95

《大中国志》
（ *Relatione della grande monarchia della Cina* ）

作　　者：［葡］曾德昭（字继元，曾名谢务禄、鲁德照，Álvaro Semedo, 1585−1658）

出　　版：罗马，斯凯乌斯（Hermann Scheus），1643 年

载体形态：4 开，VIII+324 页 +1 幅肖像版画。题名在版画框内

装　　订：犊皮软面，纸张轻度泛黄，肖像缺失，题名页有印刷皱痕和印章

版　　本：意大利文初版。本版不同于法里亚和苏萨（Faria y Sousa）的西班牙文版，其第一章补充了第 14、19 和 23 节的资料；但是其第一章第 1−8 节的文字似乎非常紧密地延续了西班牙文版第一章第 1−3 节和第二章第 1−5 节的文字。

德巴克（De Back）等版本目录学家提到该书的其他版本还有 1641 年马德里葡萄牙文版和 1642 年里斯本葡萄牙文版。曾德昭"显然在 1642 路过里斯本和马德里时将本书手稿交给了印书人，而其葡萄牙文版也随之发表于 1641 年的马德里和 1642 年的里斯本"。但今天的目录学家找不到这两个版本的踪影，并且认为 1956 年之前不曾有过葡萄牙文版。

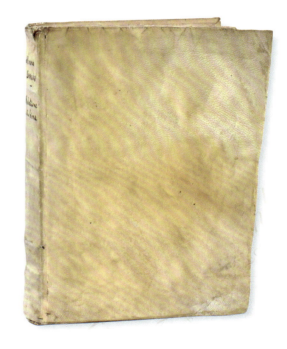

内　　容：

本书叙述了中国各地概貌、风土人情、礼仪习俗、政军治理制度以及天主教在华传播的事迹，更为特别的是本书记载了耶稣会士为确保和维持其在华传教的地位所作的努力。本书涉及的汉语言文字知识较之门多萨（1585 年）和金尼阁（1615 年）的同类著作更为丰富和全面。曾德昭将汉语与其他语言进行了比较，揭示了汉语文法简洁、表达丰富和描述生动的特点。他的这一观点使得人们相信汉语是世界各国语言的楷模，汉语也影响了整个 17 世纪的欧洲作家。曾德昭也是考察《大秦景教流行中国碑》文字的欧洲第一人，他有关景教碑的叙述也是欧洲读者见到的最早的相关印本。

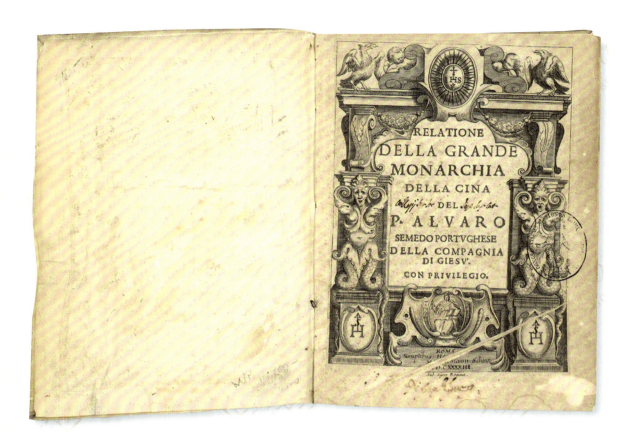

RELATIONE
DELLA GRANDE
MONARCHIA
DELLA CINA
DEL
P. ALVARO
SEMEDO PORTVGHESE
DELLA COMPAGNIA
DI GIESV.
CON PRIVILEGIO.

ROMA
Sumptibus Hermanni Scheus
M. DC.XXXXIII.
Sub Signo Reginæ.

Imprimatur, si videbitur Reuerendiss. P. Mag. Sacri Palatij
Apostolici.

Io. Baptista Alterius Episc. Camer. Vicesger.

HO con attentione letta la Relatione del Regno della
Cina scritta dal Padre Aluaro Semedo Procurator
de' Padri della Compagnia di Giesù in quel Regno. Descri-
ue egli con accuratezza il paese, esprime esattamente i costumi, riti, e il gouerno de' popoli habitanti, e minutamente
racconta i progressi della Religione Christiana in quelle
parti. Non vi hò trouata cosa che repugni alla verità della
Fede Cattolica, nè alla purità de' costumi; e perciò non po-
tendo apportar al Lettore se non notitie curiose, & vtili, la
stimo compositione degna d'esser data alle Stampe.
Il dì 8. Decembre 1642.

Pier-Battista Borghi.

Imprimatur;

Fr. Reginaldus Luccarinus Sacri Palatij Apostolici Magister.

RELA-

I

RELATIONE
DELLA GRANDE
MONARCHIA
DELLA CINA.

PROEMIO.

LO scriuere delle cose remote, hà
quasi sempre tirato seco l'incon-
ueniente di molti e non piccioli
difetti: da questo procede il ve-
dersi copiosi libri, i cui Autori
per le qualità delle persone me-
ritauano maggior credito nelle lor' opere.

Di quelli che hanno scritto della Cina, hò visto
alcuni, che lasciando in oblio quasi tutte le verità,
solamente si raggirano in cose, che son dal vero lon-
tane: perchè essendo questo Regno così remoto, &
hauendo sempre con ogni studio fuggito la communicatio-
ne co' forestieri, conseruando per se le sue cose come
proprie con particolarissima cautela, viene in conse-
guenza, che di quello solamente si sà di fuori ciò,

A   che

罗氏编号 107

《鞑靼战纪》
（De bello tartarico historia）

作　　者： ［意］卫匡国（Martino Martini，字济泰，1614−1661）

出　　版： 安特卫普，莫雷蒂（Plantiniana Balthasaris Moreti），1654 年

载体形态： 8 开，160 页＋1 幅折叠镌版地图"中华帝国各行省"

装　　订： 小牛皮面，书脊肋线烫金且标红边，封面烫金边框，衬页大理石花纹

版　　本： 拉丁文初版。该书流传甚广，自 1654 年至 1706 年之间，有 8 个国家的 25 个不同版本问世。仅 1654 年就有不少于 13 个版本用 5 种文字出版。不同的版本在正文文字、地图、插图和卷首语呈现了差异。该书的其他版本有 1654 年拉丁文科隆版和威尼斯版、荷兰文代尔夫特初版、德文慕尼黑版；1655 年荷兰拉丁文阿姆斯特丹版和乌特勒支版等等。该书还收录在卫匡国的另一部杰作《中国新图志》（Novus atlas sinensis, 1655）中，提供了权威史料的丰富性和多样性。

内　　容：

　　这是一部满族入侵和征服明帝国的历史。这段始于 17 世纪初止于 1644 年清兵入关并挥师南下的历史被称为"17 世纪的中国现代史"。该书首先提到了长城之外的北方民族鞑靼，介绍了明朝自朱元璋开国以来与女真的关系。继而记述了明万历以来辽东的战事，比较详细地介绍了天启、崇祯朝的国内政治形势，指出辽东战事、李自成流民起义和魏忠贤宦官专政是明朝灭亡的三大因素。本书还记录和保存了明清交替之际耶稣会士传教活动和中国基督教信徒的情况。

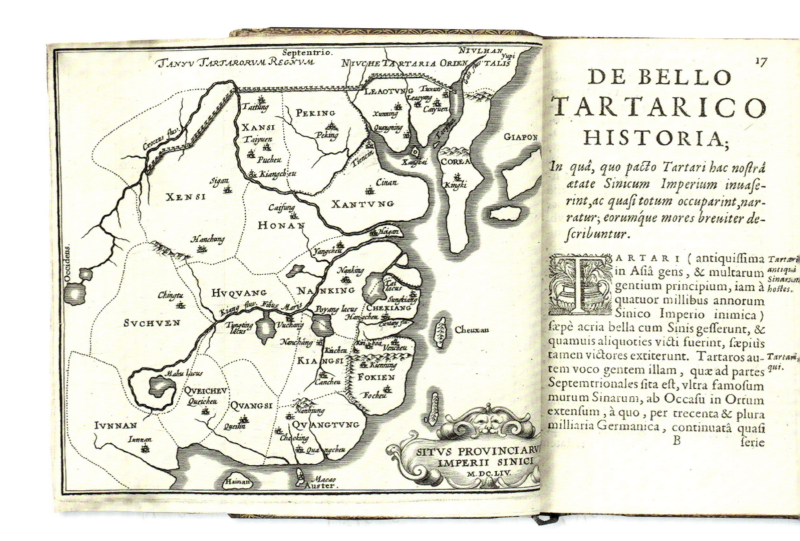

Septentrio. NIVLHAN yupi

TANYV TARTARORVM REGNVM · NIVCHE TARTARIA ORIENTALIS

SITVS PROVINCIARVM IMPERII SINICI M.DC.LIV.

DE BELLO TARTARICO HISTORIA;

In quâ, quo pacto Tartari hac nostrâ ætate Sinicum Imperium inuaserint, ac quasi totum occuparint, narratur; eorúmque mores breuiter describuntur.

TARTARI (antiquissima in Asiâ gens, & multarum gentium principium, iam à quatuor millibus annorum Sinico Imperio inimica) sæpè acria bella cum Sinis gesserunt, & quamuis aliquoties victi fuerint, sæpiùs tamen victores extiterunt. Tartaros autem voco gentem illam, quæ ad partes Septemtrionales sita est, vltra famosum murum Sinarum, ab Occasu in Ortum extensum, à quo, per trecenta & plura milliaria Germanica, continuatâ quasi

Tartari antiquæ Sinarum hostes.

Tartari, qui.

B   serie

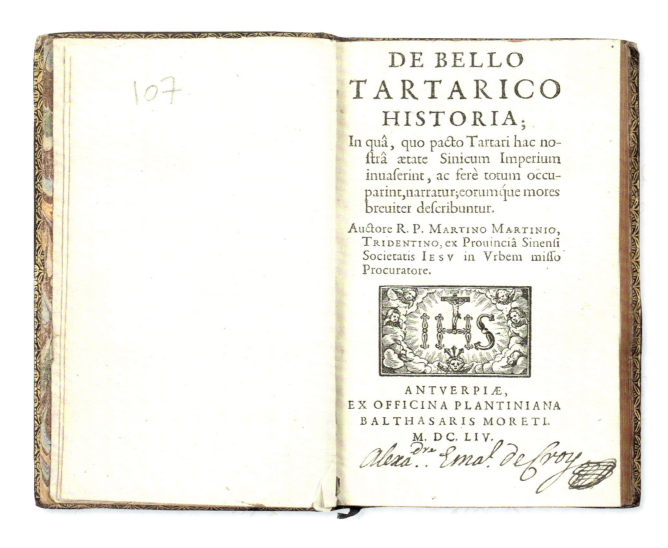

107

DE BELLO TARTARICO HISTORIA;

In quâ, quo pacto Tartari hac nostrâ ætate Sinicum Imperium
inuaserint, ac ferè totum occuparint, narratur; eorumque mores
breuiter describuntur.

Auctore R. P. MARTINO MARTINIO,
TRIDENTINO, ex Prouinciâ Sinensi
Societatis IESV in Vrbem misso
Procuratore.

ANTVERPIÆ,
EX OFFICINA PLANTINIANA
BALTHASARIS MORETI.
M. DC. LIV.

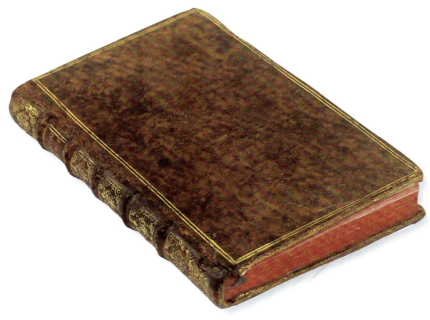

罗氏编号 **118**

《中国植物志》
（Flora sinensis, fructus floresque humillime porrigens ... ）

作　　者：[波] 卜弥格（Michal Piotr Boym，字致远，1612－1659）

出　　版：维也纳，里克蒂（Matthaei Rictii），1656 年

载体形态：对开，9+26 叶；附折叠插叶。书中包含 23 幅全页手工上色版画（21 幅左页有文字说明，折叠叶的
　　　　　左右页行文中均有木刻花饰），旁注汉文名称虽模糊，但尚能辨识

装　　订：18 世纪混色羊皮面，书脊烫金肋线，书脊上有若干虫蛀小洞，f2 叶上角有轻微撕痕，所有的蚀刻版
　　　　　画均为手工上色

版　　本：拉丁文初版。此本不包含奥格斯堡 Stadt-und Staatsbibliotek
　　　　　本中 d2 叶致卜弥格的诗歌部分，书中的 e1 叶误标为 d 叶，
　　　　　e2 叶误标为 e 叶。c2 叶右页上的导字"De"转至 e1 叶右
　　　　　页首行，而非转至 d1 叶右页首行，所以很有可能 d2 叶是
　　　　　在印刷这些起始叶并修改 e2 叶署名的时候添加的。此类错
　　　　　误与奥格斯堡及亨特郡本一致。

　　　　　　　书中的插图尤为引人注目，版画的色彩逼真地呈现了
　　　　　卜弥格手稿中的水彩画底稿的原色。

内　　容：

　　　卜弥格被誉为西方汉学研究的先锋人物，在他传奇的一生中，完
成了许多重要的科学工作，其中《中国植物志》是唯一一部在他在世
时出版的作品，也是欧洲出版的第一部介绍远东自然植物的著作。书
中列举了中国的植物约 20 种以及中国奇异动物数种。所介绍的植物中
包含了一些早期由葡萄牙人带到中国的原产自南美和中美洲的植物，
如木瓜、番石榴、腰果及菠萝等，虽然仅限于热带及亚热带物种，一
些植物还具有印度支那和马来亚的物种特征，但在 17 世纪，卜弥格的
这部著作是当时欧洲获取中国自然历史知识的最重要的途径，对随后
问世的作品有着深远的影响。

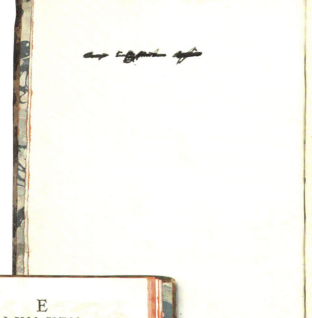

FLORA SINENSIS,

FRVCTVS FLORESQVE HVMILLIME PORRIGENS,

SERENISSIMO ET POTEN-
TISSIMO PRINCIPI, AC DOMINO,
DOMINO

EOPOLDO IGNATIO,

HUNGARIÆ REGI FLO-
RENTISSIMO, &c.

Fructus Sæculo promittenti Augustissimos,
emissa in publicum
A
R. P. MICHAELE BOYM,

Societatis IESV Sacerdote.
&

A Domo Professa ejusdem Societatis Viennæ
Majestati Suæ unà cum foelicissimi Anni apprecatione oblata.

Anno salutis

M. DC. LVI.

VIENNÆ AUSTRIÆ, *Typis Matthæi Rictij.*

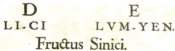

D   E
LI-CI   LVM-YEN.
Fructus Sinici.

Ici & Lumyen Arbores atque fructus, solùm apud Sinas reperiuntur, atque non nisi in aliquot Australibus Provincijs. LI-CI fructus corticem t depictum vides, in modum piniferæ Arboris ctus refert, sed Lum-yen lævissimam pelliculam ha-, vterque sapit fraga & vuas. Sinenses siccos fru-s hyemis tempore venales deferunt in alias partes. um etiam ex fructu vtroque suave conficiunt. Julio unio mensibus maturescunt; illorum nuclei inservi-t pro medicina. Sinenses pulverem ex illis factum endum præbent ægrotis. Si dicti fructus sint sylve-s, nucleos grandes & de subacida carne parum, si nsplantati nucleos exiguos, & de carne dulci pluri-m habent. Caro est coloris vnguium humanorum, autem pluribus diebus conserventur recentes, salita a depositi ex arbore asperguntur, & durant multo-n dierum spatio, abstractoque cortice, recentium saporem fructuum præstant, LI-CI creditur esse fructus calidæ qualitatis Lum-yen vero temperatæ.

C   GIAM-

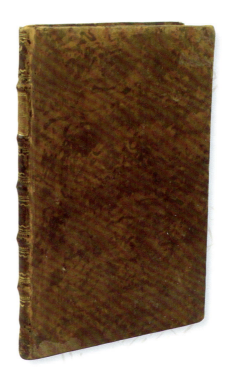

罗氏编号 **127**

《荷兰东印度公司使团初访中国记》

(L'Ambassade de la Compagnie Orientale des Provinces Unies vers l'empereur de la Chine, ou Grand Cam de Tartarie)

编 译 者：［荷］尼霍夫（Johann Neuhof）等

出　　版：莱顿，莫尔斯（Jacob de Meurs），1665 年

载体形态：对开，XVI（包括卷首插图）+116 页 +116－117 页 +117－118 页 +117－292 页 +II+136 页 +1 幅折叠地图 +1 幅肖像画 +34 幅折叠风景画和平面图，正文另包含 110 幅插图

装　　订：全小牛皮面，书脊烫金肋线和题名，原始装帧修复，地图略有泛黄

版　　本：同年早期有荷兰文初版，此本为法文初版，并增补了第二部分"中国概述"的内容。

内　　容：

　　本书提供了 1655－1657 年荷兰东印度公司使节团特使杯突高喵（郭佑，Peter Van Goyer）偕同惹诺皆色（Jacob Keyzer）来华请求朝贡贸易的记述，描述了两位荷兰特使在北京对清帝行三跪九叩礼，清廷允其每八年带四艘商船随使节来华等细节。书中有对澳门、广州、赣州、南昌、南京、安庆、芜湖、扬州等地的景致及自然历史的介绍。书中绘制的大量画稿成为西方人第一次直观地了解中国的重要材料，以致后世不断翻印或再版。

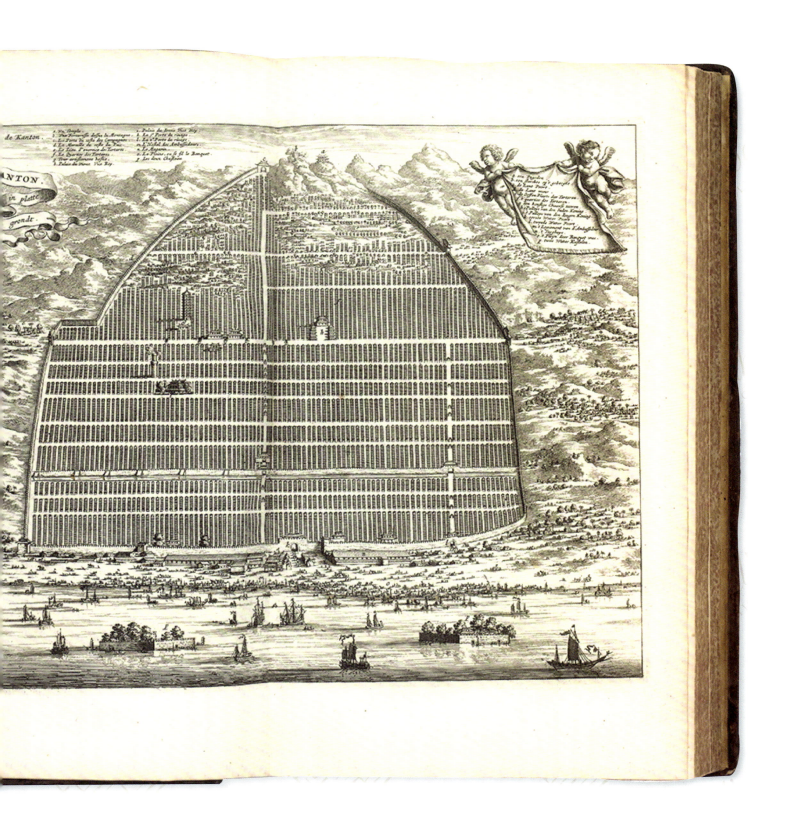

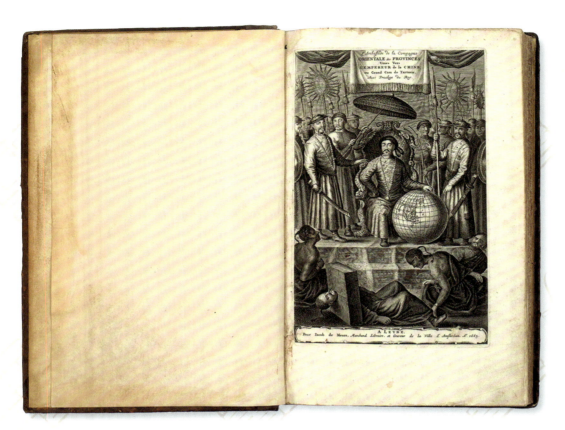

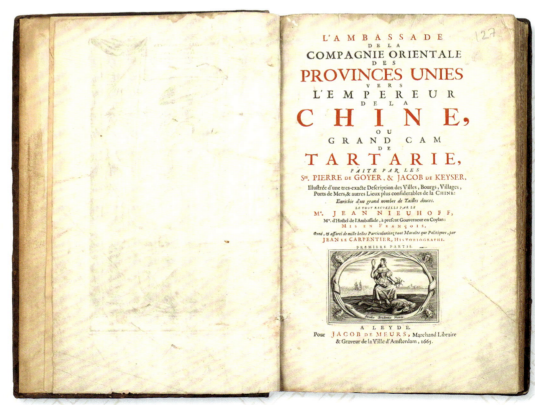

罗氏编号 128

《耶稣会中国传教史》

（Historica narratio, de initio et progressu missionis Societatis Jesu apud chinenses, ac praesertim in regia pequinensi）

编 译 者：［德］汤若望（Johann Adam Schall von Bell，字道未，
　　　　　　1592－1666）等
出　　版：维也纳，科斯默洛夫（Matthaei Cosmerovii），1665 年
载体形态：8 开，XII+268 页 +II+1 幅作者华服肖像
装　　订：犊皮面，题名页有书主题签与日期 1709 年
版　　本：拉丁文初版，第 2 版于 1672 年问世，1834 年刊行
　　　　　了德语版。

内　　容：

　　汤若望是继利玛窦之后最具影响力的耶稣会传教士。本书
叙述了他到达北京后不久即因成功预测出月食而声名鹊起，深
得崇祯皇帝赏识而被指派参与修历工作。书中还讲述了他如何
把望远镜这一欧洲的最新发明介绍到中国，并于 1630 年用中文
写成了《远镜说》，而此书的出版距伽利略首次发表介绍有关望
远镜的著作《星空使者》仅 20 年。汤若望认为中国以往天文历
算不够精确、缺乏科学性，赞扬了西方在这一领域的科学优势。

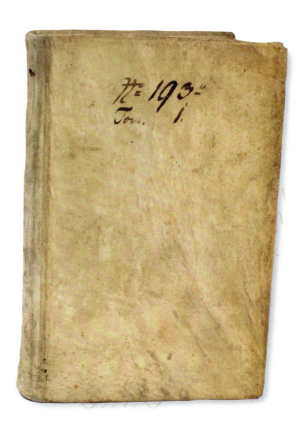

HISTORICA NARRATIO,

De

INITIO ET PROGRESSU MISSIONIS

SOCIETATIS JESU

Apud Chinenses,

Ac præsertim in Regia Pequi-
nensi,

Steph. *Nagitore*

1709

Ex Litteris

R. P. JOANNIS ADAMI SCHALL
ex eadem Societate,
Supremi ac Regij Mathematum Tribunalis
ibidem Præsidis.

Collecta

Viennæ Austriæ Anno M.DC.LXV.

1665

*Typis Matthæi Cosmerovij, Sacræ Cæsareæ Majestatis
Aulæ Typographi.*

R·P·IOANNES ADAMVS SCHALL, GERMANVS
è Societate IESV: Pequini Supremi ac Regij Mathematum Tribunalis Præses; indefessus pro Conuersione
gentium in Chinis Operarius ab annis 50. ætatis suæ 77.
Johann Steyr delin.   Mauril·Lang Sculp·Vin.

CAPUT I.

*Initia & progressus Christianæ So-
cietatis JESV ad Chinenses expeditionis.*

VLtimus laborum, quos S.
Franciscus Xaverius Christianæ Reli-
gioni apud Gentes ab orbe nostro lon-
gissimè dissitas proferendæ gloriosè
impendit, vastissimi Chinensium Im-
perij reclusus aditus fuit. Legibus illi arctiùs quàm
muro suo & Oceano conclusi pertinacissimè exte-
rorum quorumvis consuetudinem ac mores fugiunt:
Nisi legationis causâ adveneris, indubitata nex, aut
perpetuus carcer ingredi tentantem manet. Moribus autem peregrinis assuescere dedignantur, qui
superbè plus cæteris mortalibus sapere se unos cre-
dunt. Nec carent melioris indolis existimatione,
quàm ambitiosè tuentur, apud finitimos. Legem
Divinam in Japonia suadenti Xaverio reponebatur
identidem à Barbaris: iret & vicinis Chinensibus
eam persuaderet; sine morâ secuturos universim
Japones, si isti quos à sapientia suspicerent, conspi-
rarent. Itaque quos erudierat verbo, firmaturus
exemplo Indiarum Apostolus; Indis ac Japonibus
abundè in fide instructis, acceptis ab Europa etiam
                                                    socio-

A

罗氏编号 132

《中国图说》
（China monumentis）

编　　者：［德］基歇尔（Athanasius Kircher, 1601–1680）

出　　版：阿姆斯特丹，韦斯伯格和魏耶斯特拉特（Joannem Janssonium à Waesberge & Elizeum Weyerstraet），1667 年

载体形态：对开，XVI（包括卷首插图）+248 页 +1 幅汤若望肖像 +2 幅折叠地图 +23 幅版画图版（2 幅折叠）+59 幅版画插图

装　　订：混色小牛皮面，书脊烫金，折叠图版部分有衬纸，若干撕裂经修复略微影响了图画的完整性，其中 1 幅图版有虫蛀小洞以致画面有些许缺失，整本泛黄和变色

版　　本：拉丁文初版，此书是当时欧洲流行"中国热"最重要最具影响的作品，得到了神圣罗马皇帝利奥波德一世的支持和帮助。同年出现了盗版，1670 年荷语版和法语版（增加了 2 个补充部分）相继刊行，1669 年此书的英文删减版作为约翰·尼霍夫《荷兰东印度公司初访中国记》的附录出版。

内　　容：

基歇尔一生没有到过中国，但是他有机会和往来于中国的传教士进行交流并接触到他们带来的档案资料，从中获取大量有关中国的信息，这本书就是基歇尔对这些珍贵的资料进行研究整理后形成的一本汇编。本书分为 6 个部分，大部分内容是基于来华传教士卜弥格和卫匡国等人提供的材料所编写而成。基歇尔将汉字作为重要部分来介绍，通过对象形文字的解读来揭示中国文化的特质。此外最具价值的是书中有关《大秦景教流行中国碑》的研究著述，基歇尔所使用的都是当时未发表过的第一手资料，根据卜弥格和曾德昭提供的两种译本、碑文拓本，以及卜弥格对碑文逐字逐句的注音和释义，基歇尔再对全文进行了系统性的翻译并完整地报道了碑文发现的整个过程。这些工作对西方了解中文发音、对汉语的拉丁字母拼音化都有着极为重要的意义。

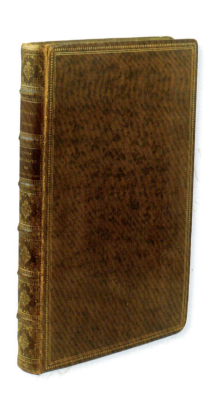

ATHANASII KIRCHERI
E Soc. JESU

CHINA
MONUMENTIS

QVA
Sacris *quà* Profanis,
Nec non variis

NATURÆ & ARTIS
SPECTACULIS,

Aliarumque rerum memorabilium
Argumentis

ILLUSTRATA,
AUSPICIIS

LEOPOLDI PRIMI
ROMAN. IMPER. SEMPER AUGUSTI
Munificentißimi Mecænatis.

A Solis Ortu   usque ad Occasui
Laudabile   Nomen Dñi.

AMSTELODAMI,
Apud *Joannem Janssonium à Waesberge & Elizeum Weyerstraet,*
ANNO cIɔ Iɔc LXVII. *Cum Privilegiis.*

罗氏编号 **150**

《中国脉理医论》

（ Les secrets de la medecine des chinois, consistant en la parfaite connoissance du pouls. Envoyez de la Chine par un françois, homme de grand merite ）

作　　者：［波］卜弥格（Michal Piotr Boym，字致远，1612-1659）

出　　版：格勒诺布尔，莎尔维斯（Philippes Charvys），［1671］年（此本的出版年份用墨水改为 1681 年）

载体形态：12 开，XII+144 页（末页空白）

装　　订：斑纹小牛皮面，以现代大理石纹书套装存

版　　本：本书题名页上年份有修改，有学者认为 1671 是印刷错误，实际可能如本册书的修改所示是 1681 年。若 1671 无误，那本书就是西方已知最早的关于中医的出版物，否则则是 1676 年米兰版的同一本著作的意大利文版，1699 年此版曾重印。

内　　容：

　　此书是西方出版的第一部有关中国医学方面的著述，其中大部分内容使用了卜弥格的手稿 Medicus Sinicus（《中国医学》）。书中介绍了魏晋时期著名医学家王叔和的《脉经》，描写了中医通过把脉来诊断病情并能预测疾病，此外还有通过查看舌苔看病的一些中国特有的行医方式。书中列出了近 300 个病例，均由卜弥格根据中国人的叙述翻译而成。此书一经出版就引起了欧洲文化界的极大关注，后世被译为多种欧洲文字刊行。

LES
SECRETS
DE LA MEDECINE
DES CHINOIS,
Consistant en la parfaite
connoissance du Pouls.

Envoyez de la Chine par un François,
Homme de grand merite.

A GRENOBLE,
Chez PHILIPPES CHARVYS,
Marchand Libraire, en la Place
de Mal-Conseil.

M. DC. LXXXI
Avec Privilege du Roy.

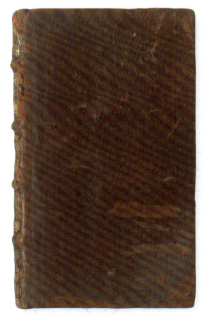

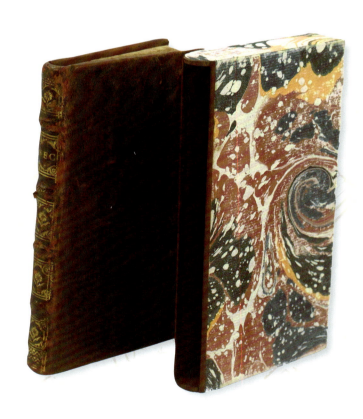

罗氏编号 154

《1581–1669 年间在华活动概述》
（ Compendiosa narratione dello stato della missione cinese, cominciádo dall'anno 1581. sino al 1669 ）

作　　者：［意］殷铎泽（Prospero Intorcetta，字觉斯，1625–1696）
出　　版：罗马，蒂佐尼（Francesco Tizzoni），1672 年
载体形态：8 开，128 页
装　　订：犊皮面
版　　本：意大利文初版，同年汤若望的《耶稣会在中国传教史》中附有此书的拉丁文版。

内　　容：

　　本书为 1581–1669 年耶稣会在华活动报告汇编。书中收有一封利类思、安文思和南怀仁神父于 1669 年 1 月 2 日寄自北京的信件和一封在华奥地利神父恩理格 1670 年 11 月 23 日寄自中国的信件。

　　殷铎泽 1657 年随重返中国的卫匡国首次来华，于 1670 年被公推去罗马会见总会长，向他陈述当时中国教区的困窘境况，并请求援助物资。此书是殷铎泽为了得到罗马总会的支援，而向总会长报告的 1581 至 1670 年天主教会在中国的付洗人数及各会圣堂、住院数量等信息。

COMPENDIOSA NARRATIONE

Dello Stato della Miſsione Cineſe, cominciádo dall'Anno 1581. fino al 1669. Offerta in Roma.

Alli Eminentiſſimi Signori Cardinali della Sacra Congregatione de Propaganda Fide.

Dal P. Proſpero Intorcetta della Compagnia di Gieſù, Miſſionario, e Procuratore della Cina : con l'aggiunta de'Prodigij da Dio operati; e delle Lettere venute dalla Corte di PeKino con feliciſſime nuoue.

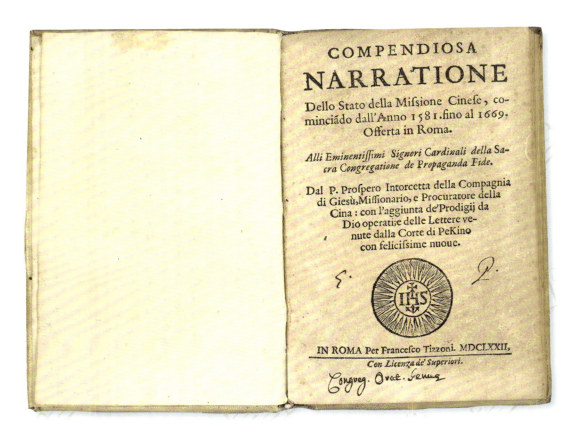

IN ROMA Per Franceſco Tizzoni. MDCLXXII,

Con Licenza de' Superiori.

Congreg. Ovat. Senug

ſegnare ai futuri, e perpetuare con ſuauità la propagatione di noſtra Sáta Fede in quei letterati campi della Cina. Mancano a me in verità per queſt'effetto le forze; perche, come accennai al principio, la noſtra Miſſione non ha Fondatore, e viue d'elemoſine mendicate dagli Europei; fra me ſteſſo però mi conſolo conſiderando l'impegno grande di Dio, e le continue preghiere, e lagrimoſi ſoſpiri della Chieſa Cineſe militante; intenta tutta à muouere la Diuina Miſericordia, e la pietà de Fedeli Europei, accioche liberali concorrano, e promuouano queſt'opera, che in ſe è ſì pia, per la Conuerſione de' Cineſi ſì neceſſaria, e per l'honor di Dio ſì glorioſa. Roma 18. d'Aprile 1671.

Proſpero Intorcetta.

CA-

CATALOGO

Dei 30. Sacerdoti, che nella Corte di Pekino furono preſentati a Giudici in queſta Perſecutione.

DELLA COMPAGNIA DI GIESV.

P Giouanni Adamo Schall Alemáno. Morì in Pekino nel tempo della perſecution & eſami.

P. Antonio di Gouuea Portugheſe.

P. Pietro Caneuari Genoueſe.

P. Ignatio da Coſta Portugheſe. Morì nell' Eſilio.

P. Michele Trigaultio Fiamengo. Morì nell' Eſilio.

P. Ludouico Buglio Siciliano.

P. Gabriele di Magaglianes Portugheſe.

C 2 P. Fran-

罗氏编号 156

《1659 年至 1666 年中华帝国政治及传教状况记》

（Relacam do estado politico e espiritval do Imperio da China, pellos annos de 1659. atè o de 1666）

作　　者：［比］鲁日满（Francois de Rougemont，字谦受，1624-1676）

出　　版：里斯本，科斯塔若阿（Ioam da Costa），1672 年

载体形态：4 开，VIII+207 页 +206-230 页

装　　订：19 世纪半摩洛哥羊皮面，首 4 叶顶部有几处不影响文字的细小修补

版　　本：葡萄牙初版，此版由马加仑神父译自拉丁文手抄本，1673 年在鲁汶刊行拉丁文版。

内　　容：

　　鲁日满 1659 年来到中国，先后在浙江省、江南省（今江苏、上海、安徽）传教，除教难期间发配广州外，直到去世，一直未远离江南地区。此书为鲁日满在广州流放期间编写，从清军入关到 1666 年征服全中国为止，涉及当时的一些社会背景和事件，这些事件对天主教会在华传教的影响，以及康熙前期辅臣摄政时期掀起的教难，在华传教士被发配关押等情况。

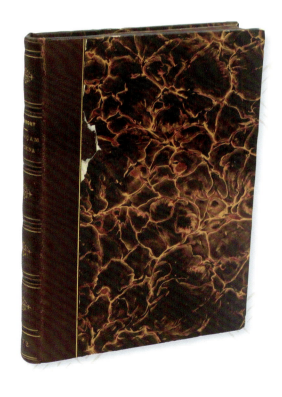
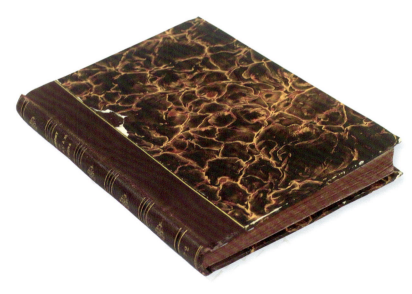

RELAÇAM
DO
ESTADO POLITICO
E ESPIRITVAL DO IMPERIO DA
China, pellos annos de 1659. atè o de 1666.

ESCRITA EM LATIM

Pello P. FRANCISCO ROGEMONT da Cópanhia
de Iesus, Flamengo, Missionario no mesmo Imperio
da China.

TRADVZIDA

Por hum Religioso da mesma Companhia de Iesus.

LISBOA.
Na Officina de IOAM DA COSTA.

M.DC.LXXII.

Com todas as licenças necessarias.

罗氏编号 182

《中国贤哲孔子》

（ Confucius sinarum philosophus, sive scientia sinensis latine exposita ... ）

编 译 者： ［比］柏应理（Philippe Couplet，字信末，1623－1693）等

出 版： 巴黎，奥尔泰梅尔斯（Danielem Horthemels），［1686］－1687 年

载体形态： 对开，CXXIV 页（包括 1 幅通页肖像）+108+24 页（末页空白）+160；+XX+20+8 页 +21－108 页 + 105－108 页 +1 幅地图，4 幅护身符图

装 订： 大开本，法国红色摩洛哥羊皮面，上有烫金路易十四纹章，书脊肋线烫金，烫金略有磨损，书脊底 部开裂，书缘有虫蛀

来 源： 题名页上复制有巴黎法国皇家图书馆的红色纹章，上有 "double vendu" 字样；扉页上有铅笔写的 "Britwell Court Library, March 1926"，应为 1926 年 3 月 15 日英国苏富比拍卖拍品中的一件，随后由 英国 Mersey 子爵收藏，并贴有 Bignor Park 书标

版 本： 拉丁文欧洲初版。

内 容：

　　本书主要由柏应理、殷铎泽、恩理格和鲁日满 4 位神父译著，内 容包括了中国经典著作及其主要注释、释道教派、诸子百家等，对《周 易》64 卦图像有较为详细的介绍和说明。书中还有一部拉丁文版《孔 子》，其中包括了《大学》《中庸》《论语》和孔子生平以及中国历史、 宗教的简介，另载有一张首次在欧洲出版物中刊印的孔子画像。因为 印刷技术的限制，柏应理只能在《大学》《论语》的第一部分中对汉语 文字作简单的介绍。在本书最后附有柏应理整理的第一份标有公元纪 年的《中华帝国年表》和他据卫匡国本所绘的中国 15 行省图。《中国 贤哲孔子》是第一部比较完整地向西方介绍中国传统文化的书籍，对 当时的欧洲产生了较大影响，在欧洲汉学史上具有启蒙意义和先驱 作用。

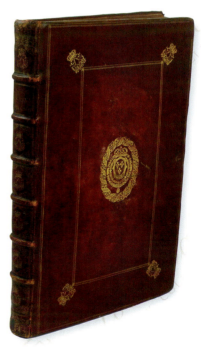

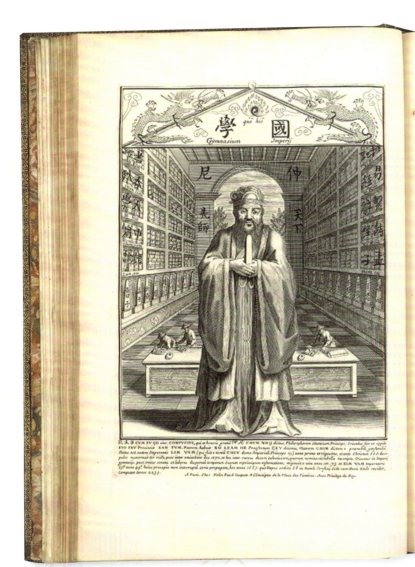

PHILOSOPHORUM SINENSIUM
PRINCIPIS
CONFUCII
VITA

CUM FU CU, *sive* Confucius quem Sinenses uti Principem Philosophiæ suæ *sequuntur*, & colunt, *vulgari vel domestico potius nomine* Kicu *dictus*; cognomento Chum nhi, natalem habuit sedem in Regno Lu, (quod Regnum hodie Xantum dicatur) in pago ceu ye territorij Cham pim, quod ad civitatem Kio seu pertinet; hæc autem civitas paret urbi Yen cheu dictæ. Natus est anno 21. Imperatoris Lim vam. Fuit hic tertius & vigesimus è tertia Familiâ, seu domo Imperatoria, Cheu dictâ, cycli 36 anno 47. Kem sio dictâ; secundo item & vigesimo anno Siam cum Regis, qui ea tempestate Regnum Lu obtinebat : die 13. undecimæ lunæ Kem çi dictæ, sub b ram nostis secundam, annos ante Christi ortum 551. Mater ei fuit Chim, è Familia prænobili Yen oriunda; Pater Xo leam he, qui non solum primi ordinis Magistratum, quem gessit in Regno Sum, sed generis quoque nobilitate fuit illustris; Hirpem quippe duxit (uti Chronica Sinensium testantur, & tabula genealogica, quæ annalibus inseritur, perspicuè docet) ex 27. sive penultimo Imperatore Ti ye è 2. familiâ Xam. Porro natus est Confucius Patre jam septuagenario, quem adeo triennius infans mox amisit; sed Mater pupillo deinde superstes fuit per annos unum & viginti, consigne in monte Tum sam Regni Lu sepulto. Puer jam sexennis præmatura quadam maturitate, avito, quàm puero similior, cum æqualibus nunquam visus est lusitare. Oblata edulia non ante delibabat, quàm priso ritu, qui çu teu nuncupatur, cælo venerabundus obtulisset. Annorum quindecim adolescens totum se dedit capit priscorum libris evolvendis, & rejectis iis, quæ minus utilia videbantur, optima quæque

c g

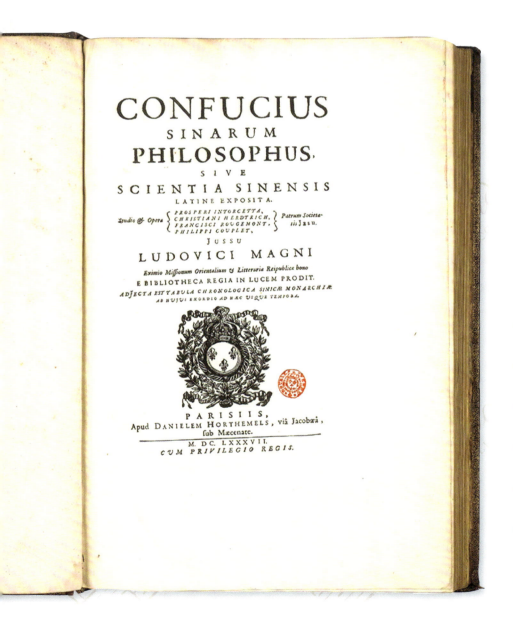

CONFUCIUS
SINARUM
PHILOSOPHUS,
SIVE
SCIENTIA SINENSIS
LATINE EXPOSITA.

Studio & Opera { PROSPERI INTORCETTA, CHRISTIANI HERDTRICH, FRANCISCI ROUGEMONT, PHILIPPI COUPLET, } Patrum Societatis JESU.

JUSSU
LUDOVICI MAGNI

Eximio Missionum Orientalium & Litterariae Reipublicae bono

E BIBLIOTHECA REGIA IN LUCEM PRODIT.

ADJECTA EST TABULA CHRONOLOGICA SINICAE MONARCHIAE
AB HUJUS EXORDIO AD HAEC USQUE TEMPORA.

PARISIIS,
Apud DANIELEM HORTHEMELS, viâ Jacobeâ,
sub Maecenate.

M. DC. LXXXVII.
CUM PRIVILEGIO REGIS.

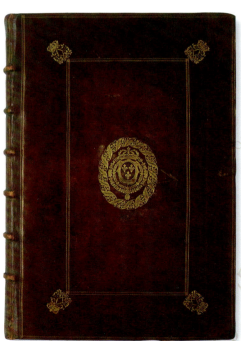

罗氏编号 185

《欧洲天文学》

（Astronomia europaea sub imperatore tartare sinico Cám Hy）

编　　者：［比］南怀仁（Ferdinand Verbiest，字敦伯，1623－1688）、柏应理
　　　　　（Philippe Couplet，字信末，1623－1693）

出　　版：迪林根，邦卡尔德（Joannis Caspari Bencard），1687 年

载体形态：4 开，VIII+128 页 +1 幅展示了德国绘画家 Melchior Haffner 绘制的北
　　　　　京天文台的观像仪器折叠图版

装　　订：现代棕色摩洛哥羊皮面，由伦敦 Sangorski & Sutcliffe 公司装订，未切
　　　　　割毛边本，图版折叠处有轻微的破损

版　　本：拉丁文欧洲初版，附有 1581－1681 年间来华传教的耶稣会士名录及其
　　　　　著述情况的目录，此目 1686 年曾在巴黎 R.J.B. de la Caille 单独出版。
　　　　　1993 年出版了由比利时历史学家诺尔英文释评的凸字锌版。

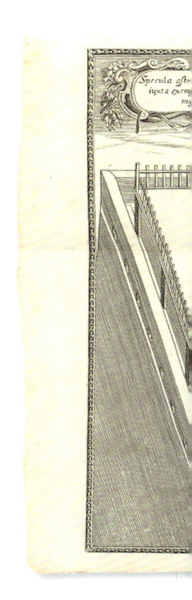

内　　容：

　　此书是南怀仁最著名的西文著作，于 1679 至 1680 年间编著，后由柏应理将此书手稿带回欧洲。本书的第一部分是关于天文历法方面的历史性记述，反映了欧洲天文学在经历"历法之争"后，在中国重新得到承认并恢复其优势地位的整个过程。南怀仁的记述从"历狱"开始，到他进呈永年历并受诰封止。内容包括：1668 年指出历法中的错误，1668 年末和 1669 年初的观测和推算，在钦天监负责治理历法的工作，钦天监机构及其任务，关于中国的天文历法的情况，进呈永年历、南怀仁本人及祖辈和父辈的受封，关于天文观测和仪器的说明；第二部分记述了 1668－1679 年间北京的耶稣会士在与数学和力学等有关的各种应用科学实践活动中的成就，并总结了以天文和数学为代表的西方科学在中国的影响。此外本书还收录了南怀仁之前所著《测验纪略》《仪象志》及《仪象图》的内容。

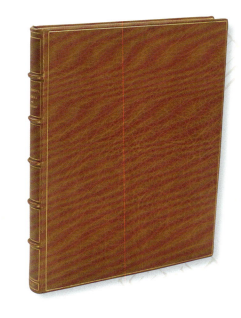

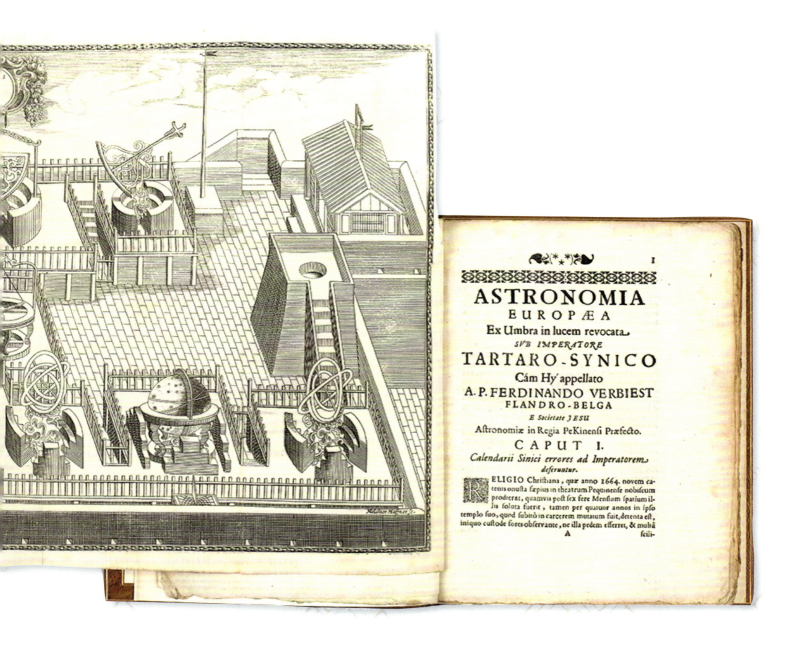

I

ASTRONOMIA
EUROPÆA
Ex Umbra in lucem revocata,
SVB IMPERATORE
TARTARO - SYNICO
Cám Hy´ appellato
A. P. FERDINANDO VERBIEST
FLANDRO - BELGA
E Societate JESU
Astronomiæ in Regia PeKinensi Præfecto.
CAPUT I.
Calendarii Sinici errores ad Imperatorem deferuntur.

RELIGIO Christiana, quæ anno 1664. novem catenis onusta sæpius in theatrum Pequinense nobiscum prodierat, quamvis post sex fere Mensium spatium illa soluta fuerit, tamen per quatuor annos in ipso templo suo, quod subitò in carcerem mutatum fuit, detenta est, iniquo custode fores observante, ne illa pedem efferret, & multâ

A

scili-

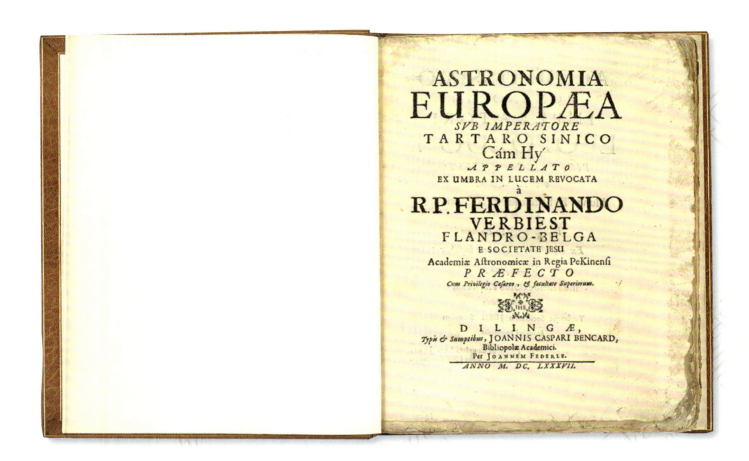

ASTRONOMIA
EUROPÆA
SVB IMPERATORE
TARTARO SINICO
Cám Hy
APPELLATO
EX UMBRA IN LUCEM REVOCATA
à
R. P. FERDINANDO
VERBIEST
FLANDRO-BELGA
E SOCIETATE JESU
Academiæ Astronomicæ in Regia PeKinensi
PRÆFECTO
Cum Privilegio Cæsareo, & facultate Superiorum.

DILINGÆ,
Typis & Sumptibus, JOANNIS CASPARI BENCARD,
Bibliopolæ Academici.
Per JOANNEM FEDERLE.
ANNO M. DC. LXXXVII.

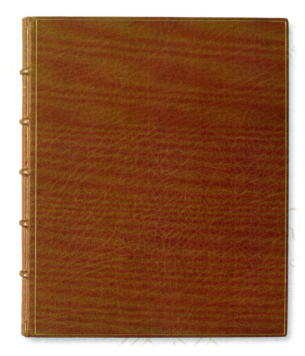

罗氏编号 189

《中国新史》

（Nouvelle relation de la Chine, contenant la description des parti-cularitez les plus considerables de ce grand empire）

作　　者：［葡］安文思（Gabriel de Magalhaes，字景明，1609－1677）

出　　版：巴黎，巴尔班（Claude Barbin），1688 年

载体形态：4 开，XXVI+396 页 +1 幅大张北京平面图

装　　订：当代重制牛皮封面，书脊书肋烫金，题名页有 2 枚印章

版　　本：法文初版，安文思于 1668 年在中国以葡萄牙文写成了
　　　　　《中国十二绝》，此手稿于 1682 年由柏应理带回欧洲并呈
　　　　　递给红衣主教，1688 年在巴黎首版，在随后的两年间不
　　　　　断重印，并被译为英文。

内　　容：

　　此书是西方早期汉学史上的一部重要作品。安文思在书中从中
国的版图、历史、语言文字、典籍、人民素养、交通、公共设施、
工艺技术、物产、政体、君主、都城及孔子的儒家思想这 12 个方面
赞扬了中国。安文思在书中对汉语的语音和字形篇章中的介绍比曾
德昭更为详细，该篇摘录了《大学》开篇的 16 个汉字，即"大学之
道，在明明德，在亲民，在止于至善"，称此"可能是中国文章摘录
首次呈现给欧洲读者"。

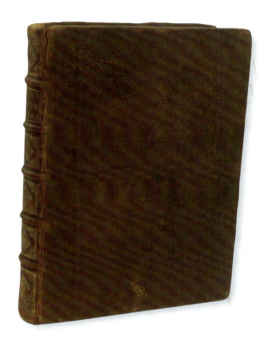

TABLE DES MATIERES.

Tribunal qui a soin du Sceau de l'Empereur.   p. 234
Tribunal des Mandarins de la Garde Royale.   p. 235, 236
Tribunal des droits d'entrée de Pe kim.   p. 237
Tribunal du Grand Prevoſt.   p. 237
Tribunal des Gouverneurs de Pekim.   p. 238, 239
Tribunal des Grands de la Famille Royale.   p. 240
Tribunal des parens du Roy du côté des femmes.   p. 241
Tribunaux des Provinces.   p. 244
Tribunal Suprême de chaque Province.   p. 244, 245
Tribunal Civil de chaque Capitale.   p. 246
Tribunal Criminel de chaque Capitale.   p. 247
Tribunal ou Mandarin Inſpecteur de chaque diſtrict d'une province.   p. 247
Tribunal de chaque Cité du premier Ordre.   p. 247, 248
Tribunal de chaque Cité du ſecond Ordre.   p. 248
Tribunal de chacune des autres Villes.   p. 249
Tribunal dans chaque Ville pour juger les gens de lettres.   p. 252
Tribunal du Sel ou de la Gabelle & autres Tribunaux. p. 253, 254

V.

Vie du Pere Gabriel de Magaillans. p. 371. Son arrivée à Goa & à Macao, ſon entrée dans la Chine, & ſon voyage à la province de Su chuen. p. 371. perſecution excitée par les Bonzes contre luy & contre le pere Buglio. p. 373. peril que leur fit courir le Tiran *Cham hien chum*, p. 374, 375, 376. Ils ſont bleſſez par les Tartares & menez à Pe kim. p. 377. Son ſéjour à la Cour & ſes occupations, p. 375, 378. Nouvelle perſecution & ſa delivrance. p. 379. Sa mort. p. 380. Eloge de ce pere fait par l'Empereur. p. 381. Son Enterrement magnifique fait par l'ordre de ce Prince. p. 382 & ſuivantes.
Uſangué, Royaume, ce que c'eſt. p. 31.

Fin de la Table des Matiéres.

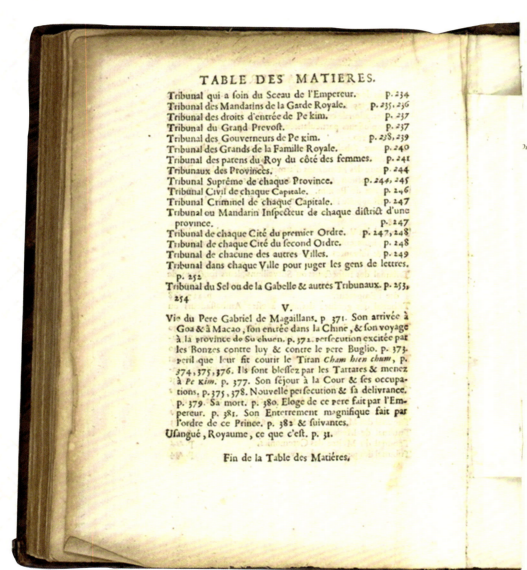

PLAN DE LA VILLE DE

Echelle de dix Stades Chinois qui valent 2730 pas Geometriques.

EXPLICAON du plan de la ville de PEKIM

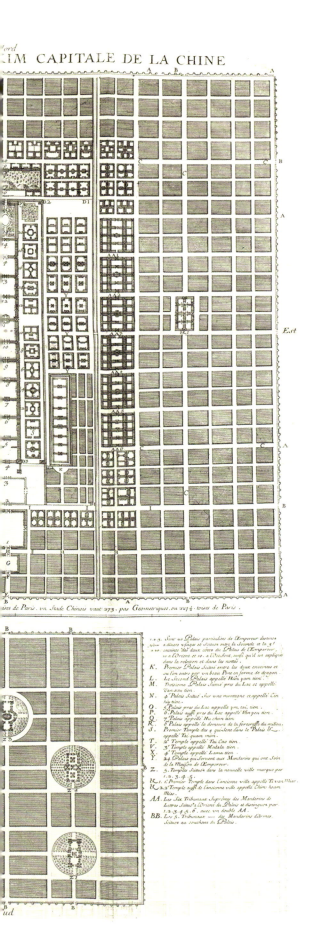

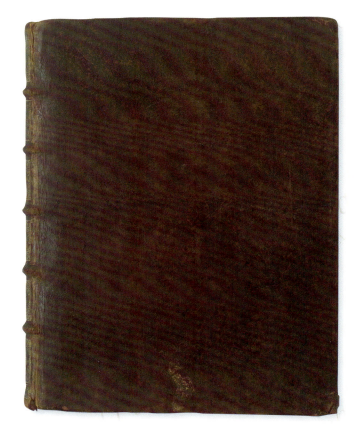

NOUVELLE RELATION DE LA CHINE,

Contenant la description des particularitez les plus considerables de ce grand Empire.

Composée en l'année 1668. par le R. P. Gabriel de Magaillans, de la Compagnie de JESUS, *Miſſionnaire Apostolique.*

Et traduite du Portugais en François par le S B.

A PARIS,

Chez CLAUDE BARBIN au Palais ſur le ſecond Perron de la Sainte Chappelle.

M. DC. LXXXVIII.

AVEC PRIVILEGE DV ROY.

罗氏编号 **214**

《中国近事报道》
（ Nouveaux mémoires sur l'état présent de la Chine ）

作　　者：［法］李明（Louis Le Comte，字复初，1665－1728）

出　　版：巴黎，阿尼松（Jean Anisson），1696 年

载体形态：12 开，XXVIII+508 页；+IV+536 页 +1 幅首页肖像 +20 幅图版（2 幅折叠）+1 幅折叠表格

装　　订：当代重制牛皮封面，烫金书脊，题名页的剪切和修补略微影响到木刻的花纹图案

版　　本：法文初版，这是一本李明寄给法国知名学者们的有关于中国的信件汇编，它的出现将欧洲关于中国礼仪问题的争论推向了高潮，一经出版便引起了巨大的关注，在 1702 年之前就已至少重印了 7 次，另还有若干种英文版以及德文、荷兰文版。

内　　容：

　　李明对中国的研究贡献涵盖了地理观测、服饰、民俗和文化等领域，本书还首次条理性地评述了中式建筑。在天文观测方面，李明使用了南怀仁著述中的天文仪器图和北京天文台全景图。

　　本书分为上下两卷，上卷是李明致信叙述自己中国之行的见闻，描述了他觐见皇帝的经过，中国的建筑工程，中国的气候、土壤、河流和物产的介绍，中国的民族特性和历史风俗，中国的语言文字和伦理道德等；下卷是李明致信红衣主教、国家议员等人的有关中国的政治、宗教、天主教在中国的创建和进展以及在华传教的注意事项等的汇报。下卷内容意在为在华耶稣会士辩护，出版 4 年后即 1700 年，索邦神学院对李明发出责难，认为其"虚假的、鲁莽的、丑闻性的、错误的、并给天主教的名誉带来巨大的损害"的著述必须封禁，此后，中西发生了大规模的礼仪之争。

P. 143.

Sphere Armillaire Zodiacale
1. Machine.

à leurs entreprises, ils demandoient alors à leurs sujets ce qu'il y avoit à réformer en leurs propres personnes, persuadez que tous les malheurs publics venoient toûjours de leur mauvais gouvernement. On en lit dans l'histoire un exemple celebre, que je ne puis m'empescher de raporter.

La sterilité ayant esté generale dans toutes les Provinces durant sept années consecutives, (ce temps ne paroist pas éloigné des sept années de sterilité dont parle l'Ecriture, & peut-estre que ce point bien examiné servira à réformer ou à confirmer nostre Chronologie *) le peuple fut réduit à la derniere extremité ; & les prieres, les jeûnes, les autres penitences ayant esté inutilement employées, l'Empereur ne sçachant plus par quel moyen il pourroit mettre fin à la misere publique, après avoir offert à Dieu plusieurs sacrifices pour appaiser sa colére, il ré-

* Cet Empereur mourut 1753. ans avant la naissance de J. C. Et la 7. an. de sterilité, selon l'écriture, arriva 1743. ans avant la mesme naissance.

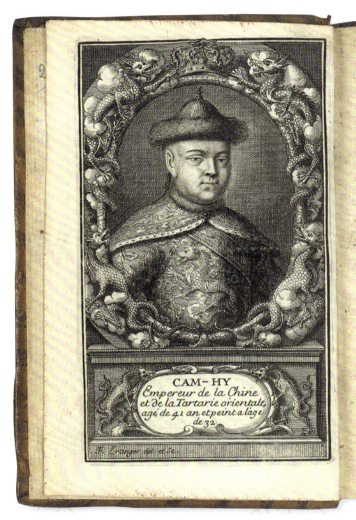

CAM-HY
Empereur de la Chine
et de la Tartarie orientale,
age de 41 an et peint a l'age
de 32.

F. Enungen del. et Sc.

NOUVEAUX
MEMOIRES
SUR
L'ETAT PRESENT
DE
LA CHINE.

Par le P. Louis Le Comte de la Compagnie de Jesus, Mathématicien du Roy.

TOME PREMIER.

A PARIS,
Chez JEAN ANISSON Directeur de l'Imprimerie Royale, ruë de la Harpe, au dessus de
S. Cosme, à la Fleur-de-Lis de Florence.

M. DC. XCVI.
Avec Privilege du Roy.

《东方游记合集》

（ Relations de divers voyages curieux,qui n'ont point esté publiées, et qu'on a traduit ou tiré des originaux des voyageurs françois, espagnols, allemands, portugais, anglois, hollandois, persans, arabes & autres orientaux, données au public ）

编 译 者：［法］特维诺（Melchisedech Thevenot, 1620−1692）

出　　　版：巴黎，莫埃特（Thomas Moëtte），1696 年

载体形态：对开，2 卷 5 部分，总题名红黑两色印刷，若干图版以及地图，多为折叠版画，正文中有木刻花纹

装　　　订：半小牛皮面

版　　　本：巴黎法文版，此本缺第 2 部分的 "Beaulieu 将军东印度旅行记"图版及第 5 部分 "Adelantado Alvaro de Mendaña 旅行记"的 a1−a2，c1−c2 叶及一些补充摘录。

　　　　这是作者身后出版的旅行记汇编，另新增了一些以前未曾提出过的记述内容。第 1 部分发行于 1663 年，第 2 部分发行于 1664 年，第 3 部分发行于 1666 年，第 4 部分发行于 1672−1674 年间。在整套书的发行期间，已发行的部分又以新题名重新刊行，导致了整套书各种版本刊行说明和收录内容存在不少差异。

内　　　容：

　　　　本套合集分上下两卷，共 5 个部分，有 25 篇内容涉及中国，3 幅地图、4 幅图板及若干插图。在上卷的第 1 部分里，有一篇关于 1661 年 7 月 5 日郑成功收复台湾的法文记述，此篇译自荷兰文，叙述了郑成功率领将士击溃荷兰东印度公司军队并收复其占领的领地。

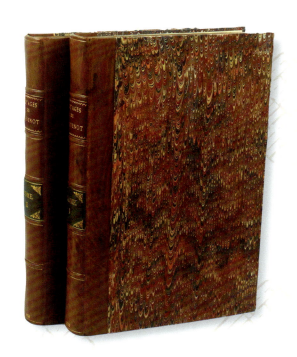

RELATIONS
DE DIVERS
VOYAGES
CURIEUX,
QUI N'ONT POINT ESTE PUBLIE'ES,

Et qu'on a traduit ou tiré des Originaux des Voyageurs François, Espagnols, Allemands, Portugais, Anglois, Hollandois,
Persans', Arabes & autres Orientaux, données au public
par les soins de feu

M. MELCHISEDEC THEVENOT.

LE TOUT ENRICHI DE FIGURES, DE PLANTES
non décrites, d'Animaux inconnus à l'Europe, & de Cartes Geogra-
phiques, qui n'ont point encore été publiées.

NOVVELLE EDITION,

Augmentée de plusieurs Relations curieuses.

TOME PREMIER.
CONTENANT LA I. ET II. PARTIE.

A PARIS,
Chez **Thomas Moette** Libraire, ruë de la Bouclerie, à saint Alexis,

M. DC. XCVI.
AVEC PRIVILEGE DE SA MAJESTE'.

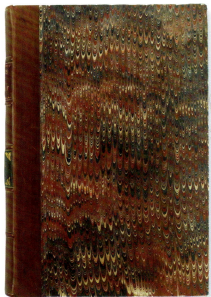

bruſé de cette eau , traitté par leurs Medecins , puis expoſé de nouueau aux meſ-
mes tourmens , y perdit enfin la vie.

Ils n'ont pas eſpargné les femmes , ils les ont tourmentées par d'autres manie-
res de ſupplices auſſi rigoureux ; car les veſues qui eſtoient paruenuës à vne grande
vieilleſſe ont eſté enuoyées à ces eaux infernalles , & pour les jeunes filles , & les femmes de moyen âge , ils les ont obligées de marcher par la ville toute nuës ſur les pieds
& ſur les mains comme des beſtes , & il s'en eſt trouué qui l'ont entrepris auec vne
ferme reſolution de le faire ; mais ſouffrir cette honte ; & s'il s'en eſt trouué quel-
ques-vnes qui s'y ſoient reſoluës , elles n'en ont pourtant pas eu meilleur marché,
pour auoir ſurmonté cette honte ; mais on leur a fait ſouffrir , ou des tourmens plus
cruels , ou des ſpectacles plus odieux , juſqu'à ce qu'enfin elles ayent eſté contraintes
d'abandonner la Foy.

Nous auons conu vne veſue Chreſtienne fort ſage & fort delicate , auec qui Mon-
ſieur Sanſwort auoit eu vne grande amitié,elle n'auoit qu'vn ſeul fils , pour lors âgé de
18. ans ou enuiron ; les Tyrans employerent toutes auec ſa mere en preſence des
Iuges;la mere & le fils furent ſi eſpouuétez , de cette execrable & abominable cruauté,
qu'ils ne ſçauoient que dire ny que penſer , ſi eſt-ce toutesfois qu'on ne pût , par quelque moyen que ce fuſt , les reſoudre à commettre vne ſi horrible meſchanceté, quelques menaces & tourmens qu'on leur fit : les Iuges aſſuroient , que ſi ils n'obeys-
ſoient , on ne les tiendroit plus pour Chreſtiens , mais pour veritables apoſtats : la
mere ny le fils ne pouuant ſupporter le des-honneur d'vn nom ſi deteſtable , s'of-
froient l'vn & l'autre de mourir de la plus cruelle mort , qu'il leur plairoit ordonner,
pluſtoſt que d'en venir là , mais cela ne leur ſeruit de rien ; car les Iuges voyans qu'ils
n'auançoient rien auec toutes leurs menaces , ordonnerent que l'on menaſt cette veſ-
uë à vn talon , & que luy ayant attaché les pieds & les mains , on la luy expoſaſt
pour en eſtre ſouillée en preſence de ſon fils,& on luy fit apres pluſieurs autres ignomi-
nies.

Enfin les Iuges voyant l'admirable conſtance de cette Dame , qui ne peût eſtre
eſbranlée par aucune menace, ny par leur ſaletez & des-honneſtetez , ny par le conſeil
& l'exhortation de ſes amis les plus conſiderables , la condamnerent auec ſon fils d'eſtre menée aux eaux infernalles , où eſtans arriuées ils ordonnerent au fils de puiſer
de cette eau bouïllante , & d'en verſer ſur le corps de ſa mere , & à la mere d'en faire
autant à ſon fils en telle quantité qu'ils commanderoient;que la mere & le fils ayans
reciproquement refuſé, bien qu'ils euſſent eux-meſmes puiſé de ces eaux dans les ar-
rouloirs , & ſe les euſſent mis entre les mains l'vn de l'autre , & que de plus l'vn de
ces bourreaux tint en main vne eſpée nuë & vn couteſas de l'autre , auec quoy il les
menaçoit , les iniuriât auec les plus ſales & vilaines paroles qu'il pouuoit pro-
noncer contre eux. Enfin cette femme deſolée voyant qu'elle ne pouuoit mourir comme elle eut bien vouly, ny eſtre deſiurée des tourmens qu'elle ne pouuoit plus ſouffrir,
renonça à ſa Religion. I'ay jugé à propos d'eſcrire vn peu au long cette hiſtoire , affin
que chaſcun puiſſe apprendre de-là toutes les autres actions horribles de cruauté qu'ils
ont exercées ſur les Chreſtiens.

En vn mot le Gouuerneur Onemandonne en quarante cinq ou ſix iours extirpa
tous les Chreſtiens ſans effuſion de ſang ny meurtre , (à l'exception de ce ieune gar-
çon dont i'ay cy-deuant parlé,) que les autres Gouuerneurs n'auoient auparauant
peû faire par toute ſorte de morts durant ſeize ans : pour y paruenir , & affin qu'il
s'en peût donner la gloire toute entiere , il ne voulut point pour l'execution de tous
ces tourmens appeller l'aſſiſtance d'aucuns des Iuges de Nangaſacque , ny d'Arrima
pour y eſtre preſens , & il n'a point eſpargné la vie des Chreſtiens pour aucune bien-
veillance qu'il eut pour eux , ny qu'il fit conſcience de les faire mourir , mais ſeulement

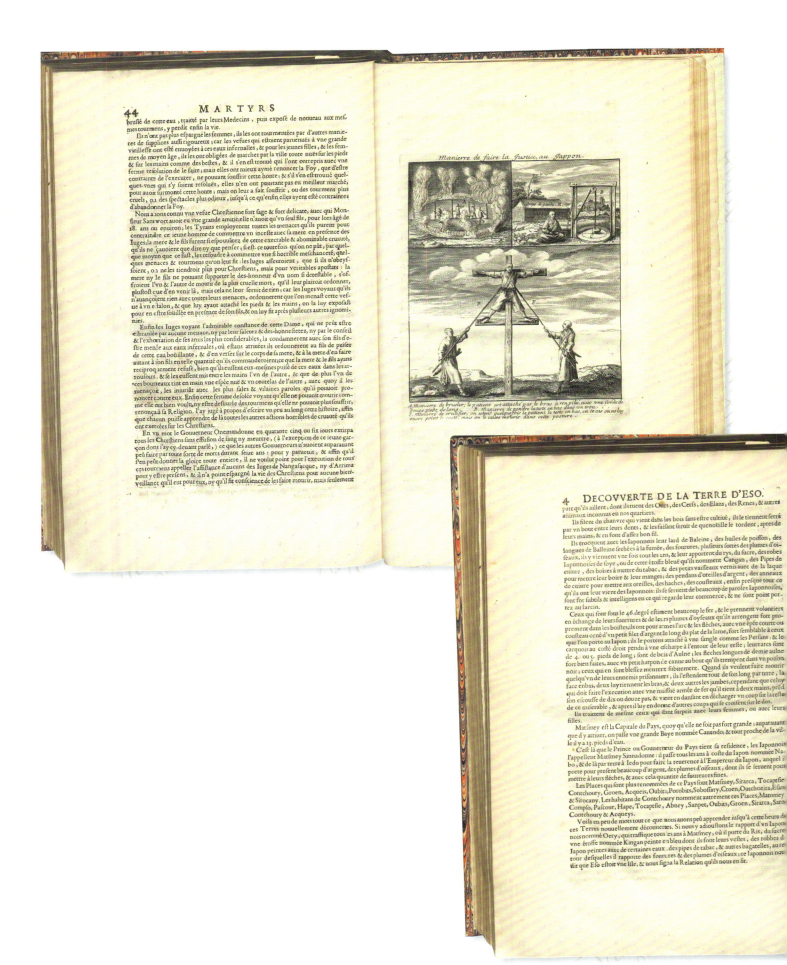

Manierre de faire la Iuſtice, au Iappon.

A Manierre de bruſler; le patiét ſert attaché par le bras à vn pile , auec vne corde de
douze pieds de long . B. Manierre de pendre la teſte en bas dans vn trou . P.
E. Manierre de crucifier; on ardent quelquefois le patient la teſte en bas, en ce cas on ne luy
ouure point le coſté , mais on le laiſſe mourir dans cette poſture .

part qu'ils aillent , dont ils tuent des Ours , des Cerfs , des Elans , des Renes , & autres
animaux inconnus en nos quartiers.

Ils filent du chanvre qui vient dans les bois ſans eſtre cultiué , ils le tiennent ſerré
par vn bout entre leurs dents , & les faiſant ſeruir de quenotille le tordent , apres
leurs mains , & en font d'aſſez bon fil.

Ils troquent auec les Iapponois leur lard de Baleine , des huiles de poiſſon , des
langues de Balleine ſechées à la fumée, des fourures , pluſieurs ſortes des plumes d'oiſeaux, ils y viennent vne fois tous les ans, & leur apportent du rys, du ſucre, des robes
Iapponoiſes de ſoye , ou de cette eſtoffe bleuë qu'ils nomment Cangan , des Pipes de
cuiure , des boites à mettre du tabac , & des petits vaiſſeaux vernis auec de la laque
pour mettre leur boire & leur manger; des pendans d'oreilles d'argent , des anneaux
de cuiure pour mettre aux oreilles , des haches , des couſteaux , enfin preſque tout ce
qu'ils ont leur vient des Iapponois: ils ſe ſeruent de beaucoup de paroles Iaponnoiſes,
ſont fort ſubtils & intelligens en ce qui regarde leur commerce , & ne ſont point por-
tez au larcin.

Ceux qui ſont ſous le 46.degré eſtiment beaucoup le fer , & le prennent volontiers
en échange de leurs fourrures & de leurs plumes d'oyſeaux qu'ils arrengent fort pro-
prement dans les boiſtes;ils ont pour armes l'arc & les fleſches , auec vne eſpée courte ou
couſteau orné d'vn petit filet d'argent le long du plat de la lame , fort ſemblable à ceux
que l'on porte au Iapon ; ils le portent attaché à vne ſangle comme les Perſans , & le
carquois au coſté droit pendu à vne eſcharpe à l'entour de leur reſte ; leurs arcs ſont
de 4. ou 5. pieds de long , ſont de bois d'Aulne ; les fleſches longues de demie aulne
fort bien faites , auec vn petit harpon ce canne au bout qu'ils trempent dans vn poiſon
noir ; ceux qui en ſont bleſſez meurent ſubitement. Quand ils veulent faire mourir
quelqu'vn de leurs ennemis priſonniers , ils l'eſtendent tout de ſon long par terre , la
face enbas , deux luy tiennent les bras,& deux autres les jambes, cependant que celuy
qui doit faire l'execution auec vn maſſue armée de fer qu'il tient à deux mains , prẽd
ſon eſcouſſe de dix ou douze pas , & vient en danſant en décharger vn coup ſur la teſte
de ce miſerable , & apres luy en donne d'autres coups qui ſe croiſent ſur le dos.

Ils traittent de meſme ceux qui ſont ſurpris auec leurs femmes , ou auec leurs
filles.

Matſmey eſt la Capitale du Pays , quoy qu'elle ne ſoit pas fort grande ; auparauant
que d'y arriuer, on paſſe vne grande Baye nommée Cauundo, & tout proche de la ville il y a 30. pieds d'eau.

C'eſt là que le Prince ou Gouuerneur du Pays tient ſa reſidence , les Iapponois
l'appellent Matſmey Sinnadonne : il paſſe tous les ans à coſte du Iapon nommée Na-
bo , & de là par terre à Iedo pour faire la reuerence à l'Empereur du Iapon , auquel il
porte pour preſent beaucoup d'argent, des plumes d'oiſeaux, dont ils ſe ſeruent pour
mettre à leurs fleſches , & auec cela quantité de foureures fines.

Les Places qui ſont plus renommées de ce Pays ſont Matſmey, Sirarca, Tocapſie,
Contchoury, Groen, Acqueis, Oubit, Porobits, Sobioſſary, Croen, Outchoeira, Eſan
& Sirocany. Les habitans de Contchoury nomment autrement ces Places, Matoniey,
Compſo, Paſcour, Hape, Tocapſie, Abney, Sanpet, Oubits, Groen, Sirarca, Saro,
Contchoury & Acqueys.

Voila en peu de mots tout ce que nous auons peû apprendre juſqu'à cette heure de
ces Terres nouuellement découuertes. Si nous y adiouſtons le rapport d'vn Iaponnois nommé Oery , qui traffique tous les ans à Matſmey , où il porte du Ris , du ſucre,
vne eſtoffe nommée Kingan peinte en bleu dont ils font leurs veſtes , des robbes de
Iapon peintes auec de certaines eaux , des pipes de tabac , & autres bagatelles , au re-
tour deſquelles il rapporte des fourures & des plumes d'oiſeaux ce Iaponnois nous
dit que Eſo eſtoit vne iſle , & nous ſigna la Relation qu'il nous en fit.

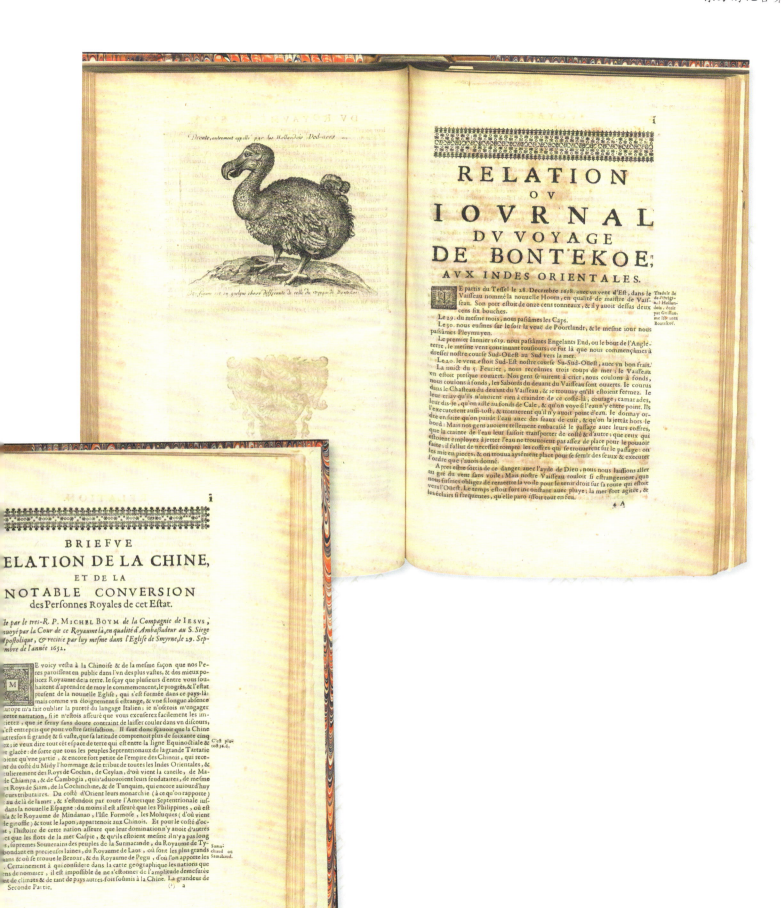

Dronte, autrement appellé par les Hollandois Ded-aers

Cette figure est en quelque chose differente de celle du voyage de Bontekoe.

RELATION OV IOVRNAL DV VOYAGE DE BONTEKOE, AVX INDES ORIENTALES.

Traduit de l'Original Hollandois, écrit par Guillaume Isbrantz Bontekoe.

IE partis du Teffel le 28. Decembre 1618. auec vn vent d'Eft, dans le Vaiffeau nommé la nouuelle Hoorn, en qualité de maiftre de Vaiffeau. Son port eftoit de onze cens tonneaux, & il y auoit deffus deux cens fix bouches.

Le 29. du mefme mois, nous paffames les Caps.

Le 30. nous eufmes fur le foir la veuë de Poortlande, & le mefme iour nous paffames Pleymuyen.

Le premier Ianuier 1619. nous paffames Engelants End, ou le bout de l'Angleterre, le mefme vent continuant toufiours, ce fut là que nous commençames à dreffer noftre courfe Sud-Oüeft au Sud vers la mer.

Le 20. le vent eftoit Sud-Eft noftre courfe Su-Sud-Oüeft, auec vn bon frais.

La nuict du 5. Feurier, nous receumes trois coups de mer; le Vaiffeau en eftoit prefque couuert. Nos gens fe mirent à crier, nous coulons à fonds, nous coulons à fonds, les Sabords du deuant du Vaiffeau font ouuerts. Ie courus dans le Chafteau du deuant du Vaiffeau, & ie trouuay qu'ils eftoient fermez. Ie leur criay qu'ils n'auoient rien à craindre de ce cofté-là, courage; camarades, leur dis-je, qu'on aille au fonds de Cale, & qu'on voye s'il n'y entre point. Ils l'executent auffi-toft, & trouuerent qu'il n'y auoit point d'eau. Ie donnay ordre en fuite qu'on puifat l'eau auec des feaux de cuir, & qu'on la iettaft hors du bord: Mais nos gens auoient tellement embaraffé le paffage auec leurs coffres, que la crainte de l'eau leur faifoit tranfporter de cofté & d'autre; que ceux qui eftoient employez à ietter l'eau ne trouuoient pas affez de place pour le pouuoir faire; il fallut de neceffité rompre les coffres qui fe trouuerent fur le paffage: on les mit en pieces, & on trouua ayfément place pour fe feruir des feaux & executer l'ordre que i'auois donné.

Apres eftre fortis de ce danger auec l'ayde de Dieu, nous nous laiffions aller au gré du vent fans voile; Mais noftre Vaiffeau rouloit fi eftrangement, que nous fufmes obligez de remettre la voile pour le tenir droit fur fa route qui eftoit vers l'Oüeft. Le temps eftoit fort inconftant auec pluye; la mer fort agitée, & les éclairs fi frequentes, qu'elle paroiffoit tout en feu.

4 A

BRIEFVE RELATION DE LA CHINE, ET DE LA NOTABLE CONVERSION des Personnes Royales de cet Estat.

...te par le tres-R. P. MICHEL BOYM de la Compagnie de IESVS, ...nuoyé par la Cour de ce Royaume là, en qualité d'Ambaffadeur au S. Siege ...poftolique, & recitée par luy mefme dans l'Eglife de Smyrne, le 29. Septembre de l'année 1652.

IE voicy veftu à la Chinoife & de la mefme façon que nos Peres paroiffent en public dans l'vn des plus vaftes, & des mieux policez Royaume de la terre. Ie fçay que plufieurs d'entre vous fouhaitent d'apprendre de moy le commencement, le progrés, & l'eftat prefent de la nouuelle Eglife, qui s'eft formée dans ce pays-là; mais comme vn éloignement fi eftrange, & vne fi longue abfence ...urope m'a fait oublier la pureté du langage Italien; ie n'oferois m'engager ...cette narration, fi ie n'eftois affuré que vous excuferez facilement les im...riétez; que ie feray fans doute contraint de laiffer couler dans vn difcours, ...'eft entrepris que pour voftre fatisfaction. Il faut donc fçauoir que la Chine ...utresfois fi grande & fi vafte, que la latitude comprenoit plus de foixante cinq ...ez; ie veux dire tout cét efpace de terre qui eft entre la ligne Equinoctiale & ...er glacée: de forte que tous les peuples Septentrionaux de la grande Tartarie ...oient qu'vne partie, & encore fort petite de l'empire des Chinois, qui rece...nt du cofté du Midy l'hommage & le tribut de toutes les Indes Orientales, & ...ticulierement des Roys de Cochin, de Ceylan, d'où vient la canelle, de Ma...de Chiampa, & de Cambogia, qui s'adouoient leurs feudataires, de mefme ...s Roys de Siam, de la Cochinchine, & de Tunquim, qui encore auiourd'huy ...leurs tributaires. Du cofté d'Orient leur monarchie (à ce qu'on rapporte) ...au delà de la mer, & s'eftendoit par toute l'Amerique Septentrionale iuf...dans la nouuelle Efpagne: du moins il eft affuré que les Philippines, où eft ...la & le Royaume de Mindanao, l'Ifle Formofe, les Moluques (d'où vient ...de giroffle) & tout le Iapon, appartenoit aux Chinois. Et pour le cofté d'oc...at, l'hiftoire de cette nation affure que leur domination n'auoit d'autres ...es que les flots de la mer Cafpie, & qu'ils eftoient mefme il n'y a pas long ...s, fupremes Souuerains des peuples de la Surmacande, du Royaume de Ty...bondant en precieufes laines, du Royaume de Laos, où font les plus grands ...ans & où fe trouue le Bezoar, & du Royaume de Pegu, d'où l'on apporte les ...Certainement à qui confidere dans la carte geographique les nations que ...ens de nommer, il eft impoffible de ne s'eftonner de l'amplitude demefurée ...nt de climats & de tant de pays autresfois foûmis à la Chine. La grandeur de

Seconde Partie.

罗氏编号 234

《中国近事》2 卷

（Novissima sinica historiam nostri temporis illustratura. Secunda editio. Accessione partis posterioris aucta. 1−2）

编　　者：［德］莱布尼茨（Gottfried Wilhelm Leibniz, 1646−1716）

出　　版：出版地不详（汉诺威或莱比锡），出版社不详，1699 年

载体形态：8 开，XXXVIII+176 页；XII+128 页 + 卷首 2 幅康熙皇帝肖像

装　　订：小牛皮面，书脊书肋烫金，有标签，封面上有虫蛀小孔

版　　本：增订再版，初版于 1697 年问世。

内　　容：

　　本书的序言部分是莱布尼茨有关中国的最主要著述，这段文字被视为他对中国礼仪之争、新教入中国之必要性以及俄国在中国与欧洲之间充当调停人的最权威言论。本书中莱布尼茨发表了以下 7 份资料：

　　1. 一位在北京的葡萄牙传教士于 1692 年撰写的有关康熙皇帝所颁赦令的介绍（卷 1，第 1−149 页）；

　　2. 在康熙皇帝关照下南怀仁神甫在中国发表的有关天文学的著作（《欧洲天文学史》）的片段（卷 1，第 149−155 页）；

　　3. 闵明我神甫致莱布尼茨的信，寄自果阿，1693 年 12 月 6 日（卷 1，第 156−158 页）；

　　4. 比利时安多神甫致莱布尼茨的信，寄自北京，1695 年 11 月 12 日（卷 1，第 159−163 页）；

　　5. 布兰特（Adam Brandt）《莫斯科使团于 1693、1694、1695 年在中国的旅行记事》；

　　6. 负责与莫斯科人讲和的张诚神甫 1689 年 9 月 2 日和 3 日就中俄冲突所写的信（关于中俄《尼布楚条约》的报告）的片段；

　　7. 白晋神甫献给法皇路易十四的《康熙皇帝传》的拉丁文缩略版（卷 2，VII+128 页 + 康熙皇帝肖像）。

　　本书是当时的欧洲思想和文化界主流对东方文化和中国文化的系统介绍，是欧洲本土学者编辑出版的最早汉学研究论文集。书中莱布尼茨预见了开辟一条经俄罗斯道往中国的陆路交通的可能性；对欧洲国家和中国所签订的第一份外交条约向欧洲人做了系统报道；再版中加收的《康熙皇帝传》是当时唯一一本专门向欧洲介绍康熙皇帝的著作。

CAM-HY
*Empereur de la Chine
et de la Tartarie Orientale,
Agé de 91 an et peint alagé
de 32.*

NOVISSIMA
SINICA

HISTORIAM NOSTRI TEM-
PORIS ILLUSTRATURA

In quibus

DE CHRISTIANISMO

Publica nunc primum autorita-
te propagato missa in Europam rela-
tio exhibetur, deqve favore scientiarum Europæarum ac
moribus gentis & ipsius præsertim Monarchæ, tum & de
bello Sinensium cum Moscis ac pace constituta,
multa hactenus ignota explicantur.

Edente G. G. Leibniz

Indicem dabit pagina versa.
Secunda Editio.
Accessione partis posterioris aucta.

ANNO M DC XCIX.

罗氏编号 **361**

《数学概要》2 卷

（Synopsis mathematica complectens varios tractatus quos hujus scientiae tyronibus et missionis sinicae candidatis breviter et clare concinnavit. 1－2）

作　　者：［比］安多（Antoine Thomas，字平施，1644－1709）

出　　版：杜埃，德尔贝（Carolum Ludovicum Derbaix），1729 年

载体形态：8 开，IV+498 页；IV+550 页 +38 幅折叠图版

装　　订：小牛皮面，书脊书肋烫金

版　　本：再版，初版于 1685 年问世。

内　　容：

　　比利时耶稣会士安多 1682 年抵达澳门，1685 年应召前往北京，协助南怀仁在钦天监工作，并成为康熙皇帝的宫廷教师。本书全名为《数学概要：由这门科学的不同论著组成，简明、清晰地为初学者和到中国传教候选人而写》，凡 2 册，第 1 册为算术、初等几何、实用几何、球体、地理、水力学、音乐等八章，第 2 册为光学、静力学、钟表、球面三角、星盘、历法、天文学等七章。据学者考证，康熙皇帝的御用数学教科书《算法纂要总纲》即是以本书为底本编撰而成。本书 1685 年之初版并不算罕见，但 1729 年之再版却堪称孤本，弥足珍贵。

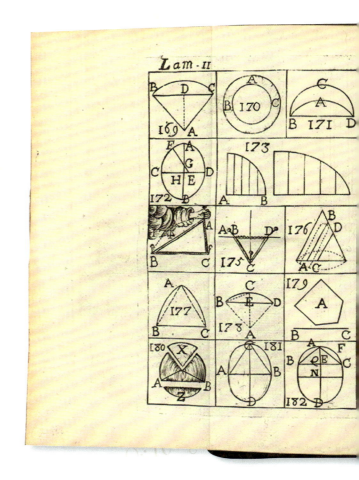

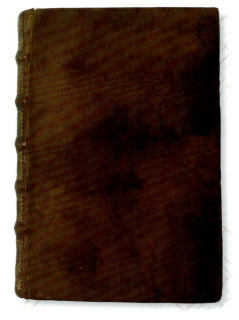

53

TRACTATUS SECUNDUS
DE GEOMETRIA ELEMENTARI.

Tractatus hic geometricus præcipuas Euclidis demonstra-
tiones complectitur, pro faciliori methodo in certum
ordinem redactas: quia tamen à Mathematicis or-
dine Euclidis citari solent, idcircò numerus libri vel
propositionis illius authoris adscriptus est.

SECTIO PRIMA.
De lineis, Angulis, Triangulis, &
Parallelogrammis.

ARTICULUS PRIMUS.
Principia libri primi Euclidis.

DEFINITIONES.

1. PUnctum est quod partibus caret.
2. Linea est longitudo sine latitudine.
3. Ejus extrema sunt puncta duo.
4. Linea recta est ab uno puncto ad alterum brevissima extensio.

D iij

SYNOPSIS
MATHEMATICA
COMPLECTENS VARIOS TRACTATUS
QUOS HUJUS SCIENTIÆ TYRONIBUS
ET MISSIONIS SINICÆ
CANDIDATIS
BREVITER ET CLARE CONCINNAVIT
P. ANTONIUS THOMAS
è Societate JESU.

PARS PRIMA

DUACI;
Apud CAROLUM-LUDOVICUM DERBAIX,
Biblio-Typographum sub signo Salamandræ. 1729

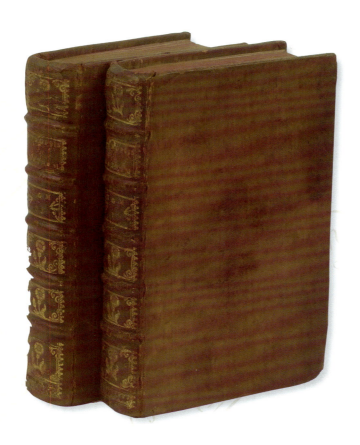

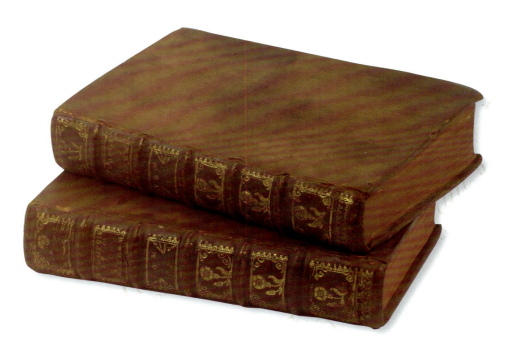

罗氏编号 364

《数学研究》3 卷
（Obeservations mathématiques，astronomiques，géographiques，chronologiques et physiques，tirées des anciens livres chinois，ou faites nouvellement aux Indes et à la Chine，par les pères de la Compagnie de Jésus. 1–3）

编 撰 者：［法］宋君荣（Antoine Gaubil，字奇英，1689–1759）、［德］戴进贤（Ignaz Kögler，字嘉宾，1680–1746）及［清］图理琛（字瑶圃，号睡心主人，1667–1740）等撰；［法］苏西埃（Etienne Souciet，1671–1744）编

出 版：巴黎，罗兰书馆（Rollin Libraire），1729–1732 年

载体形态：4 开，合 2 册，VIII+XXXII+296 页；II+XXX+188 页 +IV+374 页 +1 幅地图 +10 幅图版（8 幅折叠）

装 订：花纹牛皮面，书脊肋线烫金

版 本：初版。

内 容：

　　本书中收录了法国耶稣会士宋君荣早期著作（《中国天文学简史》《中国天文学论著》）的主体部分。卷 1 包括耶稣会士宋君荣、戴进贤等在中国所作的有关历算、天文、地理、历史和物理考察的纪录，以及宋君荣译注的清朝官吏图理琛自北京至俄国托博尔及在图尔古茨地区的日记（译自中文），这篇额外的旅行记述，1723 年在北京最早以中文出版，名为《异域录》，本书以西方语言首次收录其删减版。卷 2 收录宋君荣神甫的《中国天文学简史》，卷末有附文 5 篇：1. 论中国纪年法：干支；2.《尚书》上有关日食的记载；3.《诗经》上的记载；4. 在《春秋》上第一次日食的记载；5. 公元 31 年的日食。著作所引据的都是从中国最可靠的经典著作中摘录而来。卷 3 收录宋君荣神甫的《中国天文学论著》，论著分为前后两部分，前一部分为中国建朝以后到公元前 206 年汉高祖时代的天文学，后一部分为自汉朝起至 15 世纪止。19 世纪法国著名汉学家雷慕沙对本书的评语是："苏西埃的这部巨型汇编，包罗了科学上最精湛的资料，但编排比较杂乱，作为参考，难于按图索骥；有些札记无下文，所加注释博而不专，成为无秩序、无归类、无索引、无图表的资料堆积。"

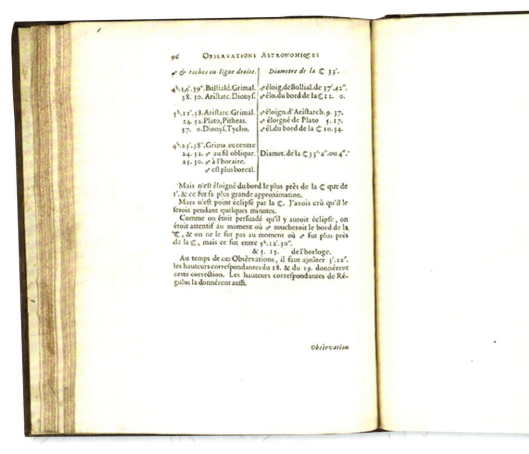

♂ & taches en ligne droite.	Diametre de la ☾ 35′.
4ʰ.16′.39″. Bulliald. Grimal.	♂ éloig. de Bulliald. de 37′.42″.
38. 30. Aristarc. Dionyſ.	♂ élo. du bord de la ☾ 12. 0.
5ʰ.11′.38. Aristarc. Grimal.	♂ éloign. d'Aristarch. 9. 37.
24. 52. Plato, Pitheas.	♂ éloigné de Plato 5. 17.
57. 0. Dionyſ. Tycho.	♂ él. du bord de la ☾ 10.34.
4ʰ.25′.38″. Grima au centre	
24. 52. ♂ au fil oblique.	Diamet. de la ☾ 35′.2″. ou 4″.
25. 30. ♂ à l'horaire.	
♂ est plus boreal.	

Mais n'est éloigné du bord le plus près de la ☾ que de 1′. & ce fut fa plus grande approximation.

Mars n'est point éclipse par la ☾. J'avois crû qu'il le feroit pendant quelques minutes.

Comme on étoit perſuadé qu'il y auroit éclipſe, on étoit attentif au moment où ♂ toucheroit le bord de la ☾, & on ne le fut pas au moment où ♂ fut plus près de la ☾, mais ce fut entre 5ʰ.12′.30″.

       & 5. 15.　de l'horloge.

Au temps de ces Obſervations, il faut ajoûter 3′.11″. les hauteurs correspondantes du 18. & du 19. donnérent cette correction. Les hauteurs correſpondantes de Régulus la donnérent auſſi.

Obſervation

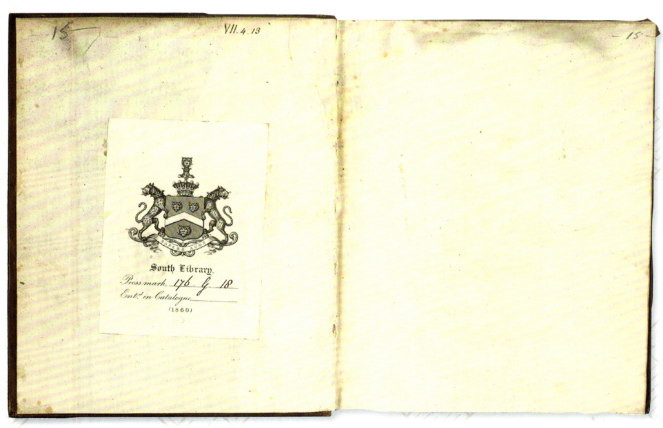

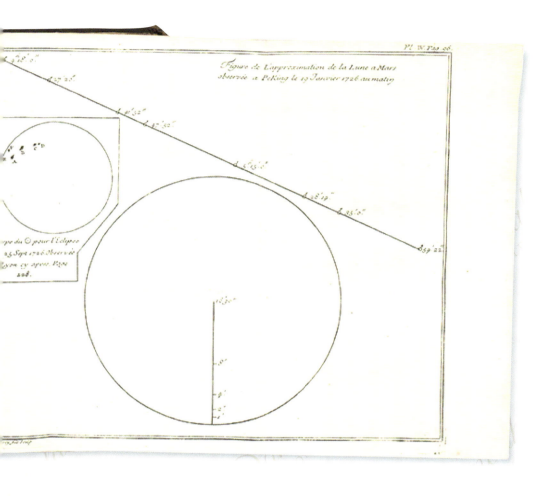

罗氏编号 394

《中华帝国全志》4 卷

(Description géographique, historique, chronologique, politique, et physique de l'empire de la Chine et de la Tartarie chinoise. 1－4)

编　者：［法］杜赫德（Jean-Baptiste du Halde, 1674－1743）

出　版：巴黎，勒梅西埃（P. G. Lemercier），1735 年

载体形态：对开，IV+VIII+LII+IV+594 页；IV+IV+728 页；IV+IV+568 页；IV+II+522 页 +53 幅地图 +42 幅平面图（折叠或跨页）+12 幅图版（10 幅跨页，1 幅乐谱，1 幅肖像）

装　订：小牛皮面，书脊肋线烫金，有红色标签

版　本：初版，1736 年法文新版（4 开 4 卷本），英文版（4 开 4 卷本），1741 年英文 3 版，1738－1741 年英语版（对开 2 卷本），1747－1749 年德文版（4 开 4 卷本），1774 年俄文删减版（前 2 卷）。

内　容：

　　本书全名《中华帝国及其鞑靼地区的地理、历史、编年、政治、物理之记述》。作者杜赫德在 1731 年的《耶稣会士书简集》第 20 卷中即已公布了他的这部新书。1735 年一经出版便引起人们注意，被称为"欧洲中国热的圣经"。本书以卫匡国《中国上古史》、李明《中国近事报道》特别是《耶稣会士书简集》为基础，较之前出现的任何一部有关中国的记述都更精致、更权威。本书付梓之前曾由在华生活 32 年之久的耶稣会士龚当信（Cyrile Contancin，字东平，1670－1733）悉心校阅，是一部百科全书式的有关中国的著作，是 18 世纪中叶欧洲人的中国知识总汇。本书是一部里程碑式的作品，它的主要成就不在于信息的准确无误、条理清晰，而在于它所提供的信息具有广泛和具体的特点，向读者全面介绍了中华帝国的神奇，以及中国人在文学、科学、哲学和艺术方面的成就。以今日的眼光看，本书在许多方面存在不足，包括地理、历史等章节，对中国政府及社会结构的描述也不尽如人意。最薄弱的当属插图，它们无一例外地使用了古怪的中国式样。

　　杜赫德编纂本书时参考了 27 位耶稣会士的作品，包括卫匡国、李明、南怀仁、柏应理、安文思、洪若翰（John de Fontaney）、白晋（Joachim Bouvet）、张诚（Jean-Francois Gerbillon）、卫方济（Francis Noël）、刘应（Claude de Visdelou）、雷孝思、马若瑟、殷弘绪（François-Xavier Dentrecolles）、赫苍璧（JulienPlacide Hervien）、龚当信、戈维里（Pierre de Goville）、夏德修（Jean-Armand Nyel）、巴多明（Dominique Parrenin）、杜德美（Pierre Jartoux）、汤尚贤（Pierre-Vincent de Tartre）、冯秉正、郭中传（Jean-Alexis de Gollet）、彭加德（Claude Jacquemin）、卜文气（Louis Porquet）、沙守信（Émeric de Chavagnac）、宋君荣和杨嘉禄（Charles-Jean Baptiste Jacques）。

　　对中国作品的选译主要分布在本书的第 1－3 卷。第 1 卷是对中国的总体介绍，从关于中华帝国的最一般知识开始，介绍中国的地理、方位，然后分别介绍中国内部各省的基本情况，还介绍了中国历史的一般线索，从

夏到清，将历代王朝一一罗列出来。此外还包含了 1693 年白晋作为康熙皇帝官方使节从北京到广州再到欧洲的部分游记内容。本卷中选译的中国作品包括朱熹和司马光的《通鉴纲目》和袁黄的《历史纲鉴》。第 2 卷介绍了中国的社会政治，从皇帝、皇宫、皇权到海关、监狱、人口、商业、物产到生活中的礼仪，包括《中国的漆器》《中国的瓷器》《中国的语言》《中国的纸、墨、笔、印刷术及中国书籍的装帧》等文章，选译的中国作品包括徐光启的《农政全书》、朱熹的《朱子全书》和《书经》《诗经》《春秋》《礼记》《大学》《中庸》《论语》《孟子》《孝经》等中国经典。第 3 卷介绍了中国的学术文化，从宗教、哲学、逻辑到数学、音乐、文学、戏剧和医学、医药，马若瑟翻译的元代纪君祥创作的杂剧《赵氏孤儿》法文全译本便收录在此卷中（第 339–378 页），另外还收录了关于中医的几篇译作，包括《长生》、王叔和的《脉经》、李时珍的《本草纲目》节译。本卷中选译的中国作品包括凌濛初、冯梦龙的《今古奇观》等。第 4 卷介绍中国与其属国、中国周边的国家及其与中国的关系、人文地理等，向西方揭示了中华文明的影响力和在亚洲的地位。内容包括《南怀仁神甫随中国皇帝至东部鞑靼游记》《法国耶稣会士张诚神甫鞑靼游记》，后者描述了张诚的 9 次鞑靼之旅。中俄《尼布楚条约》订立过程中的斡旋沟通，随着张诚日记在本卷中的刊行而传遍欧洲。

本书中的地图、平面图等在 1735 年出版过单行本，名为《中国总图》，1785 年法国耶稣会士格鲁贤又用原书铜板印行了他的《中国坤舆总图》，唐维尔（Jean-Baptiste Bourguignon d'Anville, 1697–1782）的《中国新图》中有 42 张重刻地图。

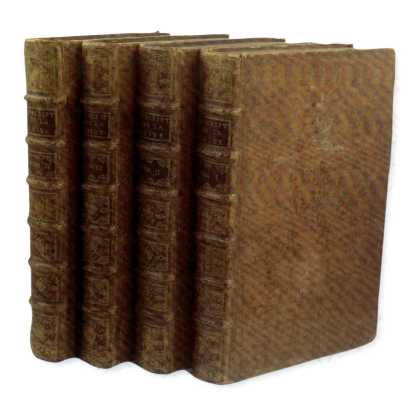

ACTEURS.

TOU NGAN COU, Premier Ministre de la Guerre.

TCHAO TUN, Ministre d'Etat, Personnage muet.

TCHAO SO, Fils de TCHAO TUN, & Gendre du Roy.

La Fille du Roy, Femme de TCHAO SO.

TCHING YNG, Médecin.

HAN KOUE', Mandarin d'Armes.

CONG LUN, ancien Ministre, retiré à la Campagne.

TCHING POEI, jeune Seigneur, qui passe pour le fils du Médecin, qui est adopté par TOU NGAN COU.

OUEI FONG, Grand Officier du Roy.

Il y a huit Personnages , quoiqu'il n'y ait que cinq Comédiens.

TCHAO CHI COU ELL'

TCHAO CHI COU ELL,
OU
LE PETIT ORPHELIN
DE LA MAISON DE TCHAO.
TRAGEDIE CHINOISE.

SIÉ TSEE,
OU PROLOGUE.

SCENE PREMIERE.
TOU NGAN COU, seul.

L'HOMME ne songe point à faire du mal au Tigre , mais le Tigre ne pense qu'à faire du mal à l'Homme. Si on ne se contente à tems , on s'en repent. Je suis *Tou ngan cou* , premier Ministre de la *Guerre* dans le Royaume de *Tse*. Le Roy *Ling cong* mon Maître avoit deux hommes, ausquels il se fioit sans reserve ; l'un pour gouverner le Peuple, c'est *Tchao tun* ; l'autre pour gouverner l'Armée, c'est moi ; nos Charges nous ont rendus ennemis : j'ai toûjours eu envie de perdre *Tchao* , mais je ne pouvois en venir à bout. *Tchao so* fils de *Tun* avoit épousé la fille du Roy, j'avois donné ordre à un assassin de prendre un poignard , d'escalader la muraille du Palais de *Tchao tun* , & de le tuer. Ce malheureux en voulant exécuter mes ordres , se brisa la tête contre un arbre , & se tua. Un jour *Tchao tun* sortit pour aller animer les Laboureurs au travail, il trouva sous un

Tome III. Ssss

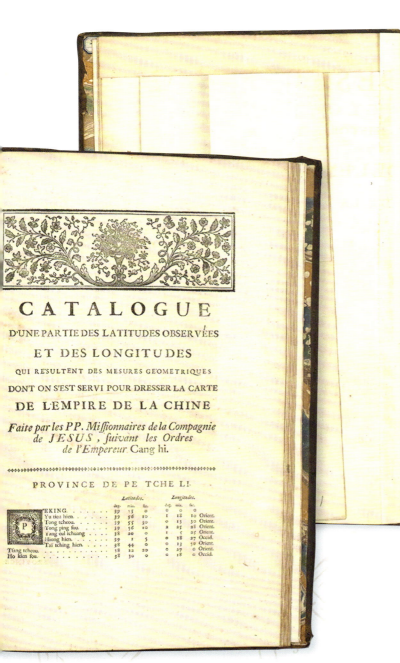

CATALOGUE

D'UNE PARTIE DES LATITUDES OBSERVÉES

ET DES LONGITUDES

QUI RÉSULTENT DES MESURES GÉOMETRIQUES

DONT ON S'EST SERVI POUR DRESSER LA CARTE

DE L'EMPIRE DE LA CHINE

Faite par les PP. Missionnaires de la Compagnie de JESUS, suivant les Ordres de l'Empereur Cang hi.

PROVINCE DE PE TCHE LI.

DESCRIPTION

GEOGRAPHIQUE

HISTORIQUE, CHRONOLOGIQUE,

POLITIQUE, ET PHYSIQUE

DE L'EMPIRE DE LA CHINE

ET

DE LA TARTARIE CHINOISE,

ENRICHIE DES CARTES GENERALES ET PARTICULIERES de ces Pays, de la Carte générale & des Cartes particulieres du Thibet, & de la Corée, & ornée d'un grand nombre de Figures & de Vignettes gravées en Taille-douce.

Par le P. J. B. DU HALDE, de la Compagnie de JESUS.

TOME PREMIER.

A PARIS,

Chez P. G. LE MERCIER, Imprimeur-Libraire, rue Saint Jacques, au Livre d'Or.

M. DCC. XXXV.

AVEC APPROBATION ET PRIVILEGE DU ROY.

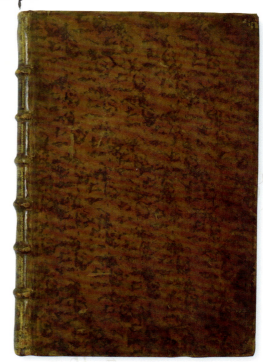

Cortège d'un Viceroy toutes les fois qu'il sort de son Palais.

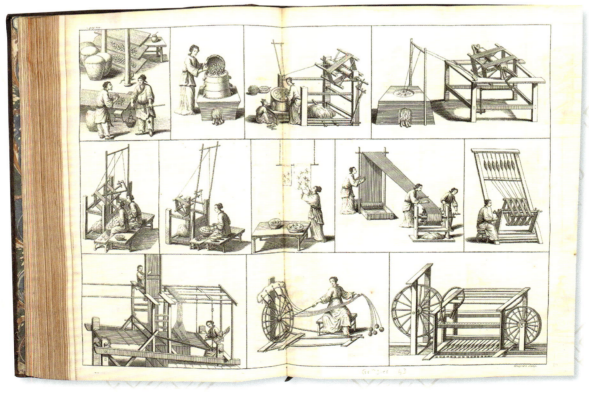

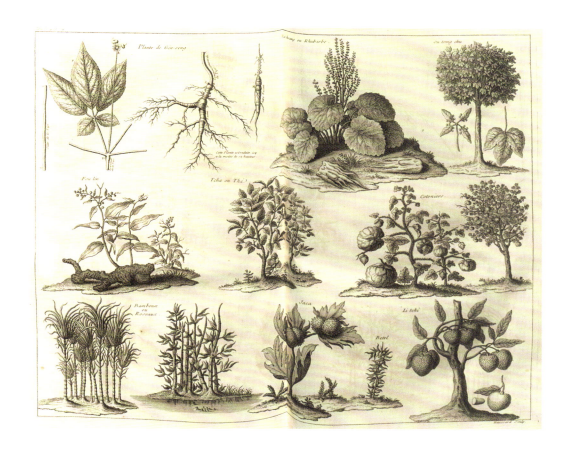

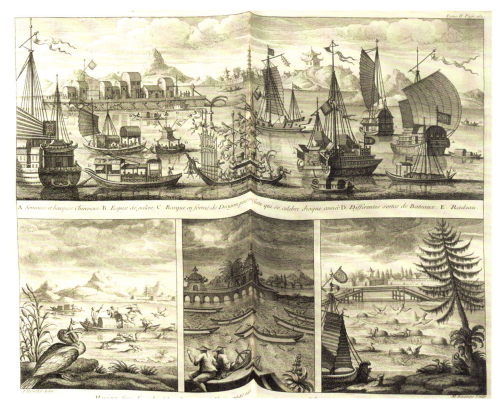

罗氏编号 486

《北狄通史》4 卷

（ Histoire générale des Huns, des Turcs, des Mogols, et des autres Tartares occidentaux, & c. Avant et depuis Jésus-Christ jusqu'à present; precede d'une introduction contenant des tables chronol. & historiques des princes qui ont regné dans l'Aise. Ouvrage tiré des livres chinois, & des manuscrits orientaux de la Bibliothèque du roi. 1: 1–2–4 ）

作　者：［法］德金（Joesph de Guignes, 1721–1800）

出　版：巴黎，德桑和莎杨（Desaint & Saillant），1756–1758 年

载体形态：4 开，CXVIII+472 页；8+XCVI+522 页；VIII+272+292 页；VIII+544 页；VIII+520 页

装　订：小牛皮面，书脊肋线烫金，有标签

版　本：初版。1824 年俄国 Osip Ivanovich Senkovskij 出版单行本附录，1768–1771 年德文版。

内　容：

　　本书作者德金是法国 18 世纪著名的东方学家、汉学家，师从当时的中文权威傅尔蒙（Étienne Fourmont, 1683–1745），1741 年成为法王路易十五的汉语翻译，1745 年接替傅尔蒙担任国王图书馆的东方语言翻译，1754 年成为法兰西学院院士。本书是德金最具影响力的一部作品，全名为《匈奴、突厥、蒙古及其他西部鞑靼通史》。这部有关内陆欧亚史的著作首次利用回教及汉语文献对蒙古人做了科学研究，首次提出入侵欧洲的匈人部落就是中国古代匈奴的后裔。这一观点在 18 世纪英国著名历史学家爱德华·吉本（Edward Gibbon）的名著《罗马帝国衰亡史》中被采纳。

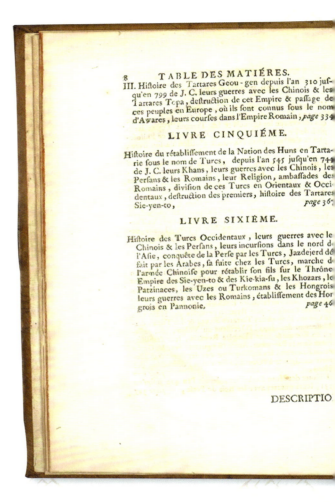

DESCRIPTION
DE LA GRANDE TARTARIE.

 A Grande Tartarie comprend à présent tous les vaftes pays qui font renfermés entre le fleuve Etel ou Volga & la mer orientale. Au midi elle eft bornée par la Chine, par le Tibet, & par le fleuve Gihon ; au nord elle confine, dans toute fon étendue, à la Siberie. Anciennement elle portoit le nom de Scythie, & elle avoit à peu près les mêmes limites, finon que, du côté du nord, les anciens Géographes ne lui en affignoient aucunes, parce que tous les pays qui compofent aujourd'hui la Siberie leur étoient inconnus.

Ptolémée divife la Scythie en deux grandes parties ; la premiere qu'il appelle Scythie en deçà de l'Imaüs ; & la feconde, Scythie au-delà de l'Imaüs. L'une étoit terminée, du côté du couchant par la Sarmatie Afiatique & par le Rha ou Volga ; au nord par des pays inconnus, qui, autant que l'on peut en juger, ne s'étendent pas jufqu'à Tobolsk en Siberie ; au midi par les Saces & les peuples du Maouarennahar ou de la Tranfoxiane, & enfin à l'orient par le mont Imaüs. L'autre, adoffée du côté du couchant à cette même montagne & au pays des Saces, s'étendoit vers le nord jufques dans des contrées dont on n'avoit alors aucune connoiffance. A l'orient elle étoit terminée par la

Tome I. a

HISTOIRE
GÉNÉRALE
DES HUNS,
DES TURCS, DES MOGOLS,
ET DES AUTRES
TARTARES OCCIDENTAUX, &c.
AVANT ET DEPUIS JESUS-CHRIST JUSQU'A PRESENT;

Précédée d'une INTRODUCTION contenant des TABLES Chronol. & Hiftoriques des Princes qui ont regné dans l'Afie.

OUVRAGE TIRÉ DES LIVRES CHINOIS,
& des Manufcrits Orientaux de la Bibliotheque du Roi.

Par M. DEGUIGNES, de l'Académie Royale des Infcriptions & Belles-Lettres, Cenfeur Royal, Interprête du Roi pour les Langues Orientales, & Membre de la Société Royale de Londres.

SUITE DES MÉMOIRES DE L'ACADÉMIE ROYALE
DES INSCRIPTIONS ET BELLES-LETTRES.

TOME PREMIER, PARTIE PREMIERE.

A PARIS,
Chez DESAINT & SAILLANT, rue S. Jean-de-Beauvais.

M. DCC. LVI.
Avec Approbation & Privilege du Roi.

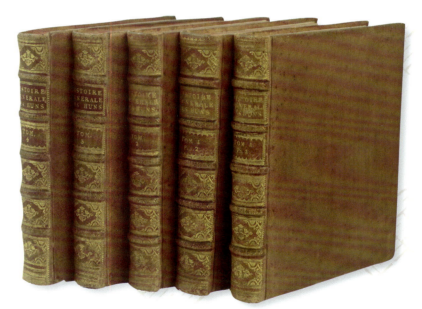

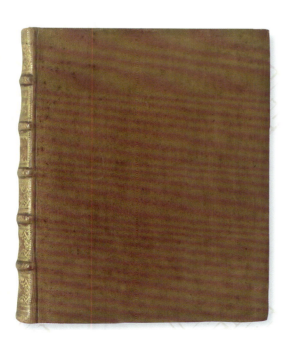

罗氏编号 497&498

《中国民用及装饰建筑》

（Chinese architecture, civil and ornamental. Being a large collection of the most elegant and useful designs of plans and elevations, & c. from the imperial retreat to the smallest ornamental building in China. Likewise their marine subjects）

《中国建筑》

（Chinese architecture. Part the second. Being a large collection of designs of their paling of different kinds, lattice work, & c.）

作　　者：［英］德克尔（Paul Decker，生卒年不详）
出　　版：伦敦，自印，1759 年
载体形态：长 4 开（23.5×29.2 mm），题名页 +24 幅图版；题名页 +12 幅图版
装　　订：小牛皮面配大理石花纹纸质书板；两书合册
来　　源：有题签 Thomas Brown 及其日期 1764 年
版　　本：英文初版。

内　　容：

　　如果建筑师保罗·德克尔真的确有其人，那么这部书则是他有记载的唯一著作。《中国民用及装饰建筑》几乎不能算是他本人的作品，因为在 24 幅号称是作者在中国绘制的"真正设计"中，有 21 幅源于 1754 年乔治·爱德华和马什·达利的《中国设计新书》中的铜版画，只是增加了一些风景背景及细小的变化。毋庸置疑的是，英国学者威廉·钱伯斯（William Chambers）1757 年出版的《中国建筑的设计》促使本书作者挑选了部分爱德华和达利的装饰图样重新印刷，配上平面图、比例尺以及风景设置等内容作为实用建筑模型。本书在 19 世纪法国著名汉学家高迪爱的《西人汉学书目》中未有收录。

CHINESE ARCHITECTURE,

Thomas Civil and Ornamental. *Brown* 1764

Being a Large

COLLECTION

OF THE

Most Elegant and Useful Designs of PLANS and ELEVATIONS, &c.

FROM THE

Imperial Retreat to the smallest *Ornamental Building* in *CHINA.*

Likewise their

MARINE SUBJECTS.

The Whole to adorn Gardens, Parks, Forests, Woods, Canals, &c.

Consisting of great Variety, among which are the following, viz.

Royal Garden Seats, Heads and Terminations for Canals, Alcoves, Banqueting Houses, Temples both open and close, adapted for Canals and other Ways, Bridges, Summer-Houses, Repositories, Umbrello'd Seats, cool Retreats, the Summer Dwelling of a Chief Bonza or Priest, Honorary Pagodas, Japaneze and Imperial Barges of CHINA.

ALSO

Those for the Emperor's Women, and principal Officers attending on the Emperor, Pleasure Boats &c.

To which are added,

CHINESE FLOWERS, LANDSCAPES, FIGURES, ORNAMENTS, &C.

The Whole neatly engraved on Twenty-Four Copper-Plates, from real Designs drawn in China, Adapted to this Climate, by

P. DECKER, Architect

Printed for the AUTHOR, and Sold by Henry Parker and Elizabeth Bakewell, opposite Birchin-lane and H. Piers and Partner, at the Bible and Crown

MDCCLIX

Royal Garden Seat.

罗氏编号 **514**

《好逑传》4 卷

（Hau-kiou choaan，or the pleasing history. A translation from the Chinese language. To which are added，I. The argument or story of a Chinese play，II. A collection of Chinese proverbs，and III. Fragments of Chinese poetry ... With notes.1－4）

作　　者：［英］魏金森（James Wilkinson，生卒年不详）译，　［英］珀西（Thomas Percy，1729－1811）编译

出　　版：伦敦，多兹利（R. and J. Dodsley），1761 年

载体形态：8 开，XXXII+340+II 页；II+292+II 页；II+272+II 页；II+256+XVI+II 页 +4 幅折叠卷首插图

装　　订：小牛皮面，书名上有所有者题字

版　　本：初版，1766 年法文版、德文版，1767 年荷文版，1842 年法文版。

内　　容：

　　《好逑传》讲述了铁中玉与水冰心的爱情故事，是转译成欧洲文字的第一部中国小说。最早的英译者魏金森是一个喜爱文学的商人，懂葡萄牙文，供职于东印度公司。他在中国无意中得到了《好逑传》的葡文译稿，返国后将葡文译成英文。英国学者托马斯·珀西从魏金森亲戚处得到此译稿，作了一些删节，添加了许多有关中国科举、历法、礼仪、官制、建筑、地理、习俗等方面的注释付梓出版，卷 3 末尾附有一些杜赫德及其他传教士采集的中国谚语和格言警句。本书展现的中国日常生活，是传教士们对中国进行的学术性研究中被忽略的。

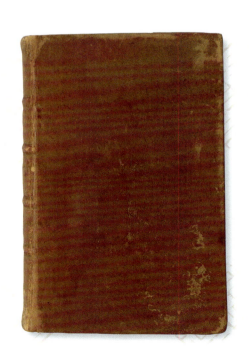

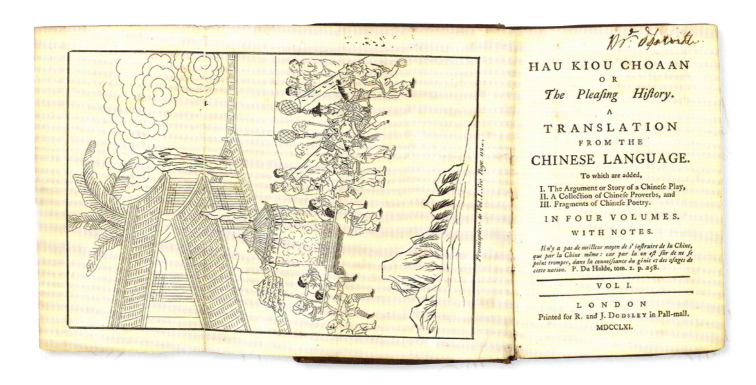

HAU KIOU CHOAAN
OR
The Pleasing History.
A
TRANSLATION
FROM THE
CHINESE LANGUAGE.

To which are added,

I. The Argument or Story of a Chinese Play,
II. A Collection of Chinese Proverbs, and
III. Fragments of Chinese Poetry.

IN FOUR VOLUMES.
WITH NOTES.

*Il n'y a pas de meilleur moyen de s'instruire de la Chine,
que par la Chine même : car par là on est sûr de ne se
point tromper, dans la connoissance du génie et des usages de
cette nation.* P. Du Halde, tom. 2. p. 258.

VOL I.

LONDON
Printed for R. and J. DODSLEY in Pall-mall.
MDCCLXI.

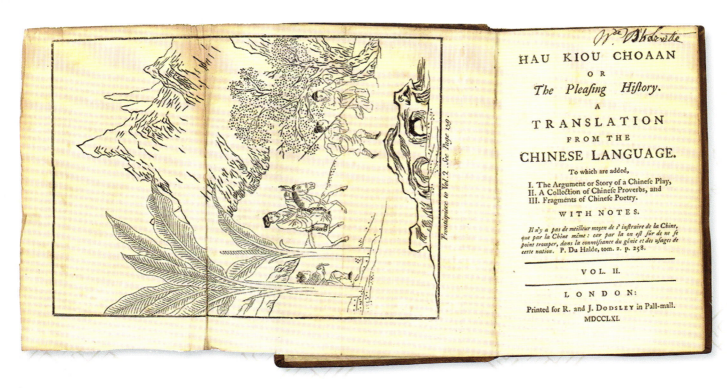

HAU KIOU CHOAAN
OR
The Pleasing History.
A
TRANSLATION
FROM THE
CHINESE LANGUAGE.

To which are added,

I. The Argument or Story of a Chinese Play,
II. A Collection of Chinese Proverbs, and
III. Fragments of Chinese Poetry.

WITH NOTES.

*Il n'y a pas de meilleur moyen de s'instruire de la Chine,
que par la Chine même : car par là on est sûr de ne se
point tromper, dans la connoissance du génie et des usages de
cette nation.* P. Du Halde, tom. 2. p. 258.

VOL. II.

LONDON:
Printed for R. and J. DODSLEY in Pall-mall.
MDCCLXI.

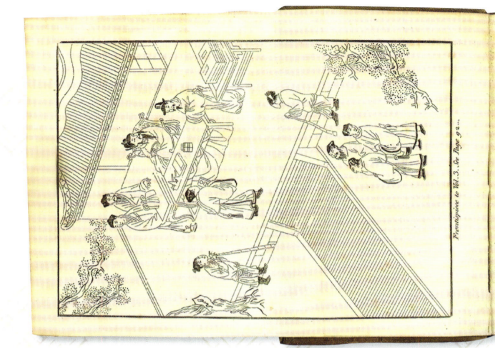

Frontispiece to Vol. 3. See Page 92.

Wᵐ Dᵈ harville

HAU KIOU CHOAAN

OR

The Pleasing History.

A

TRANSLATION

FROM THE

CHINESE LANGUAGE.

To which are added,

I. The Argument or Story of a Chinese Play,
II. A Collection of Chinese Proverbs, and
III. Fragments of Chinese Poetry.

WITH NOTES.

*Il n'y a pas de meilleur moyen de s' instruire de la Chine,
que par la Chine même: car par la on est sûr de ne se point
tromper, dans la connoissance du génie et des usages de cette
nation.* P. Du Halde, tom. 2. p. 258.

VOL. III.

LONDON:

Printed for R. and J. Dodsley in Pall-mall.
MDCCLXI.

Frontispiece to Vol. 4. See Page 98.

Wᵈ Dᵈ harville

HAU KIOU CHOAAN

OR

The Pleasing History.

A

TRANSLATION

FROM THE

CHINESE LANGUAGE.

To which are added,

I. The Argument or Story of a Chinese Play,
II. A Collection of Chinese Proverbs, and
III. Fragments of Chinese Poetry.

WITH NOTES.

*Il n'y a pas de meilleur moyen de s' instruire de la Chine,
que par la Chine même: car par la on est sûr de ne se point
tromper, dans la connoissance du génie et des usages de cette
nation.* P. Du Halde, tom. 2. p. 258.

VOL. IV.

LONDON:

Printed for R. and J. Dodsley in Pall-mall.
MDCCLXI.

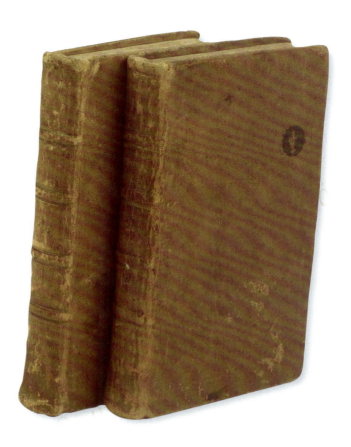

罗氏编号 552

《乾隆御制盛京赋》

（Éloge de la ville de Moukden et dee ses environs; poème composé par Kien-long, empereur de la Chine & de la Tartarie, actuellement regnant）

作　　者：爱新觉罗·弘历（1711－1799）撰，［法］钱德明（Jean-Joseph-Marie Amiot，字若瑟，1718－1793）译，［法］德金（Joesph de Guignes, 1721－1800）编

出　　版：巴黎，蒂亚尔（N. M. Tilliard），1770 年

载体形态：8 开，XXIV+XXXVIII+382+11 页

装　　订：小牛皮面，书脊烫金

版　　本：欧洲初版。

内　　容：

　　清朝乾隆皇帝对诗赋创作的喜好，在中国历代帝王中名列前茅。在历史上形形色色的京都赋中，乾隆的《御制盛京赋》是流传海外并产生巨大影响的赋文。《御制盛京赋》既陈述了恭谒祖陵的宗旨、感受与经过，更写出了盛京的地理位置、山川形胜、地域广阔、物产丰饶，又追怀开国时期文武功臣；再由彰显军威的围猎，延及耕桑农事、国富民殷、宫室富丽，内容丰富，显现出雄视百代的帝王文学气魄，极具历史和文献价值。本书是《御制盛京赋》的第一个欧洲译本，由法国耶稣会士钱德明根据满文译成法文，汉学家德金编辑并注释。除了翻译诗作本身外，本书还收录了乾隆皇帝颁布的命官员以 32 种字体刊印《盛京赋》的诏令，以及乾隆皇帝追念祖先和孝道的一篇序言。本书 127－197 页还收录了钱德明对中国文字的阐述，329－337 页则收录了德金翻译并加注的乾隆皇帝创作的茶诗。

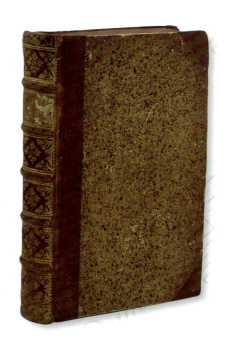

xxxviij PRÉFACE

même les Peuples, & qu'il les comble de
tous ses dons.

Instruit de tout ce qui a été dit allégo-
riquement en l'honneur de ma Patrie, &
de tous les éloges qu'on lui a donnés sous
différents noms, pourquoi ne joindrois-je
pas ma foible voix à celle de la vénérable
Antiquité ?

En faisant l'Eloge d'un lieu, on peut
l'envisager sous deux points de vue dif-
férents ; célébrer les affaires qui s'y trai-
tent, & alors c'est l'objet du Toukict-
choun *(7) ; chanter les choses qu'il pro-*
duit, ou qu'il renferme ; c'est sur quoi
principalement doit rouler le Foutchou-
roun. *Je commence par ce dernier. En*
voici les paroles.

POEME
DE L'EMPEREUR DE LA CHINE,
POUR CÉLÉBRER
MOUKDEN,
Capitale de ses anciens Etats.

LA révolution des années ayant ramené
celle qui porte le nom du sanglier (a);
dans le cours de ce mois, où l'étoile
Lieou (b) se trouvant le matin, vers le

(a) L'année qui porte le nom du *sanglier*, est
la derniere du cycle de 60. Elle s'appelle autrement *Kouei-hai*, & termine la période. J'ai subs-
titué le mot de *sanglier* à celui de *cochon*, à cause
de la délicatesse de notre langue. Cette année ré-
pond à l'an 1743 de l'ére Chrétienne, & à la hui-
tieme du règne de *Kien-long*.

(b) Dans la partie du *Ly-ki*, intitulée *Yué-*
ling, il est dit que l'étoile *Lieou*, pendant celui
des mois d'automne qui va terminer cette sai-

c iv

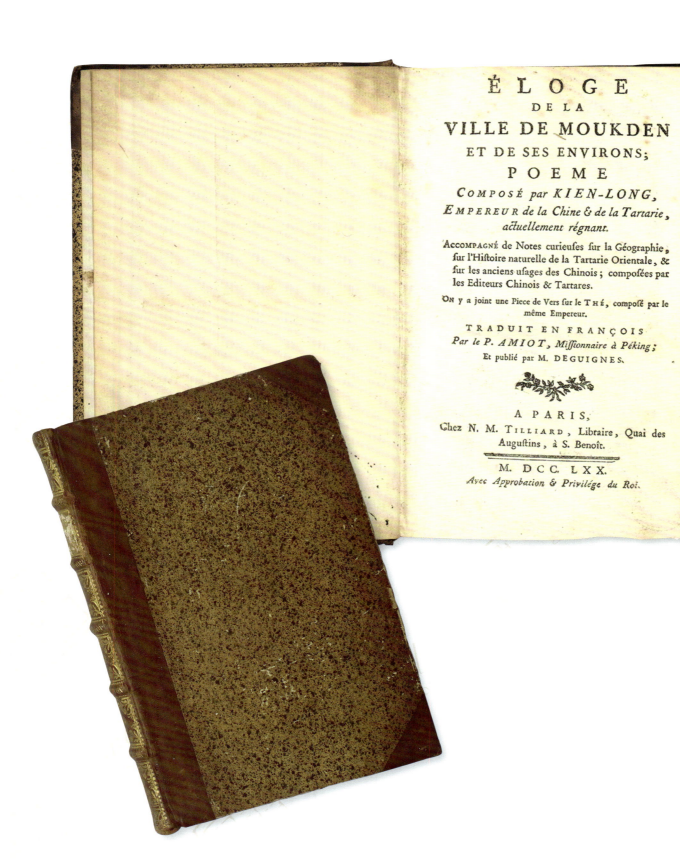

ÉLOGE
DE LA
VILLE DE MOUKDEN
ET DE SES ENVIRONS;
POEME
Composé par KIEN-LONG,
Empereur de la Chine & de la Tartarie,
actuellement régnant.

Accompagné de Notes curieuses sur la Géographie,
sur l'Histoire naturelle de la Tartarie Orientale, &
sur les anciens usages des Chinois; composées par
les Editeurs Chinois & Tartares.

On y a joint une Piece de Vers sur le Thé, composé par le
même Empereur.

TRADUIT EN FRANÇOIS
Par le P. AMIOT, Missionnaire à Péking;
Et publié par M. DEGUIGNES.

A PARIS,
Chez N. M. TILLIARD, Libraire, Quai des
Augustins, à S. Benoît.

M. DCC. LXX.
Avec Approbation & Privilége du Roi.

罗氏编号 **568**

《北京来信》

（**Lettre de Pékin, sur le genie de la langue chinoise, et la nature de leur écriture symbolique compare avec celle des anciens Égyptiens; en réponse à celle de la Société Royale des Sciences, de Londres, sur le même sujet: On y a joint l'extrait de deux ouvrages nouveaux de Mr.［Joseph］de Guignes ...**）

编　　者：［法］韩国英（Pierre-Martial Cibot，字伯督，1727－1780）、［英］尼达姆（John Turberville Needham，1713－1781）

出　　版：布鲁塞尔，布贝尔斯（J. L. de Boubers），1773 年

载体形态：4 开，XXXVIII；50+VI 页 +29 幅图版

装　　订：板面，有磨损

版　　本：初版。

内　　容：

　　本书全名为《北京来信：关于中国汉字与埃及象形字两者的比较，作为对伦敦皇家科学院有关同一主题的信的回复》。本书的第一部分是德金编辑出版的《书经》法译本节录，27 幅图版源自 1769 年英国人查尔斯·摩顿的《哲学交易》第 59 卷中的铜版画。本书的第二部分有独立的篇名《有关中国文字的信》，收录了法国耶稣会士韩国英于 1764 年 10 月 20 日在北京写的一封信，信中论及英国自然学家尼达姆有关中国汉字和埃及象形文字相似性的假设。《哲学交易》第 59 卷中收录了该信的摘要；1776 年《中国丛刊》第 1 卷 275－323 页中再次收录了该信，并加上了尼达姆的"观点"，《中国丛刊》索引中该信的作者变成了钱德明。

　　尼达姆所主张的有关中国汉字与埃及象形文字相似性的理论，在当时的欧洲古物收藏界迅速引起轰动，他本人也试图用中国汉字去破译在都林的一尊埃及伊西斯女神半身像上的象形文字。他的理论遭到了 18 世纪德国艺术史家温克尔曼（Johann Joachim Winckelmann，1717－1768）和法国东方学家、汉学家德金等人的反驳。

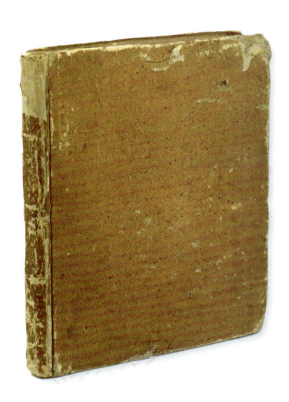

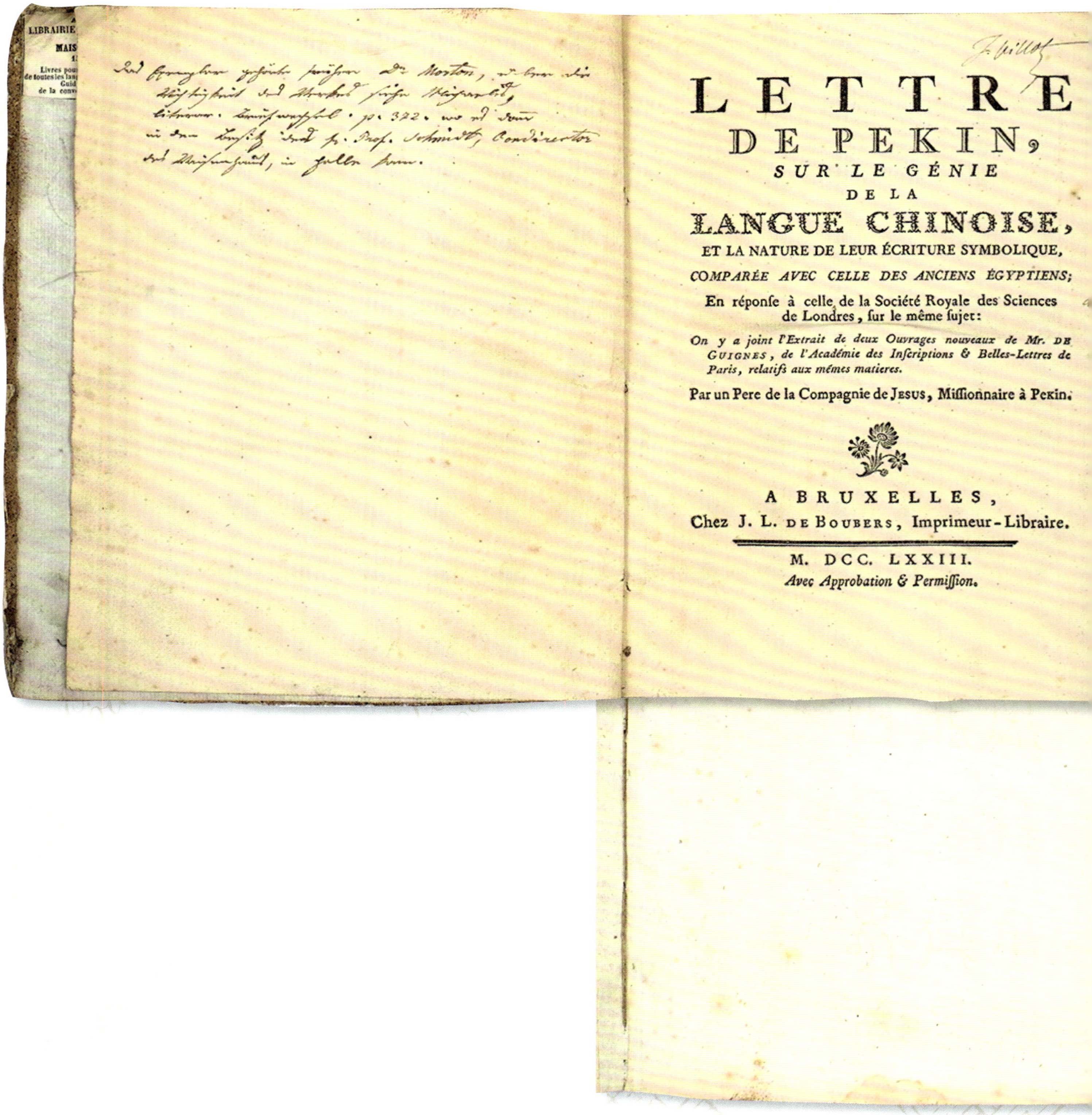

[handwritten annotation in German cursive, partly illegible]

Der Ethnograph gehörte zwischen der Morton, … der Morton, … das Beschreibung der Werke siehe Weizenbel, Litteratur. Zeitschwechsel. p. 322. wo … das in der Ansicht steht p. Prof. Schmidt, Condirector des Weisenheit, … füllen …

LETTRE
DE PEKIN,
SUR LE GÉNIE
DE LA
LANGUE CHINOISE,
ET LA NATURE DE LEUR ÉCRITURE SYMBOLIQUE,

COMPARÉE AVEC CELLE DES ANCIENS ÉGYPTIENS;

En réponse à celle de la Société Royale des Sciences de Londres, sur le même sujet:

On y a joint l'Extrait de deux Ouvrages nouveaux de Mr. DE GUIGNES, de l'Académie des Inscriptions & Belles-Lettres de Paris, relatifs aux mêmes matieres.

Par un Pere de la Compagnie de JESUS, Missionnaire à Pekin.

A BRUXELLES,
Chez J. L. DE BOUBERS, Imprimeur-Libraire.

M. DCC. LXXIII.
Avec Approbation & Permission.

Philos.Trans.Vol.LIX.TAB.XX. p.504.

The character called Tchouen Tsée.

J.Mynde sculp.

罗氏编号 599

《中国通史》12 卷

（Historie générale de la Chine, ou annals de cet empire; traduites du Tong-Kien-Kang-Mou. 1−12）

编 译 者：［法］冯秉正（Joseph-Marie-Anne de Moyriac de Mailla, 字端友，1669−1748）、［法］格鲁贤（Jean-Baptiset-Gabriel-Alexandre Grosier, 1743−1823）、［法］德奥特雷（Michel-Ange-André le Roux Deshautesrayes，生卒年不详）

出 版：巴黎，皮埃雷斯和克鲁西耶（Pierres & Clousier），1777−1783 年

载体形态：4 开，LXXII+CC+352 页；IV+592 页；XII+588 页；IV+596 页；VIII+564 页；IV+588 页；VIII+484 页；IV+664 页；VI+660 页；IV+580 页；IV+612 页；XXIV+196+348 页 +16 幅图版（1 幅折叠）+3 幅折叠彩色勾线地图 +5 幅折叠表格

装 订：小牛皮面统一装帧，书脊烫金，有红、绿色标签，书名上有印章

版 本：初版，1777−1781 年有意文版 35 卷（译自法文版前 11 卷）。

内 容：

　　本书作者法国耶稣会士冯秉正 1703 年来华，1748 年卒于北京。从本书的全名《中国通史或译自〈通鉴纲目〉的中国编年史》可知，本书内容主要取材于朱熹的《通鉴纲目》，但冯秉正是从康熙皇帝钦定的满文译本摘译的，并用了明代商辂的《续通鉴纲目》补《通鉴纲目》之不足，清史部分冯秉正写到康熙帝（本书第 11−12 卷是根据较近期资料编纂的明清史）。冯秉正在序言中详尽介绍了包括《竹书纪年》在内的中国各个时代的中国史书。第 1 卷中收录了他与著名学者尼古拉斯·弗雷莱就中国历史交换意见的 13 封信件。书稿于 1737 年寄到巴黎，尼古拉斯·弗雷莱便为其出版事宜积极奔走，但法国耶稣会对中国历史始于何时意见不一，出版事宜遂被搁置。1763 年，耶稣会被解散，存放于里昂耶稣会学校的书稿落入政府手中，1775 年辗转出让给了时任巴黎阿森纳尔图书馆馆长的格鲁贤，格鲁贤将原稿加以整理，分成 12 册陆续出版。本书第 12 卷包含了一个字母索引及 3 个附录：宋君荣的《交趾支那历史笔记》《东京历史记忆》及《〈尼布楚条约〉签订前俄国首个对华贸易公司的历史笔记》。本书问世时，"中国热"已近尾声，但由于此书第一次向欧洲人提供了由中国人编写的详尽的中国历史，所以依然受到了各界精英的关注。

Échelle

Lis communs de la Chine.

Lieues d'une heure.

INDICATION

● Villes du 1er. ordre . . . . fou

• Villes du 2e . . . . tcheou

• Villes du 3e. . . . . hien

N°. La terminaison de quelques villes du
de celle du 2e. cette derniere est conser

HISTOIRE
GÉNÉRALE
DE LA CHINE,
OU
ANNALES DE CET EMPIRE;

TRADUITES DU TONG-KIEN-KANG-MOU,

Par le feu Père JOSEPH-ANNE-MARIE DE MOYRIAC DE MAILLA,
Jésuite François, Missionnaire à Pékin:

Publiées par M. l'Abbé GROSIER,

Et dirigées par M. LE ROUX DES HAUTESRAYES,
Conseiller-Lecteur du Roi, Professeur d'Arabe au Collège Royal
de France, Interprète de Sa Majesté pour les Langues Orientales.

OUVRAGE enrichi de Figures & de nouvelles Cartes Géographiques de la Chine ancienne
& moderne, levées par ordre du feu Empereur KANG-HI, & gravées pour la
première fois.

TOME PREMIER.

A PARIS,

Chez { PH.-D. PIERRES, Imprimeur du Grand-Conseil du Roi, & du
Collège Royal de France, rue Saint-Jacques.
CLOUSIER, Imprimeur-Libraire, rue Saint-Jacques.

M. DCC. LXXVII.

AVEC APPROBATION, ET PRIVILÉGE DU ROI.

---

114 HISTOIRE GÉNÉRALE

AVANT L'ERE
CHRÉTIENNE.
2221.
Chun.

» rain entreprend quelque affaire, il doit examiner avec soin
» les motifs qui l'y déterminent, & suivre toujours le parti
» de la paix & de la douceur; la chose est-elle facile? Ses
» ministres doivent être humbles, soumis, droits & capables
» de remplir ses intentions pour le bien général; s'ils ne sont
» pas tels, il les a mal choisis. Il doit toujours se ressouvenir
» qu'il n'est que le dépositaire de l'autorité qu'il a en main;
» que c'est du Chang-ti qu'il l'a reçue, & que son bonheur
» dépend d'exécuter ponctuellement sa volonté. Un prince,
» accablé de tant de soins, peut-il être sans crainte «?

» Cela est vrai, dit l'empereur, je compare mes ministres
» à mes voisins qui me doivent leur secours. Vous êtes mes
» yeux & mes oreilles, vous êtes mes pieds & mes mains;
» nous ne faisons qu'un corps; vous m'aidez à gouverner
» l'empire par vos lumières & vos conseils; voilà ce que vous
» devez être. Si l'œil ne voit pas, si l'oreille n'entend pas,
» si les bras & les pieds sont sans mouvement, que peuvent
» la tête & le cœur quelque éclairés qu'ils soient?

» Je me rappelle notre ancien habit de cérémonie: sur
» celui de dessus, on voit peints le soleil, la lune & les
» étoiles, les montagnes, le dragon & le faisan: sur celui
» de dessous, on a brodé cinq sortes de couleurs, le vase (1)
» dont on use dans la salle des cérémonies pour les ancêtres,
» l'herbe aquatique, le feu, le ris blanc, la hache d'armes

(1) Ce vase, appellé *Tsong-y*, étoit une coupe ou aiguière sur laquelle étoit
ciselée, d'un côté la figure d'un tigre, & de l'autre celle d'un singe à queue fort
longue & fourchue. Lorsqu'il pleut, ce singe se suspend à une branche d'arbre à
la renverse, & bouche ses narines, soit avec sa queue, soit avec ses deux doigts.
Il étoit le symbole de la prudence, comme le tigre l'étoit de la force. Le feu dési-
gnoit la sagesse; le ris, l'obligation de nourrir le peuple. *Editeur.*

Tome I. — *Pag. 114.*

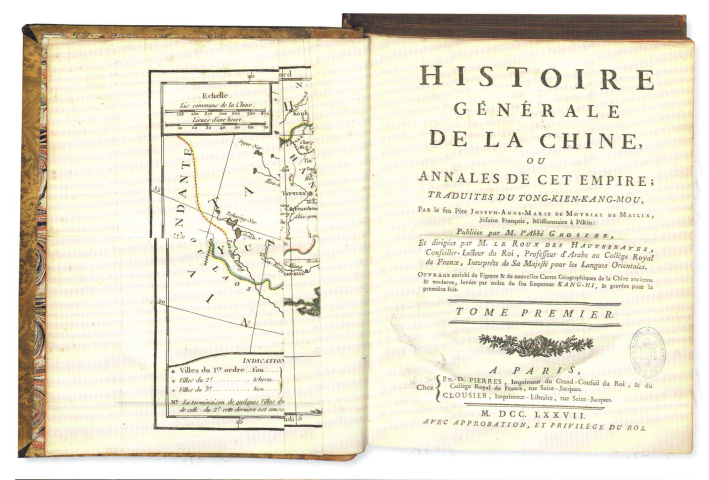

Ornemens brodés sur les habits de Cérémonie.
1. Le Soleil. 2. la Lune. 3. les Étoiles. 4. les Montagnes. 5. les Dragons. 6. le Faisan.

罗氏编号 **646**

《中国概述》
（ Description générale de la Chine ）

《中国坤舆总图》
（ Atlas general de la Chine; pour server à la Description générale de cet empire ）

作　　者：〔法〕格鲁贤（ Jean-Baptiset-Gabriel-Alexandre Grosier, 1743－1823 ）

出　　版：巴黎，穆塔尔（ Moutard〔 ... 〕& de Madame Comtesse d'Artois ），1785 年

载体形态：4 开，IV+800 页；对开，书名页 +11+53 幅地图、平面图（大多折叠）+12 幅图板（10 幅跨页，1 幅乐谱，1 幅孔子肖像）

装　　订：小牛皮面统一装帧，书脊烫金，有红、绿色标签；亦有牛皮面，大理石纹书板，书名上有书主印章（中文）

版　　本：初版，1878 年再版（8 开），1818－1820 年 3 版。

内　　容：

　　格鲁贤将自己撰写的《中国概述》作为冯秉正《中国通史》的第 13 卷付梓印行。冯秉正的《中国通史》止于康熙帝驾崩，格鲁贤在《中国概述》中将清史续写至 1780 年。本书相当一部分内容是有关自然史的，比如有 108 页是关于植物学的。

　　格鲁贤的《中国坤舆总图》，包含了杜赫德《中华帝国全志》中用到的所有地图、平面图和图版，且用了杜赫德的原版铜版印刷。

DESCRIPTION
GÉNÉRALE
DE LA CHINE,
OU
TABLEAU DE L'ÉTAT ACTUEL
DE CET EMPIRE;

CONTENANT, 1.º la Description topographique des quinze Provinces qui le composent ; celle de la Tartarie, des Isles, & autres pays tributaires qui en dépendent ; le nombre & la situation de ses Villes, l'état de sa Population, les productions variées de son Sol, & les principaux détails de son Histoire Naturelle ; 2.º un précis des connoissances le plus récemment parvenues en Europe sur le Gouvernement, la Religion, les Mœurs & les Usages, les Arts & les Sciences des Chinois.

Rédigé par M. l'Abbé GROSIER, Chanoine de S. Louis du Louvre.

A PARIS,

Chez MOUTARD, Imprimeur-Libraire de la REINE, de MADAME, & de Madame Comtesse D'ARTOIS, rue des Mathurins, Hôtel de Cluni.

M. DCC. LXXXV.
Avec Approbation, & Privilége du Roi.

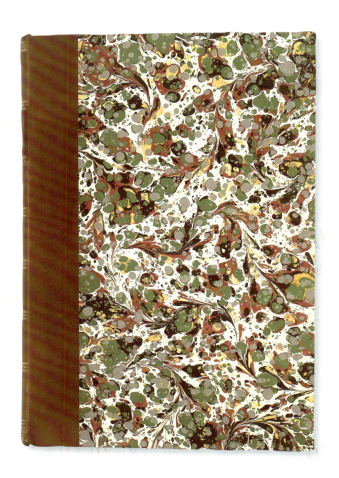

罗氏编号 647

《孔子生平事迹简介》
（ Abrégé historique des principaux traits de la vie de Confucius ... ）

作　　者：［法］赫尔曼（Isidore-Stanislas Helman, 1743－1806）
出　　版：巴黎，作者和蓬斯（L'Auteur & M. Ponce），约 1786 年
载体形态：4 开本，24 幅版画插图 +24 页描述文字
装　　订：牛皮面，磨损，书脊改装，轻微水渍
版　　本：法文版。

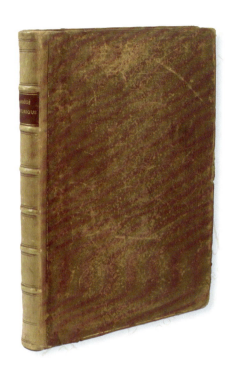

内　　容：

　　法国耶稣会神父钱德明博学多识，汉学造诣颇深。1784 年，他出版著作《孔子传》，图文并茂，广受赞誉。这些描绘孔子生平的生动木刻画，流传至巴黎，成为法国雕刻师赫尔曼刊刻《孔子生平事迹简介》的蓝本。以风俗画董声欧陆的赫尔曼，通过 24 幅精美版画，展现了孔子诞生前麒麟显现、出生求学、游历授业至圣人故去、宋真宗祭孔的一生履迹。这些珍贵的版画插图与文字说明，是早期欧洲了解孔子生平及学说的重要来源。

IIII.ᵉ ESTAMPE.

On voit l'Appartement où naquit Confucius,
et où se font les Cérémonies en usage à l'occasion
du nouveau-né. Audessus on a voulu représenter
les Chœurs de Musique et les voix celestes qui
se firent entendre au moment de sa naissance.
Ces voix lui donnoient le nom de Saint Fils; elles
attestoient que le Ciel avoit tressailli de joye à
cet évenement fortuné pour la Terre. Les Commen-
tateurs en concluent qu'un Enfant annoncé par
tant de Prodiges, ne devoit pas être un homme
ordinaire. Il seroit prudent d'être de leur avis
si l'on voyageoit à la Chine.

CONFUCIUS.

De la seule Raison salutaire interprète,
Sans éblouir le monde éclairant les esp...
Il ne parla qu'en sage et jamais en P...
Cependant on le crut, et même en fon...

ABRÉGÉ HISTORIQUE

DES PRINCIPAUX TRAITS

DE LA VIE DE CONFUCIUS

Célèbre Philosophe Chinois

Orné de 24 Estampes in 4°.

Gravées par Helman,

*d'après des Dessins Originaux de la Chine
envoyés à Paris par M.* Amiot
Missionnaire à Pékin

Et tirés du Cabinet de M. Bertin M.re et ancien S.re d'État.

À Paris

Chez l'Auteur, de l'Académie de Lille en Flandre, Rue S.t Honoré,
vis-à-vis l'Hôtel de Noailles, N.° 315.
Et chez M. Ponce, Graveur de M.gr Comte d'Artois, Rue S.te Hyacinthe N.° 19.

Prix in 4° en feuilles 12.tt et broché en Carton 13.tt 10.s
Il y a quelques Exemplaires sur grand Papier qui feront suite aux
Batailles de la Chine Prix 18.tt

I.re ESTAMPE.

*Cette Planche représente CONFUCIUS
Tel qu'il étoit anciennement exposé à la Vénération des Lettrés.*

Ce Philosophe, dont le nom Chinois est Koung-Tsée,
exerça la Magistrature dans plusieurs Royaumes,
recherchant les dignités, non pour les avantages personels
qu'elles lui procuroient, mais pour travailler au bonheur
des peuples, et pour donner à sa Doctrine cette autorité
que lui même recevoit de ses Emplois. Il s'en démettoit
aussitôt quand il n'en recevoit que de vains honneurs,
sans pouvoir être utile aux hommes.

À l'âge de 55 Ans il fut élevé au principal Ministère
dans le Royaume de LOU sa Patrie. Il y fit tout le
bien que peut faire un Sage tant qu'il est secondé
par un Roi; mais en butte aux persécutions des Cour-
tisans qui parvinrent enfin à corrompre leur Maître;
il fut réduit à s'éloigner, en pleurant, du Pays dont il
avoit fait le bonheur. Il parcourut différens États,
toujours égal à lui même dans l'adversité comme dans
la prospérité. Il mourut à l'âge de 73 Ans. On a
conservé ses dernières paroles. »Les Rois, dit-il,
»n'observent pas ce que j'enseigne; aucun d'eux ne suit
»mes principes; il ne me reste plus qu'à mourir» il reçut

罗氏编号 697

《英使谒见乾隆纪实》

（An authentic account of an embassy from the King of great Britain to the Emperor of china ... ）

作　　者：［英］斯当东（Sir George Leonard Staunton, 1737-1801）

出　　版： 伦敦，布尔默（W. Bulmer），1797 年

载体形态： 4 开本。两卷。卷一 II+XXXIV+518 页；卷二 XX+626+2 幅卷首肖像 +1 幅版画。文中插有 26 幅版画。附地图册（57×44 厘米），含 44 幅地图及图版（1 幅折叠，6 幅双页）

装　　订： 19 世纪小牛皮面，卷一书脊顶部破损，轻微书边虫蛀，纸板角损坏，大理石纹纸磨损褪色，有 Chester 图书馆纹章书票

版　　本： 伦敦英文初版，1798 年重印，1799 年美国英文再版。

内　　容：

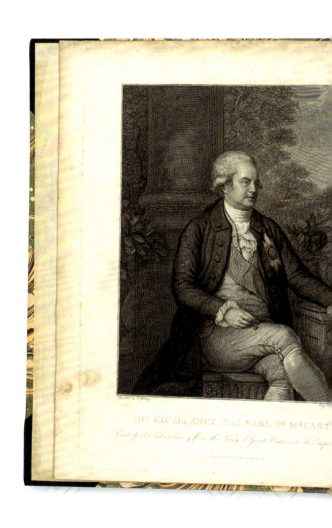

1793 年（乾隆五十八年）英王全权特使马戛尔尼伯爵（George Macartney, 1737-1806）率英国使团造访中国，旨在缔结中英商业联系。关于这一重要的外交事件，使团副使乔治·斯当东进行了详细记述。作为"从开始就熟悉这次远征中的细节，后来又在全部过程中亲自参与其事的人"，斯当东向英国公众介绍了此次访华情况，并对谒见乾隆时发生的诸多插曲加以描绘。这部纪实为研究 18 世纪中英关系史乃至探究清朝社会提供了第一手资料。

全书主要取材于马戛尔尼伯爵、使节团指挥官高尔爵士（Sir Erasmus Gower, 1742-1814）及使团其他成员的个人文件。分章记载派遣使团的缘起、筹备，英船"狮子号"及"印度斯坦号"进入黄海渤海、使团抵京、观光长城、谒见皇帝、游历杭州、到访广澳的一系列经过，所附地图册则完整呈现当时地理情况，具有极大参考价值。

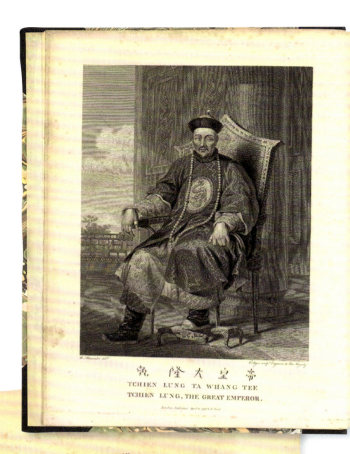

乾隆大皇帝
TCHIEN LUNG TA WHANG TEE
TCHIEN LUNG, THE GREAT EMPEROR.

AN

AUTHENTIC ACCOUNT

OF

AN EMBASSY

FROM

THE KING OF GREAT BRITAIN

TO THE EMPEROR OF CHINA;

INCLUDING

CURSORY OBSERVATIONS MADE, AND INFORMATION OBTAINED, IN TRAVELLING THROUGH
THAT ANCIENT EMPIRE, AND A SMALL PART OF CHINESE TARTARY.

TOGETHER WITH A RELATION OF

THE VOYAGE UNDERTAKEN ON THE OCCASION

BY HIS MAJESTY'S SHIP THE LION, AND THE SHIP HINDOSTAN, IN THE EAST
INDIA COMPANY'S SERVICE, TO THE YELLOW SEA, AND GULF OF PEKIN;
AS WELL AS OF THEIR RETURN TO EUROPE;

WITH

NOTICES OF THE SEVERAL PLACES WHERE THEY STOPPED IN THEIR WAY OUT AND HOME;
BEING THE ISLANDS OF MADEIRA, TENERIFFE, AND ST. JAGO; THE PORT OF RIO DE
JANEIRO IN SOUTH AMERICA; THE ISLANDS OF ST. HELENA, TRISTAN
D'ACUNHA, AND AMSTERDAM; THE COAST OF JAVA, AND SUMATRA,
THE NANKA ISLES, PULO CONDORE, AND COCHIN-CHINA.

TAKEN CHIEFLY FROM THE PAPERS OF

His Excellency the EARL OF MACARTNEY, Knight of the Bath, His Majesty's
Embassador Extraordinary and Plenipotentiary to the Emperor of China; Sir ERASMUS GOWER,
Commander of the Expedition, and of other Gentlemen in the several departments of the Embassy.

By SIR GEORGE STAUNTON, BARONET,

Honorary Doctor of Laws of the University of Oxford, Fellow of the Royal Society of London, his Majesty's
Secretary of Embassy to the Emperor of China, and Minister Plenipotentiary in the absence of the Embassador.

In Two Volumes, with Engravings; beside a Folio Volume of Plates.

VOL. I.

LONDON:

PRINTED BY W. BULMER AND CO.
FOR G. NICOL, BOOKSELLER TO HIS MAJESTY, PALL-MALL.
MDCCXCVII.

AN

AUTHENTIC ACCOUNT

OF

AN EMBASSY

FROM

THE KING OF GREAT BRITAIN

TO THE EMPEROR OF CHINA;

INCLUDING

CURSORY OBSERVATIONS MADE, AND INFORMATION OBTAINED, IN TRAVELLING THROUGH
THAT ANCIENT EMPIRE, AND A SMALL PART OF CHINESE TARTARY.

TOGETHER WITH A RELATION OF

THE VOYAGE UNDERTAKEN ON THE OCCASION

BY HIS MAJESTY'S SHIP THE LION, AND THE SHIP HINDOSTAN, IN THE EAST
INDIA COMPANY'S SERVICE, TO THE YELLOW SEA, AND GULF OF PEKIN;
AS WELL AS OF THEIR RETURN TO EUROPE;

WITH

NOTICES OF THE SEVERAL PLACES WHERE THEY STOPPED IN THEIR WAY OUT AND HOME;
BEING THE ISLANDS OF MADEIRA, TENERIFFE, AND ST. JAGO; THE PORT OF RIO DE
JANEIRO IN SOUTH AMERICA; THE ISLANDS OF ST. HELENA, TRISTAN
D'ACUNHA, AND AMSTERDAM; THE COASTS OF JAVA, AND SUMATRA,
THE NANKA ISLES, PULO CONDORE, AND COCHIN-CHINA.

TAKEN CHIEFLY FROM THE PAPERS OF

His Excellency the EARL OF MACARTNEY, Knight of the Bath, His Majesty's
Embassador Extraordinary and Plenipotentiary to the Emperor of China; Sir ERASMUS GOWER,
Commander of the Expedition, and of other Gentlemen in the several departments of the Embassy.

By SIR GEORGE STAUNTON, BARONET,

Honorary Doctor of Laws of the University of Oxford, Fellow of the Royal Society of London, his Majesty's
Secretary of Embassy to the Emperor of China, and Minister Plenipotentiary in the absence of the Embassador.

In Two Volumes, with Engravings; beside a Folio Volume of Plates.

VOL. II.

LONDON:

PRINTED BY W. BULMER AND CO.
FOR G. NICOL, BOOKSELLER TO HIS MAJESTY, PALL-MALL.
MDCCXCVII.

VIEW of one of the WESERN GATES of the CITY of PEKIN.

A FRONT VIEW of the HALL of AUDIENCE at the PALACE of YUEN-MIN-YUEN.

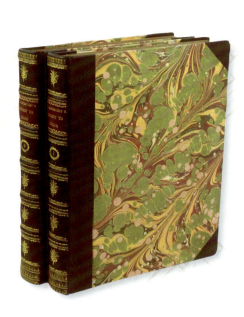

《中国服饰》

（The costume of China, illustrated by sixty engravings: with explanations in English and French）

作　　者：［英］梅森（George Henry Mason）

出　　版：伦敦，米勒（W. Miller），1800 年

载体形态：对开本，法文题名 + 英文题名 +X 页 +60 幅手工上色点刻画 + 英法对照说明文字

装　　订：直纹绯红摩洛哥羊皮面，烫金，大理石纹衬纸，版刻藏书票

版　　本：英文初版，1804 年重印，1806 年再版。

内　　容：

　　作者英军 102 团少校梅森曾私藏一系列中国题材画作，这些作品大多出自署名"蒲呱"（Pu-Quà）的广州画匠之手。官员贵妇，平民走卒，画家妙笔之下，尽显世态风情。1800 年，作者将画作配文出版，达德利（J.Dadly）刻版，作为米勒出版社服饰系列丛书的第一本。

　　付梓发行的英法对照图文版，选取了中国社会各阶层的 60 种人物肖像，除部分清廷官员外，大部分为平民百姓。剃头匠、制鞋匠、铁匠、渔夫、屠户、木匠、农民，这些原本被忽视的绘画题材，在这本《中国服饰》中得到栩栩如生的呈现。而编撰者梅森，也借由此书，达到"对遥远东方人民经济及社会生活的生动描绘"。此书的成功，带动了此后一系列东方文化书籍在欧洲的热销，同时，也为后世留下了珍贵的图像资料。

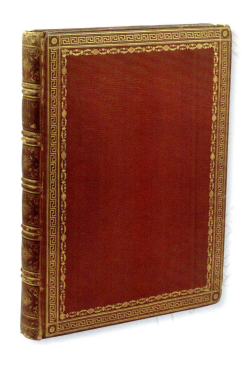

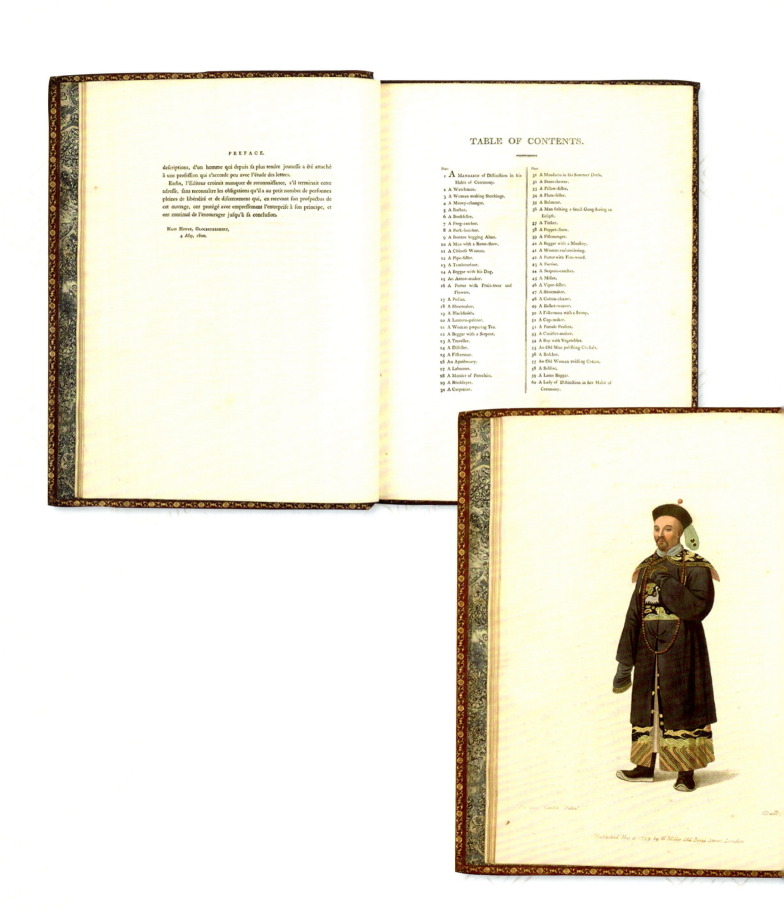

PREFACE.

descriptions, d'un homme qui depuis fa plus tendre jeuneffe a été attaché à une profeffion qui s'accorde peu avec l'étude des lettres.

Enfin, l'Editeur croirait manquer de reconnaiffance, s'il terminait cette adreffe, fans reconnaître les obligations qu'il a au petit nombre de perfonnes pleines de libéralité et de difcernement qui, en recevant fon profpectus de cet ouvrage, ont protégé avec empreffement l'entreprife à fon principe, et ont continué de l'encourager jufqu'à fa conclufion.

Nass House, Gloucestershire,
4 May, 1800.

TABLE OF CONTENTS.

Plate
1 A Mandarin of Diftinction in his Habit of Ceremony.
2 A Watchman.
3 A Woman making Stockings.
4 A Money-changer.
5 A Barber.
6 A Bookfeller.
7 A Frog-catcher.
8 A Pork-butcher.
9 A Bonze begging Alms.
10 A Man with a Razor-fhow.
11 A Chinefe Woman.
12 A Pipe-feller.
13 A Tambourier.
14 A Beggar with his Dog.
15 An Arrow-maker.
16 A Porter with Fruit-trees and Flowers.
17 A Pedlar.
18 A Shoemaker.
19 A Blackfmith.
20 A Lantern-painter.
21 A Woman preparing Tea.
22 A Beggar with a Serpent.
23 A Traveller.
24 A Diftiller.
25 A Fisherman.
26 An Apothecary.
27 A Labourer.
28 A Mender of Porcelain.
29 A Bricklayer.
30 A Carpenter.

Plate
31 A Mandarin in his Summer Drefs.
32 A Stone-hewer.
33 A Pillow-feller.
34 A Flute-feller.
35 A Balancer.
36 A Man ftriking a fmall Gong during an Eclipfe.
37 A Tinker.
38 A Puppet-fhow.
39 A Fishmonger.
40 A Beggar with a Monkey.
41 A Woman embroidering.
42 A Porter with Fire-wood.
43 A Furrier.
44 A Serpent-catcher.
45 A Miller.
46 A Viper-feller.
47 A Shoemaker.
48 A Cotton-cleaner.
49 A Basket-weaver.
50 A Fisherman with a Scoop.
51 A Cap-maker.
52 A Female Peafant.
53 A Cunifter-maker.
54 A Boy with Vegetables.
55 An Old Man polishing Cryftals.
56 A Butcher.
57 An Old Woman twirling Cotton.
58 A Soldier.
59 A Lame Beggar.
60 A Lady of Diftinction in her Habit of Ceremony.

THE

COSTUME

OF

CHINA,

ILLUSTRATED

BY

SIXTY ENGRAVINGS:

WITH

EXPLANATIONS

IN

ENGLISH AND FRENCH.

BY

George Henry Mason, Esquire,

MAJOR OF HIS MAJESTY's (LATE) 102D REGIMENT.

LONDON:

PRINTED FOR W. MILLER, OLD BOND STREET,

BY S. GOSNELL, LITTLE QUEEN STREET, HOLBORN.

M.DCC.C.

PLATE I.

REPRESENTS

A MANDARIN OF DISTINCTION,

IN HIS HABIT OF CEREMONY.

THE dress of a Chinese is suited to the gravity of his demeanour. It consists, in general, of a long vest extending to the ankle: the sleeves are wide at the shoulder, are gradually narrower at the wrist, and are rounded off in the form of a horse-shoe, covering the whole hand when it is not lifted up. No man of rank is allowed to appear in public without boots, which have no heels, and are made of satin, silk, or calico. In full dress he wears a long silk gown, generally of a blue colour and heavily embroidered; over this is placed a fur-coat of silk, which reaches to the hand, and descends below the knee. From his neck is suspended a string of costly coral beads. His cap is edged with satin, velvet, or fur, and on the crown is a red ball with a peacock's feather hanging from it: these are badges of distinction conferred by the emperor. The embroidered bird upon the breast is worn only by mandarins high in civil rank, while the military mandarins are distinguished by an embroidered dragon. All colours are not suffered to be worn indiscriminately. The emperor, and the princes of the blood only, are allowed to wear yellow; although violet colour is sometimes chosen by mandarins of rank on days of ceremony. The common people seldom wear any other than blue or black, and white is universally adopted for mourning.—The Chinese carefully avoid every word or gesture which may betray either anger or any violent emotion of the mind. They entertain the highest reverence for their parents, and respect for the aged. They are enthusiastic admirers of virtue, and venerate the memory of such of their nation as have been celebrated for a love of justice and of their country. With this singular people neither riches nor birth can ever establish the smallest claim to honours. Personal merit is the sole basis upon which any man can raise himself to distinguished rank. Talents and virtue are indispensably requisite for those in power; and where they are deficient, every adventitious or hereditary pretension is totally disallowed.

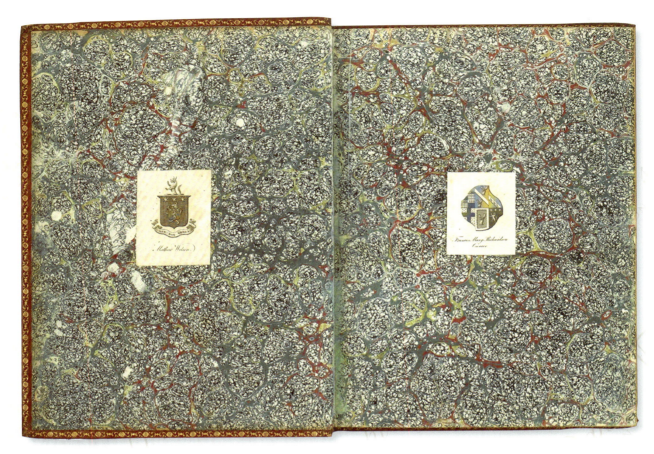

罗氏编号 **715**

《中国酷刑》

（ The punishments of China, illustrated by twenty-two engravings: with explanations in English and French ）

作　　者：［英］梅森（George Henry Mason）

出　　版：伦敦，米勒（W. Miller by W. Bulmer），1801 年

载体形态：对开本，法文题名 + 英文题名 +6 页 +22 幅手工上色点刻画 + 英法对照说明文字

装　　订：绿色摩洛哥羊皮面，烫金

版　　本：英文初版，1804 年、1808 年、1830 年重印。

内　　容：

　　继《中国服饰》之后，作者梅森 1801 年在伦敦出版了姐妹篇《中国酷刑》，仍由署名"蒲呱"（Pu-Quà）的广州画匠绘制。画作精美，人物鲜活，受刑者神情悲苦，形态扭曲，阅者无不触目惊心。

　　此书的 22 幅彩色插图描绘了中国法律中的 22 种常见刑罚，如杖刑、夹指、示众、负枷、断筋、绞刑等，通过图文并茂的形式，展现当时的刑罚体系。梅森在配文中解释了惩罚适用对象及行刑方法，堪称西方读者了解中国刑罚的入门读本。此书的出版，推进了西方学界对中国刑罚的研究进程。

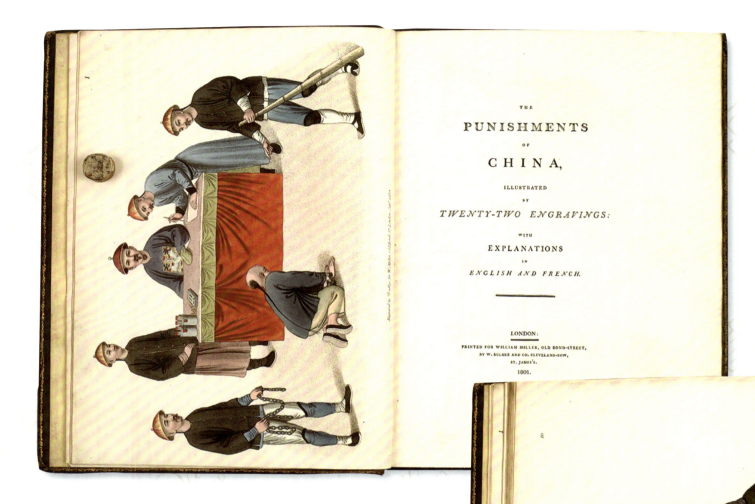

THE

PUNISHMENTS

OF

CHINA,

ILLUSTRATED

BY

TWENTY-TWO ENGRAVINGS:

WITH

EXPLANATIONS

IN

ENGLISH AND FRENCH.

LONDON:

PRINTED FOR WILLIAM MILLER, OLD BOND-STREET,
BY W. BULMER AND CO. CLEVELAND-ROW,
ST. JAMES'S.
1801.

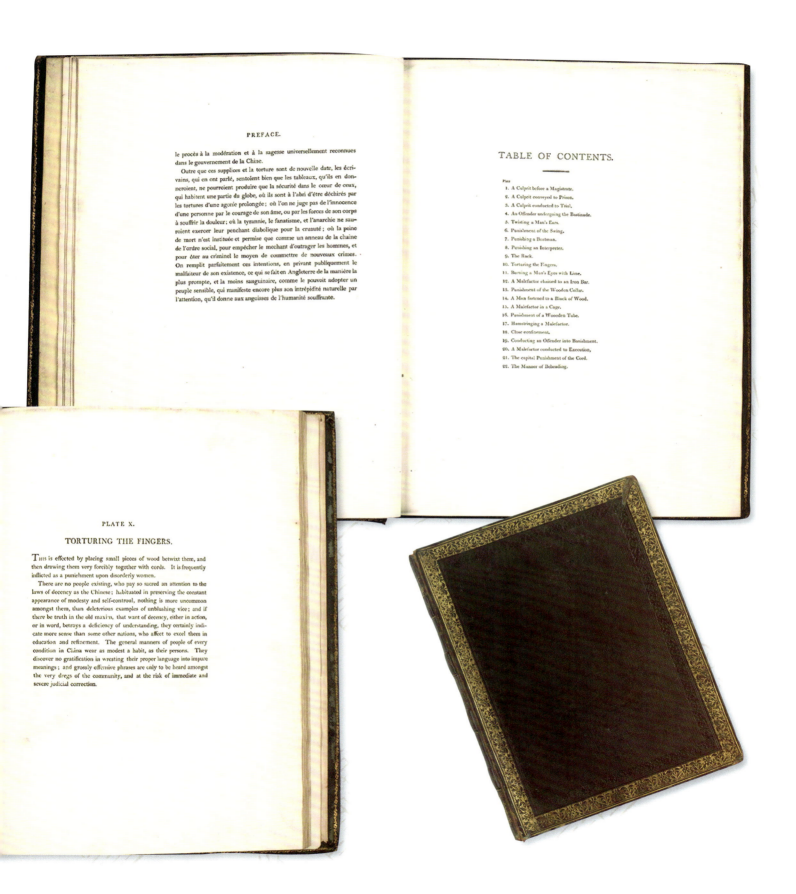

PREFACE.

le procès à la modération et à la sagesse universellement reconnues dans le gouvernement de la Chine.

Outre que ces supplices et la torture sont de nouvelle date, les écrivains, qui en ont parlé, sentoient bien que les tableaux, qu'ils en donneroient, ne pourroient produire que la sécurité dans le cœur de ceux, qui habitent une partie du globe, où ils sont à l'abri d'être déchirés par les tortures d'une agonie prolongée; où l'on ne juge pas de l'innocence d'une personne par le courage de son âme, ou par les forces de son corps à souffrir la douleur; où la tyrannie, le fanatisme, et l'anarchie ne sauroient exercer leur penchant diabolique pour la cruauté; où la peine de mort n'est instituée et permise que comme un anneau de la chaine de l'ordre social, pour empécher le mechant d'outrager les hommes, et pour ôter au criminel le moyen de commettre de nouveaux crimes. On remplit parfaitement ces intentions, en privant publiquement le malfaiteur de son existence, ce qui se fait en Angleterre de la manière la plus prompte, et la moins sanguinaire, comme le pouvoit adopter un peuple sensible, qui manifeste encore plus son intrépidité naturelle par l'attention, qu'il donne aux angoisses de l'humanité souffrante.

TABLE OF CONTENTS.

Plate

1. A Culprit before a Magistrate.
2. A Culprit conveyed to Prison.
3. A Culprit conducted to Trial.
4. An Offender undergoing the Bastinade.
5. Twisting a Man's Ears.
6. Punishment of the Swing.
7. Punishing a Boatman.
8. Punishing an Interpreter.
9. The Rack.
10. Torturing the Fingers.
11. Burning a Man's Eyes with Lime.
12. A Malefactor chained to an Iron Bar.
13. Punishment of the Wooden Collar.
14. A Man fastened to a Block of Wood.
15. A Malefactor in a Cage.
16. Punishment of a Wooden Tube.
17. Hamstringing a Malefactor.
18. Close confinement.
19. Conducting an Offender into Banishment.
20. A Malefactor conducted to Execution.
21. The capital Punishment of the Cord.
22. The Manner of Beheading.

PLATE X.

TORTURING THE FINGERS.

THIS is effected by placing small pieces of wood betwixt them, and then drawing them very forcibly together with cords. It is frequently inflicted as a punishment upon disorderly women.

There are no people existing, who pay so sacred an attention to the laws of decency as the Chinese; habituated in preserving the constant appearance of modesty and self-controul, nothing is more uncommon amongst them, than deleterious examples of unblushing vice; and if there be truth in the old maxim, that want of decency, either in action, or in word, betrays a deficiency of understanding, they certainly indicate more sense than some other nations, who affect to excel them in education and refinement. The general manners of people of every condition in China wear as modest a habit, as their persons. They discover no gratification in wresting their proper language into impure meanings; and grossly offensive phrases are only to be heard amongst the very dregs of the community, and at the risk of immediate and severe judicial correction.

罗氏编号 **743**

《论语》
（**The works of Confucius; containing the original text, with a translation**）

作　者：［英］马士曼（Joshua Marshman, 1768－1837）译

出　版：塞兰坡，差会出版社（Mission Press），1809 年

载体形态：4 开本，IV+IV+IV 页 +XL 页（"孔子生平"）+IV+CXIV 页 + 勘误页 +5 幅折叠表（"基本汉字"与"汉语单字"）+726 页 +18 页（补遗）+IV 页（勘误页）

装　订：四分之一牛皮面，书脊肋线烫金，大理石纹板，书页有污渍，遗失若干勘误页

来　源：有格雷格（Walter W. Greg）藏书票，题名页背面有 "1821. Presented by Mr. A. H. Hamilton" 等字样的题签。

版　本：英文初版。

内　容：

《论语》作为儒家经典，自春秋以来，传承千年。把握中国传统文化精髓，从研读并了解这部经典开始。

早在 1687 年，比利时汉学家柏应理在其编撰的《中国贤圣孔子》（罗氏编号 182）中，出版了由耶稣会士翻译的拉丁文版《论语》，1691 年英国人泰勒（Randal Taylor）将其中内容改编转译为英文。然而，《论语》真正从中文翻译成英文，要归功于英国浸礼会牧师马士曼。

马士曼 1809 年出版的《论语》，是第一部汉语直译的英译本。此书包含孔子生平介绍、基本汉字图表、《论语》的前半部分，以及一篇《关于汉语汉字与声调的论文》。

全书采用汉字旁标注音标及汉字序号的方式，译文后附评注，便于读者理解。

此书的英文原名为《孔子著作卷一》，而事实上包含的只是《论语》的节译本，此后译者也未完成剩下部分，但这部作品毕竟为后来的《论语》英译起到了示范和参考作用，开《论语》英文译本先河。虽然马士曼坦言："此类开创性翻译存在问题在所难免，尤其是翻译像汉语这样的语言。"但他的严谨精神与为汉学传播所做出的努力已足为人称道。

THE

WORKS

OF

CONFUCIUS;

CONTAINING

THE ORIGINAL TEXT,

With a Translation.

VOL. I.

TO WHICH IS PREFIXED

A DISSERTATION
ON THE CHINESE LANGUAGE AND CHARACTER.

By J. MARSHMAN.

SERAMPORE:
PRINTED AT THE MISSION PRESS.
1809.

REMARKS ON THE CHARACTERS.

1. *Yaou*, to have, and sometimes, to be. Its key is *gnut*, a month, which forms the lower part of the character. The two transverse strokes which form the upper part, are part of *cho*, the left hand.

2. *P'hang*, a friend; here, perhaps, an admirer, or a disciple. It is however constantly used to denote a friend. This character is composed of *gnut*, a month, repeated, which is also the key.

3. *Chee*, from, has two meanings. Here, it signifies from: but in many places it denotes self. It is one of the key characters, under which, in the dictionaries, are classed 10 other characters.

4. *Eün*, far, distant; distance, &c. The right side of this character is composed above, of *t'hoo*, the earth, and underneath, of *ee*, apparel. The left side, which is drawn underneath the other part, is *chook*, motion, &c. an obsolete character, used only as a key, as in this instance.

5. *Fong*, room, place, part, region. It is a simple character, and a key, under which are placed 68 characters.

6. *Loi*, to arrive, to come, to approach, is composed of *mook*, wood, and *yun*, man, on each side, placed below the horizontal stroke. The key is *yun*.

7. *Put*, not. See Remark 8. Sentence 1st.

8. *Yek*. See 9, in the former sentence.

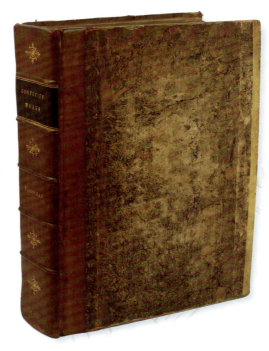

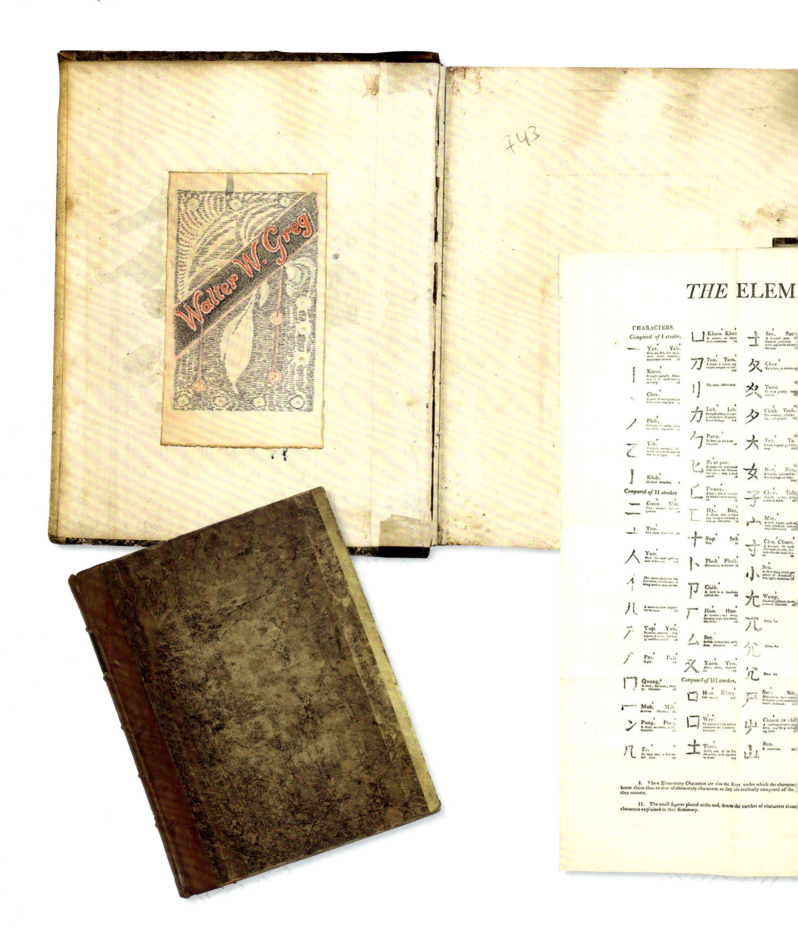

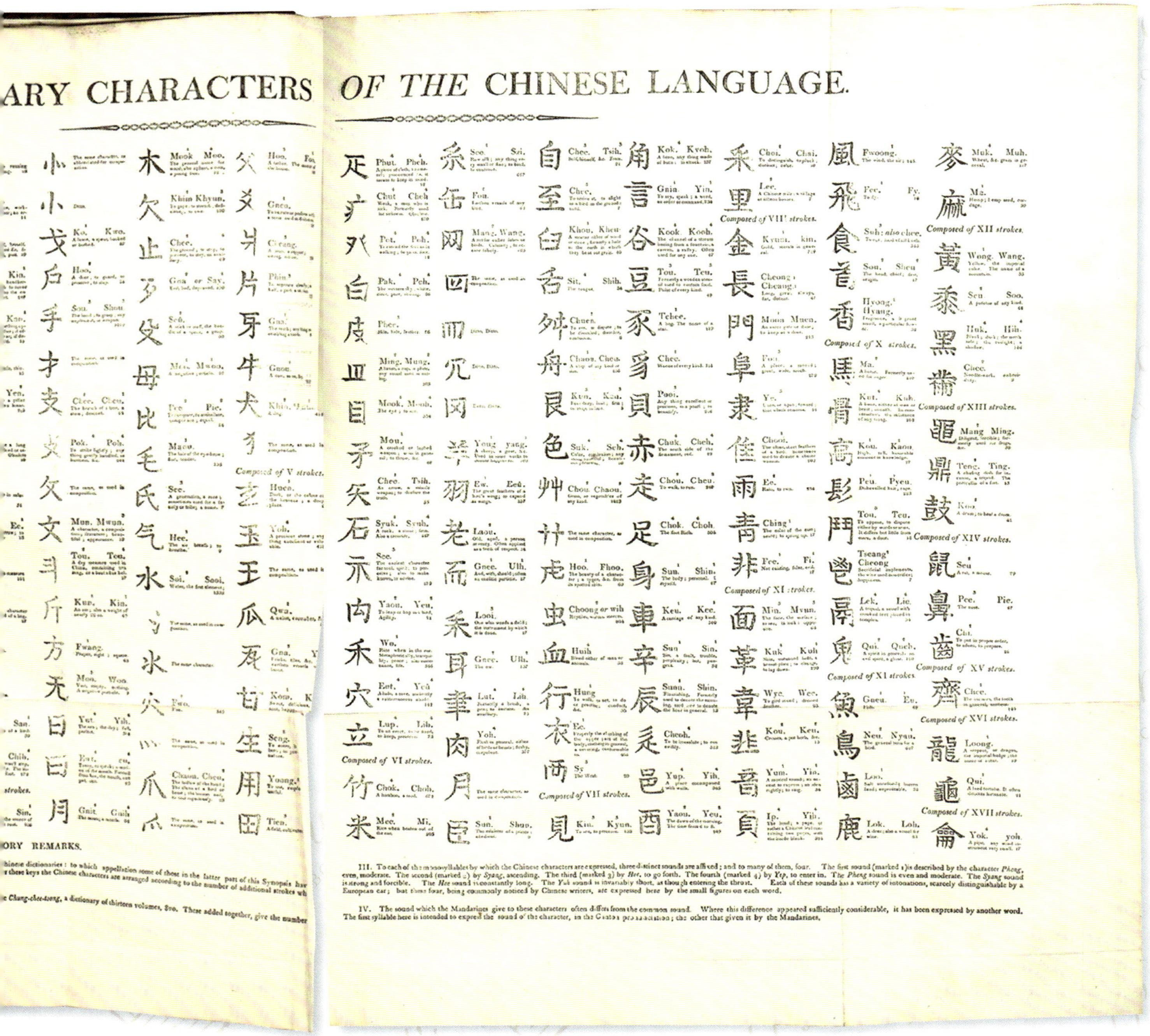

ARY CHARACTERS OF THE CHINESE LANGUAGE.

（本页为《中国语言文字表》之一页，以偏旁部首按笔画数排列，并附广东音与官话音之罗马拼音。字体细小，多不可辨。）

Composed of V strokes.

玄 玉 瓜 瓦 甘 生 用 田

Composed of VI strokes.

疋 疒 癶 白 皮 皿 目 矛 矢 石 示 肉 禾 穴 立

竹 米 糸 缶 网 羊 羽 老 而 耒 耳 聿 肉 月 臣

Composed of VII strokes.

自 至 臼 舌 舛 舟 艮 色 艸 虍 虫 血 行 衣 西

言 谷 豆 豕 豸 貝 赤 走 足 身 車 辛 辰 辵 邑 酉

角

Composed of VII strokes.

金 長 門 阜 隶 隹 雨 青 非

Composed of X strokes.

面 革 韋 韭 音 頁 風 飛 食 首 香

Composed of XI strokes.

馬 骨 高 髟 鬥 鬯 鬲 鬼

Composed of XII strokes.

魚 鳥 鹵 鹿 麥 麻

Composed of XIII strokes.

黃 黍 黑 黹 黽 鼎 鼓 鼠

Composed of XIV strokes.

鼻 齊

Composed of XV strokes.

齒

Composed of XVI strokes.

龍 龜

Composed of XVII strokes.

龠

III. To each of the monosyllables by which the Chinese characters are expressed, three distinct sounds are affixed; and to many of them, four. The first sound (marked 1) is described by the character *Pheng*, even, moderate. The second (marked 2) by *Syang*, ascending. The third (marked 3) by *Her*, to go forth. The fourth (marked 4) by *Yep*, to enter in. The *Pheng* sound is even and moderate. The *Syang* sound is strong and forcible. The *Her* sound is constantly long. The *Yeh* sound is invariably short, as though entering the throat. Each of these sounds has a variety of intonations, scarcely distinguishable by a European ear; but these four, being commonly noticed by Chinese writers, are expressed here by the small figures on each word.

IV. The sound which the Mandarines give to these characters often differs from the common sound. Where this difference appeared sufficiently considerable, it has been expressed by another word. The first syllable here is intended to express the sound of the character, in the Canton pronunciation; the other that given by the Mandarines.

罗氏编号 763

《汉法拉字典》

（ **Dictionnaire chinois, français et latin, publié d'après l'ordre de sa majesté l'empereur et roi Napoléon le Grand** ）

编　　者：［法］小德金（Chrétien-Louis-Joseph de Guignes, 1759-1845）

出　　版：巴黎，皇家印刷所（Imprimerie impériale），1813 年

载体形态：对开本，VIII+LVI+1112 页 +II 页（勘误页）

装　　订：树样花纹小牛皮面，磨损，上部书脊槽缺损，空白页缺失

版　　本：巴黎初版。

内　　容：

　　小德金为著名汉学家德金之子，1794-1795 年间随同荷兰特使抵京，觐见乾隆皇帝，庆祝乾隆登基六十周年。返法后出版的这部《汉法拉字典》，为"拿破仑敕撰"，获得极大的社会反响。但后来据法国汉学家雷慕沙考证，这部作品其实并非小德金的原创，而是始自意大利方济各会传教士叶尊孝（Basilio de Glemona Brollo, 1648-1704）《汉字西译》手稿。1694 年至1699 年间，叶尊孝在南京编成第一部汉拉词典，囊括 7 000 单字与释义，该词典一直以手抄形式流传。

　　1813 年面世的这部《汉法拉字典》，可以说是叶尊孝字典的首印本。全书采用汉语大字，旁注法语与拉丁文对应解释，排版清晰明了。

　　虽然雷慕沙及德国东方学家克拉普洛特（Julius Heinrich Klaproth, 1733-1835）已确认此书作者实为叶尊孝，但这并不影响此书的刊印价值，它的出版为学习与研究汉学者提供了指路门径。

漢

HÁN

字

TSÉ

西

SY

譯

Y

TRADUCTION EN LANGUE EUROPÉENNE,

DES CARACTÈRES CHINOIS.

SINICORUM CHARACTERUM

EUROPÆA INTERPRETATIO.

TABLE DES CLEFS.

lvj

CLEFS DE DOUZE TRAITS.	CLEFS DE TREIZE TRAITS.	鼠 Chū. (208) Page 921.	CLEFS DE QUATORZE TRAITS.	CLEFS DE QUINZE TRAITS.	CLEFS DE SEIZE TRAITS.	CLEF DE DIX-SEPT TRAITS.
黃 Hoâng. (201) Page 914.	黽 Mĭng. (205) Page 919.	鼻 Pĭ. (209) Page 923.	齒 Tchĭ. (211) Page 926.	龍 Lóng. (212) Page 929.	龠 Yŏ. (214) Page 931.
黍 Chù. (202) Page 915.	鼎 Tĭng. (206) Page 920.	齊 Tsĭ. (210) Page 925.	龜 Kouēy. Page 930.	龜 Kouēy. (213) Page 930.	
黑 Hĕ. (203) Page 916.	鼓 Kôu. (207) Page 920.	鼐 Ĕ.			
黹 Tchĭ. (204) Page 918.					

DICTIONNAIRE
CHINOIS,
FRANÇAIS ET LATIN.

CLEFS D'UN SEUL TRAIT.

PREMIÈRE CLEF.

1.re Clef.

一 Ý. (1)

CLEF de l'unité, de la priorité et de la perfection : un, unité, parfait.

Clavis unitatis, prioritatis et perfectionis : unus, primus. Tý-x (a) primus, perfectum, æquale, simile ; x-tĕ, cœlum ; x-sēng, per totam vitam ; x-sīn, toto corde ; x-x, singillatim.

CARACTÈRES JOINTS À LA CLEF.

1 TRAIT.

丁 Tīng. (2)

Porter, fort, robuste.

Gestare, fortis, robustus, substituere loco alterius ; littera temporaria inter chĭ-hâi. Mĭ-ouï, plebs ; pīng-x, milites ; kōg-x, pupillus omnibus destitutus ; x-hiĕu, triennii tempus quo filii ob mortem parentum cessant à muneribus publicis ; tchīng-x, complere annum ætatis 16 vel 18 ; x-hiāng, caryophyllum.

七 Tsĭ. (3)

Sept.

Septem, numerus septimus. Tý-x, septimus.

2 TRAITS.

1.re Clef.

万 Ouán. (4)

Dix mille.

Decem millia.

丈 Tchàng. (5)

Mesure de dix pieds Chinois.

Mensura decem pedum Sinensium. x-foŭ, maritus ; xgín vel yŏu, socer ; fûng, Bonziorum domus ; tâu, mutuò pugnare.

三 Sān. (6)

Trois.

Numerus tres. Tý-x, tertius ; tsâ-x, repetitis vicibus, seu efficaciter. Legitur etiam Sán, iterùm : x-sê, diù cogitare ; tsâ-x, multoties.

上 Chàng. (7)

En haut, dessus, suprême, parfait, aller.

Suprà, superior, nobilis, rex, altus, ascendere, pluris æstimare, ire. Tý-x, supremus ; hoâng, imperator ; x-pên, libellum imperatori porrigere ; x-chĕ, olim ; x-où, meridies ; x-tý, cœli moderator. Legitur etiam Chàng, à loco inferiori ad superiorem ascendere : x-chēng, tonus tertius.

(a) Par-tout où l'on trouvera un x, cet x annonce qu'il remplace le caractère principal : ainsi Tý-x est la même chose que Tý-ý ; ainsi de suite.

A

罗氏编号 785

《华英字典》
（ A dictionary of the Chinese language, in three parts ）

编　　者：［英］马礼逊（Robert Morrison, 1782–1834）

出　　版：澳门，英属东印度公司出版社（Honorable East India Press），1815–1823 年（卷一：1815–1823 年；卷二：1819–1820 年；卷三 1822 年）

载体形态：三卷。卷一分卷一 VI+XVIII+930 页 +II，卷一分卷二 II+884，卷一分卷三 II+908+II；卷二分卷一 XX+II+400 页 +405–1090 页，卷二分卷二 VI+178+306 页；卷三 IV+VI+480 页

装　　订：绿色半摩洛哥山羊皮，书脊题名烫金，略有污渍及修补，缺少第一卷第一部分末页，第二卷第二部分 128 页至 131 页间有一叶未标页码

版　　本：澳门初版，1817 年重印本，1865 年伦敦重印本。

内　　容：

　　英国伦敦会传教士马礼逊是基督教新教来华传教的先驱。他汉学造诣深厚，1812 年完成《汉语语法》，此后，又编纂《华英字典》，成为历史上第一部汉英字典，被后世汉英字典编撰者奉为圭臬。

　　马礼逊的《华英字典》，主要依据《康熙字典》及《汉字西译》，同时参引其他古籍，卷帙浩繁，计三卷六部分，于 1815 年至 1823 年间由隶属于英国东印度公司的澳门印刷厂印制。第一卷分三部分：以部首排列的汉英字典，收录汉字四万余个；第二卷分两部分：以字母音序排列的汉英字典；第三卷：英汉字典，包含汉语单字、词语及句子的对译。

　　马礼逊的《华英字典》，不仅仅是汉字的西译，还包括了例句、相关的历史文化知识及人物介绍，可谓中西文化的百科全书。在这部字典中，马氏也加入了自己对中国文化艺术如戏曲等的见解。

　　马礼逊编撰《华英字典》的初衷，是便于传教士了解中国语言从而利于传播福音，而此书一经出版即风靡欧陆，让更多西人了解中国语言与文化，对中西文化交流与传播意义重大。同时，其中存留的关于中国语言文化、社会风俗等的描述也为后世留下了宝贵的历史资料。

字典

A

DICTIONARY

OF THE

CHINESE LANGUAGE,

IN THREE PARTS.

PART THE FIRST; CONTAINING

CHINESE AND ENGLISH, ARRANGED ACCORDING TO THE RADICALS;

PART THE SECOND,

CHINESE AND ENGLISH ARRANGED ALPHABETICALLY;

AND PART THE THIRD,

ENGLISH AND CHINESE.

BY THE REV. ROBERT MORRISON.

博雅好古之儒有所據以爲考究斯亦著讀書者之一大助

"THE SCHOLAR WHO IS WELL READ, AND A LOVER OF ANTIQUITY, HAVING AUTHENTIC MATERIALS SUPPLIED HIM TO REFER TO AND INVESTIGATE;—EVEN THIS, IS A VERY IMPORTANT ASSISTANCE TO THE SKILFUL STUDENT."　　WANG-WOO-TAOU.

VOL. I.—PART I.

MACAO:

PRINTED AT THE HONORABLE EAST INDIA COMPANY'S PRESS,

BY P. P. THOMS.

1815.

A DICTIONARY

OF THE

CHINESE LANGUAGE.

First Radical. Yih 一

FIRST RADICAL.

一 YIH.† 弓 S.C. ↑ A. V.

One. 第一 Te yih. "Order one," i. e. the first. 同｜般 Tung yih pan; or ｜樣 Yih yang. "The same as." 都是｜樣 Too she yih yang. "It is all the same, or they are all alike." 畫｜ Hwă yih. "To draw one line." e. i. to reduce all to the same rule. To place in order. 不能畫｜ Pŭh năng hwă yih. "The same cannot be affirmed of all; or they cannot be managed alike." Repeated, Yih yih, singly, One by one. 好語似珠穿｜｜ Haou yu sze choo, chuen yih yih. "Good sayings are like pearls strung one by one."

Yih is often rendered by "A," as 個人 Yih ko jin. "A man."

｜口水 Yih k'how shwúy. "A draught of water." Also by "Once, when once, as soon as." As, 視色事如鴆毒｜入口即立死 She yih sze joo chin tih, yih jŭh k'how tseih leih sze. "View illicit pleasure as you would poison, which, as soon as it enters the mouth, causes instant death." 專｜ Chuen yih. "Application to one object, undivided attention."

Yih, often denotes the whole of a thing, as 心｜ Yih sin. "One heart;" i. e. the whole heart. 生｜ Yih shng. "The whole life." 總｜ Yih tsung, and 概｜ Yih kae, or 切｜ Yih tse. All denote the whole number of persons or things; there is, however, a peculiarity in the use of each. 不能｜概而論 Pŭh năng yih kae urh lun. "Cannot affirm the same of all." 領

RADICALS.

SHEWING THEIR ORDER AND MEANING.

Characters formed by One Stroke of the Pencil.		Characters formed by Two Strokes.	
1. 一	Yĭh.* One.	7. 二	Urh. Two.
2. 丨	Kwăn. To descend; C.	8. 亠	Tow. (Undefined;) C.
3. 丶	Choo. A point.	9. 人	Jin. A man; C 亻
4. 丿	Pĕĭh. Bent out; C.	10. 儿	Jin. A man; C.
5. 乙	Yĭh. One.	11. 入	Jĭh, or Jŭh. To enter.
6. 亅	Keŭĕ. Hooked; C.	12. 八	Pă. Eight.

---

* The form of these Radicals, and of the large Characters throughout the work, is taken from an excellent Dictionary, first Published in the Reign of Keen-lung. The latest Edition was Published in the Eleventh year of the present Emperor, Kea-king; and prefaced with flattering recommendations from Persons of the first rank and learning in the State. It was not, however, Published by Imperial Authority. The work is called 佩文備覽 E-wăn-pe-lan, and. is contained in Forty-two volumes, Octavo. The Author's name is 沙木 Sha-mŭh. He was Thirty years engaged in writing it.

VOL. I.

B

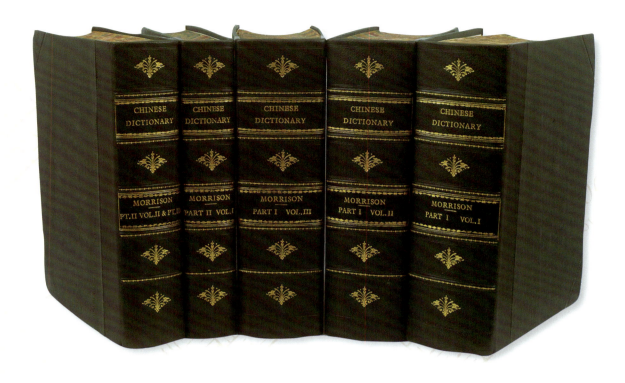

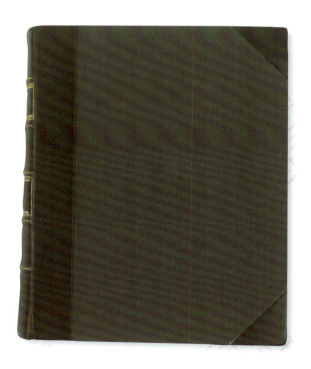

罗氏编号 851

《玉娇梨》
（Iu-kiao-li, ou les deux cousines; roman chinois 1–4）

译　　者：［法］雷慕沙（Jean-Pierre Abel-Rémusat, 1788–1832)

出　　版：巴黎，穆塔迪耶（Moutardier），1826 年

载体形态：12 开本。四卷。卷一 IV+256 页；卷二 IV+172 页；卷三 IV+196 页；卷四 IV+239 页。每卷卷首有
插图。

装　　订：蓝色四分之一摩洛哥山羊皮面，书脊烫金，大理石纹板

版　　本：法文初版，1827 年英文版，1827 年德文版，1829 年荷兰文版，1858 年丹麦文版。

内　　容：

　　《玉娇梨》又名《双美奇缘》，是中国明末清初的长篇小说，讲述青年才子苏友白与宦家小姐白红玉、卢梦梨之间的爱情纠葛，以有情人终成眷属的大团圆收尾。

　　这部典型的中国才子佳人小说，却在遥远的西方产生极大反响，法、德、英、荷等国相继出版，鲁迅称"此书在外国特有名，远过于其在中国"。缘何欧人对此宠爱有加，不得不提到《玉娇梨》的第一位西文译者，法国汉学家雷慕沙。

　　雷慕沙可谓 19 世纪最杰出的汉学家之一，他曾出版多部关于汉语语言及文学的论著。因其在汉学领域作出的贡献，雷氏荣聘法兰西学院汉学教授，并在皇家图书馆负责汉籍工作。雷慕沙除了出版如《汉文简要》之类的学术著作，还将一些中国的文学作品译为法语，其中最著名的莫过于此部《玉娇梨》。

　　在全书的第 1 至 82 页，包含了雷慕沙关于中国小说的重要文章。当读者了解了中国小说的基本脉络后，译者将这部经过"错中错各不遂心"到最后"锦上锦大家如愿"的爱情喜剧呈现在读者眼前。通过雷氏妙笔迻译，这部东方爱情小说牢牢抓住了西方读者的心。

sur ma traduction, celui qui concernera l'original en est tout-à-fait indépendant : je serais surpris que ce dernier fût très-sévère, et j'espère que la faveur du public s'étendra du sujet, qui ne m'appartient pas, à mon travail particulier. Il est arrivé quelquefois que des écrits donnés pour solides ont été réputés superficiels, et que des essais où l'on n'avait en vue que l'agrément ont été trouvés fastidieux. La nature mixte de cet ouvrage-ci doit le garantir de ce double danger. Si des hommes graves le jugeaient frivole, on leur représenterait que ce n'est qu'un roman, une production légère qui ne mérite pas les honneurs d'une critique approfondie; et s'il était médiocrement goûté des gens du monde, on les prierait de remarquer qu'il s'agit d'une composition exotique, traduite d'une langue savante très-difficile, et que la peine qu'elle a coûtée au traducteur lui donne de grands droits à leur indulgence. Ces précautions suffiront pour la faire accueillir avec une approbation universelle.

IU-KIAO-LI,

OU

LES DEUX COUSINES.

CHAPITRE PREMIER.

UNE JEUNE LETTRÉE COMPOSE DES VERS A LA PLACE DE SON PÈRE.

C'est le cœur humain qui est le fondement de nos livres classiques.
Railleries, injures, le style embellit tout.
Le monde est un vaste théâtre, où se joue une longue comédie,
Maintenant comme jadis, nos débats en sont le spectacle.
Ce n'est pas pour rien que les royaumes de Tching et de Weï revivent dans les Odes :
Les désordres racontés par Confucius pourraient-ils se reproduire ?
Il y a des Tseu-Yun, qui vivent encore après mille années
Et qui doivent à l'harmonie les succès de leur vie, et la gloire dont ils jouissent après leur mort.

ON RACONTE que dans les années de la *droiture universelle* (1), il y avait un lettré qui occupait une grande charge de magistrature. Son nom de famille était Pe, son surnom, Hiouan, et

(1) De 1436 à 1450. — C'est un de ces noms que les empereurs de la Chine donnent aux années de leur

IU-KIAO-LI,

OU

LES DEUX COUSINES;

Roman Chinois,

TRADUIT

PAR M. ABEL-RÉMUSAT;

PRÉCÉDÉ D'UNE PRÉFACE

OÙ SE TROUVE UN PARALLÈLE DES ROMANS DE LA CHINE
ET DE CEUX DE L'EUROPE.

———

TOME PREMIER.

———

PARIS,

MOUTARDIER, LIBRAIRE,

RUE GÎT-LE-COEUR, N° 4.

1826.

罗氏编号 **873**

《诗经》
（Confucii Chi-king sive liber carminum. Ex latina）

译　　者：［法］孙璋（Alexandre de la Charme，字玉峰，1695-1767）
出　　版：斯图加特与蒂宾根，科塔（J.G.Cottae），1830 年
载体形态：8 开本，XXII+322+XVI 页
装　　订：红色四分之一摩洛哥山羊皮面，书脊肋线烫金，上书边烫金
版　　本：拉丁文初版。

内　　容：

　　《诗经》为我国第一部诗歌总集，被尊为儒家五经之一。《诗经》中的优美诗篇，为历代所传颂。

　　西方译介《诗经》，早在 16 世纪就已开始，耶稣会神父金尼阁、马若瑟都曾选译过《诗经》，而《诗经》的全译本，则由法国耶稣会神父孙璋译出并刊行欧洲。

　　此书全名《孔子诗经》，除译文外，附有大量注释。译者 1733 年始译，以渊博知识与坚韧毅力，独自完成了《诗经》的全部译文，然而直至 1830 年才由德国东方学家莫尔（Julius von Mohl，1800-1876）编辑成书。

　　此书对后世《诗经》的翻译产生极大影响。德国诗人吕克特（F. Ruckert，1788-1866）的德译本即参照孙璋译本转译，在德语世界大受欢迎。著名的理雅各（James Legge，1815-1897）英译本，也参照孙译而来。在《诗经》乃至儒家经典的传播史上，本书占据重要地位。

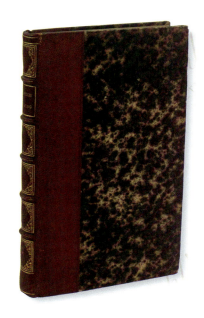

num Ping et in tonum Tche alternatim; deinceps primus in tonum Tche, alter in tonum Ping, tertius in tonum Tche et sic de caeteris. Sinarumque prosodia his hodie verbis fere continetur Ping, tche, ping. Ping, ping, tche, Ping, tche, ping, tche. Tche, ping, tche. Aliis aliorum temporum regulis nihil immoror.

Quoad numerum verborum sive syllabarum in quolibet versu, aliae etiam aliis temporibus fuerunt regulae. Nunc temporis versus impari numero gaudent et quinque aut septem vocibus constant. Tempore dynastiae Ming quae hanc proxime praecessit, versus pari numero gaudebant, et quatuor aut sex vocibus constabant.

Liber autem Chi-king modo has, modo illas regulas sequitur; alii versus tonum Ping habent in medio, alii in fine, alii initio versus; et hoc dixisse satis erit: ipsi sinae litterati poësin antiquam non bene norunt.

De poësi hodierna dicam praeterea, quas nuper accepi regulas supra dictas magis esse pro cantilenis quam pro vera poësi, cujus hae sunt regulae. Cantus est octo versuum; quilibet versus septem verbis constat, primum tertium, quintum est ad libitum; secundum autem, quartum et sextum in primo versu sunt ping, tche, ping, in secundo tche, ping, tche; in tertio ut in secundo; in quarto ping, tche, ping; in quinto ut in quarto; in septimo tche, ping, tche; in octavo ping, ping, ping primus versus cum secundo versu, cum quarto, sexto et octavo in eundem sonum rythmicum definit

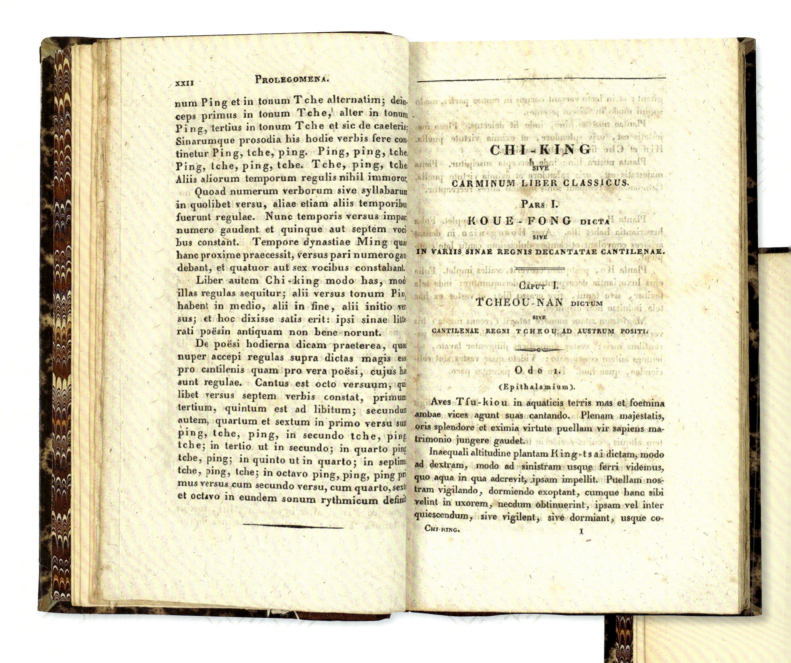

CHI-KING
SIVE
CARMINUM LIBER CLASSICUS.

PARS I.
KOUE-FONG DICTA
SIVE
IN VARIIS SINAE REGNIS DECANTATAE CANTILENAE.

CAPUT I.
TCHEOU-NAN DICTUM
SIVE
CANTILENAE REGNI TCHEOU AD AUSTRUM POSITI.

Ode 1.
(Epithalamium).

Aves Tsu-kiou in aquaticis terris mas et foemina ambae vices agunt suas cantando. Plenam majestatis, oris splendore et eximia virtute puellam vir sapiens matrimonio jungere gaudet.

Inaequali altitudine plantam King-tsai dictam, modo ad dextram, modo ad sinistram usque ferri videmus, quo aqua in qua adcrevit, ipsam impellit. Puellam nostram vigilando, dormiendo exoptant, cumque hanc sibi velint in uxorem, necdum obtinuerint, ipsam vel inter quiescendum, sive vigilent, sive dormiant, usque co-

CONFUCII CHI - KING

SIVE

LIBER CARMINUM.

———

EX LATINA

P. LACHARME INTERPRETATIONE

EDIDIT

JULIUS MOHL.

———

STUTTGARTIAE et TUBINGAE,

Sumptibus J. G. Cottae.

1830.

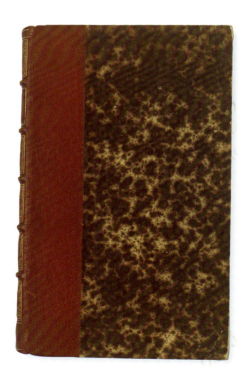

罗氏编号 **883**

《汉语札记》
（Notitia linguae sinicae）

作　　者：［法］马若瑟（Joseph Henri-Marie de Prémare，1666–1736）

出　　版：马六甲，英华书院（Academiae Anglo-Sinensis），1831 年

载体形态：4 开本，II+264 页（最后一页为空白页）+28 页（索引）

装　　订：布面。题名页有曾任职英华书院的基德（Samuel Kidd）的题词

版　　本：拉丁文初版，1847 年英文版，1893 年香港拉丁文重印版。

内　　容：

　　马若瑟的《汉语札记》是这位精通汉学的法国耶稣会神父最重要的代表作，也是他最受称赞的作品。马若瑟从入华开始，就尽心学习汉语，对他而言，汉语不仅是传教的工具，同时他也试图从来自遥远东方的古籍中寻找上帝的话语。

　　马若瑟一直强调，汉语与拉丁语不同，不应用拉丁语的概念解释并归纳汉语，汉语实践比理论更重要。因此，为了体现实用性的原则，马氏使用了一种不同于以往汉语语法的编撰体系。

　　全书引言部分，介绍了有关中国书籍的概念及阅读方法，第一部分论通俗语言和常用语体，第二部分则专论当时的书面语言及经典篇目。这样一本雅俗并存的汉语语法著作，在当时具有体例上的创新性。

　　虽然此书命运多舛，马氏过世百年后才得以付梓，但正如法国汉学家雷慕沙所说："这是马若瑟神父著作中最受称道和最重要的作品，毫无疑问，也是在所有西欧人士同类作品中最优秀之作。"

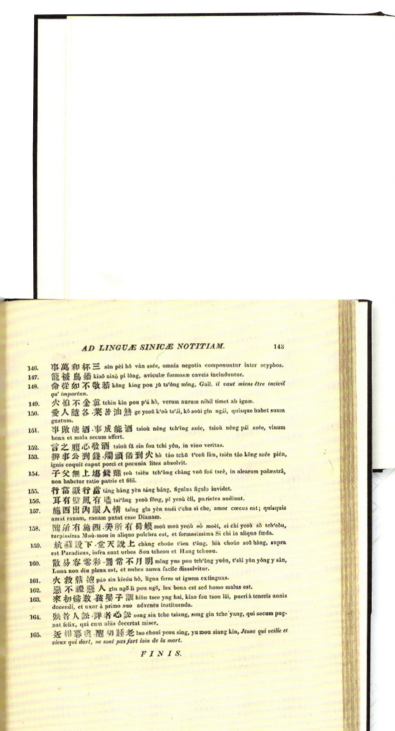

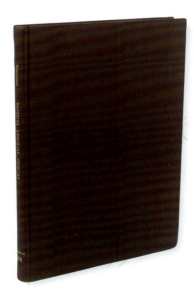

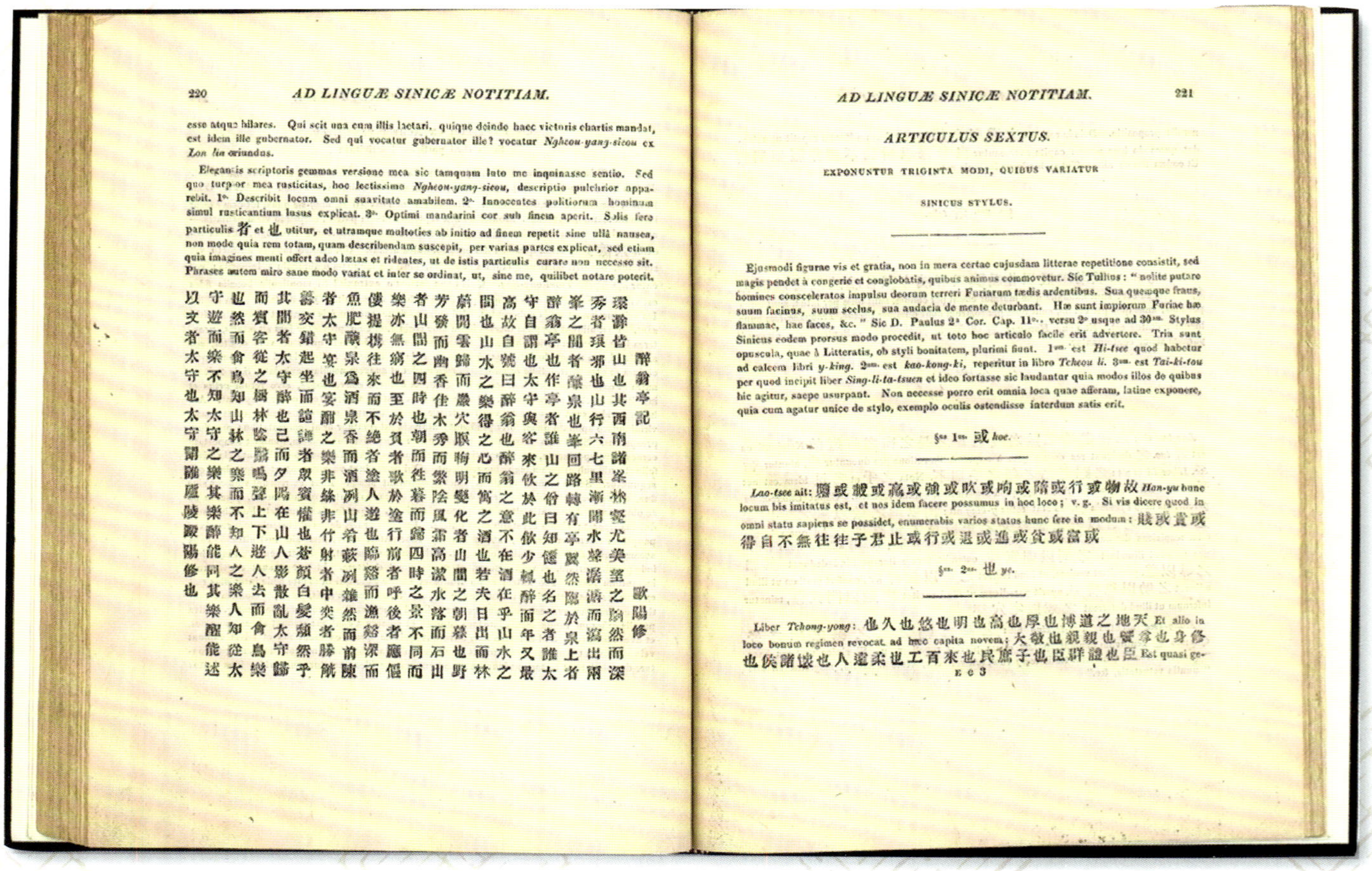

220 *AD LINGUÆ SINICÆ NOTITIAM.*

esse atque hilares. Qui scit una cum illis lætari, quique deinde haec victoris chartis mandat, est idem ille gubernator. Sed qui vocatur gubernator ille? vocatur *Nghcou-yang-sicou* ex *Lou lin* oriundus.

Elegantis scriptoris gemmas versione mea sic tamquam luto me inquinasse sentio. Sed quo turpior mea rusticitas, hoc lectissimo *Nghcou-yang-sicou*, descriptio pulchrior apparebit. 1°. Describit locum omni suavitate amabilem. 2°. Innocentes politiorum hominum simul rusticantium lusus explicat. 3°. Optimi mandarini cor sub finem aperit. Solis fere particulis 者 et 也 utitur, et utramque multoties ab initio ad finem repetit sine ullâ nausea, non modo quia rem totam, quam describendam suscepit, per varias partes explicat, sed etiam quia imagines menti offert adeo lætas et ridentes, ut de istis particulis curare non necesse sit. Phrases autem miro sane modo variat et inter se ordinat, ut, sine me, quilibet notare poterit.

醉翁亭記 歐陽修

環滁皆山也其西南諸峯林壑尤美望之蔚然而深秀者瑯琊也山行六七里漸聞水聲潺潺而瀉出兩峯之間者釀泉也峯回路轉有亭翼然臨於泉上者醉翁亭也作亭者誰山之僧曰知僊也名之者誰太守自謂也太守與客來飲於此飲少輒醉而年又最高故自號曰醉翁也醉翁之意不在酒在乎山水之間也山水之樂得之心而寓之酒也若夫日出而林霏開雲歸而巖穴暝晦明變化者山間之朝暮也野芳發而幽香佳木秀而繁陰風霜高潔水落而石出者山間之四時也朝而往暮而歸四時之景不同而樂亦無窮也至於負者歌於塗行前者呼後者應傴僂提携往來而不絕者滁人遊也臨谿而漁谿深而魚肥釀泉爲酒泉香而酒洌山肴蔌洌雜然而前陳者太守宴也宴酣之樂非絲非竹射者中奕者勝觥籌交錯起坐而諠譁者衆賓懽也蒼顏白髮頹然乎其間者太守醉也已而夕陽在山人影散亂太守歸而賓客從之樹林陰翳鳴聲上下遊人去而禽鳥樂也然而禽鳥知山林之樂而不知人之樂人知從太守遊而樂不知太守之樂其樂醉能同其樂醒能述以文者太守也太守謂誰廬陵歐陽修也

AD LINGUÆ SINICÆ NOTITIAM. 221

ARTICULUS SEXTUS.

EXPONUNTUR TRIGINTA MODI, QUIBUS VARIATUR

SINICUS STYLUS.

Ejusmodi figurae vis et gratia, non in mera certae cujusdam litterae repetitione consistit, sed magis pendet à congerie et conglobatis, quibus animus commovetur. Sic Tullius : " nolite putare homines consceleratos impulsu deorum terreri Furiarum tædis ardentibus. Sua quemque fraus, suum facinus, suum scelus, sua audacia de mente deturbant. Hæ sunt impiorum Furiae hæ flammae, hae faces, &c. " Sic D. Paulus 2ª Cor. Cap. 11°. versu 2° usque ad 30um. Stylus Sinicus eodem prorsus modo procedit, ut toto hoc articulo facile erit advertere. Tria sunt opuscula, quae à Litteratis, ob styli bonitatem, plurimi fiunt. 1um est *Hi-tsee* quod habetur ad calcem libri *y-king*. 2um est *kao-kong-ki*, reperitur in libro *Tcheou li*. 3um est *Tai-ki-tou* per quod incipit liber *Sing-li-ta-tsuen* et ideo fortasse sic laudantur quia modos illos de quibus hic agitur, saepe usurpant. Non necesse porro erit omnia loca quae afferam, latine exponere, quia cum agatur unice de stylo, exemplo oculis ostendisse interdum satis erit.

§us 1us 或 *hoe.*

Lao-tsee ait: 故物或行或隨或呴或吹或強或羸或載或隳 *Han-yu* hunc locum bis imitatus est, et nos idem facere possumus in hoc loco ; v. g. Si vis dicere quod in omni statu sapiens se possidet, enumerabis varios status hunc fere in modum : 或貴或賤或富或貧或進或退或行或止君子往往無不自得

§us 2us 也 *ye.*

Liber *Tchong-yong* : 天地之道博也厚也高也明也悠也久也 Et alio in loco bonum regimen revocat ad hæc capita novem ; 修身也尊賢也親親也敬大臣也體群臣也子庶民也來百工也柔遠人也懷諸侯也 Est quasi ge-

E e 3

罗氏编号 905

《易经》
（Y-king antiquissimus sinarum liber ... ）

译　　者：［法］雷孝思（Jean-Baptiste Régis，字永维，1663–1738）
出　　版：斯图加特与图宾根，科塔（J. G. Cottae），1834–1839 年
载体形态：8 开本，两卷。卷一 XVIII+474 页；卷二 II+590 页，附四幅平版图
装　　订：原纸板面，书脊烫金，磨损，有红色铅笔下划线
版　　本：拉丁文初版。

内　　容：

　　法国汉学家雷慕沙曾评论《易经》"是最古老的、最真实的，也是最隐晦、最难理解的中国古典著作之一"。即使对中国人而言，《易经》亦属古奥艰涩。

　　而法国耶稣会士雷孝思神父在综合并借鉴了前人的研究成果之后，译著了这部《易经》的拉丁文本。

　　全书共两卷，分三大部分。在引言部分，探讨《易经》及其作者，以及《易经》的评价、意义及地位。第二部分，原文的翻译和附注。第三部分，原文的补遗和评论。

　　此书之翻译约在 1698 年至 1723 年前后，是《易经》的第一个西文译本，而付梓出版则是在 1834 年。此书对以后欧洲的《易经》其他语种翻译创造了有利条件。

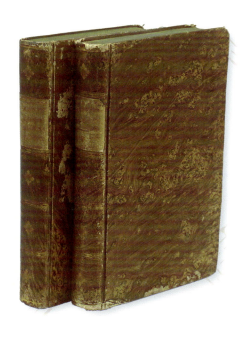
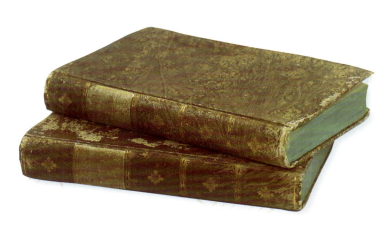

toto divisis nesciatur, intelligi ab illis non potest, quid pictura, quid verba, convenientiae leporisque habeant; 2) ipsam exponimus figuram quae in Y-king rei naturalis semper imago est, adductis etiam philosophorum physicis explicationibus; 3) sententiae quanam ratione figurae congruant, soleantque ex ea traduci ad moralia ac politica praecepta facto historico accommodata, ostendimus ex interpretibus omnium aetatum, qui in regii typi (anni 1715) recentibus commentariis laudantur plusquam ducenti. Sub familia regia Han decem octo; sub Tang undecim; sub Song nonaginta octo; sub Yuen viginti duo; sub Ming sexaginta duo etc.; et qui proinde habendi sunt tanquam perpetui sensus Sinici libri Y-king testes.

DE EXPLICATIONE TEXTUUM
LIBRI Y-KING
A FIGURA I. PRINCIPIS FO-HI AD LXIV.

CAPUT PRIMUM.

$$\text{Kien} \left\{ \begin{array}{l} \underline{\hspace{3cm}} \quad \text{coelum} \ldots \ldots \text{Kien.} \\ \underline{\hspace{3cm}} \quad \text{coelum} \ldots \ldots \text{Kien.} \end{array} \right.$$

EPIGRAPHE, principis OUEN-OUANG.

Magnum, penetrans, conveniens, solidum.
1.   2.   3.   4.

INTERPRETATIO.

Hac Epigraphe (inquit doctor Tchang vulgo Ko-lao dictus) princeps Ouen-ouang voluit optimi imperatoris imaginem informare, ad imitationem coelestis regiminis. Coelo autem praecipue in rerum materialium productione quatuor imprimis dotes, ex principis mente, conveniunt; debet ejus virtus esse: 1) ita magna, ut nihil non attingat; 2) ita penetrans, ut generationum omnium sit efficax; 3) ita conveniens rebus,

11 *

Y-KING

ANTIQUISSIMUS SINARUM LIBER QUEM EX LATINA INTERPRETATIONE

P. REGIS

ALIORUMQUE EX SOC. JESU P. P.

EDIDIT

JULIUS MOHL.

VOL. I.

CUM QUATUOR TABULIS.

1834.

STUTTGARTIAE et TUBINGAE.

SUMPTIBUS J. G. COTTAE.

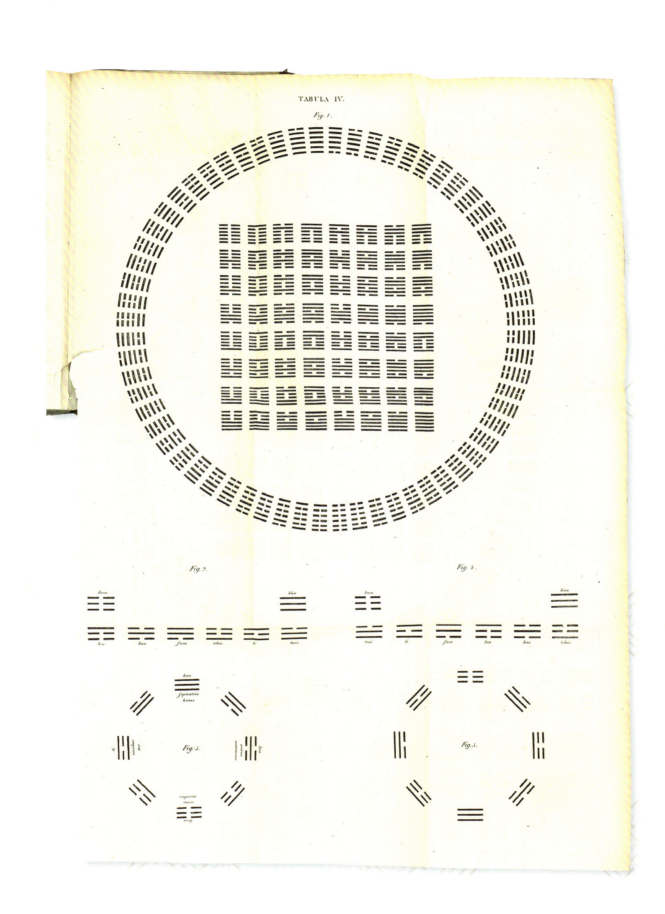

罗氏编号 912

《中国人：中华帝国及其居民概述》
（The Chinese: A general description of the Empire of China and its inhabitants）

作　　者：［英］德庇时（Sir John Francis Davis, 1795－1890）

出　　版：伦敦，Charles Knight，1836 年

载体形态：12 开本。两卷。上卷 IV+IV+420 页；下卷 IV+IV+480 页。附 3 幅木刻图版＋书中 52 幅木刻插图

装　　订：蓝色磨光牛皮烫金，大理石纹板，上部书边烫金

来　　源：上卷题名页有题词："布瓦洛夫人，作者敬赠（The Lady Catherine Boileau with the author's compts）"；
　　　　　　下卷附有一封折叠的致布瓦洛爵士（Sir John Peter Boileau）的书信及一份译稿

版　　本：伦敦英文初版，1836 年纽约版，1857 年扩充版。

内　　容：

　　英国外交家、汉学家德庇时曾任英国驻华公使、商务正监督及香港总督兼总司令。他的外交生涯广为人知，而作为汉学家的德庇时则以《中国人：中华帝国及其居民概述》一书为代表作。

　　此书分上下两卷共二十一章，包含了对中国历史、政治、风俗、宗教、艺术等的描述，内容极其庞杂。

　　上卷含引文，计十章，描述了中英关系、中国地理、历史、政治与风俗习惯。下卷共十一章，记叙中国城市、宗教、语言、艺术、科学、农业与商业情况。全书附有关于中国风土人情的插图，描绘中国社会生活的诸多细节，在当时产生了较大影响。此书关于中华帝国的描述，也深刻影响了当时英人的中国观。

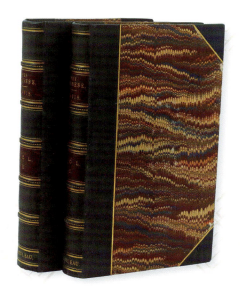

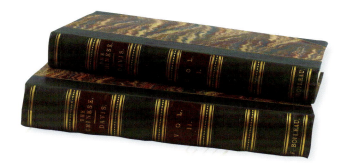

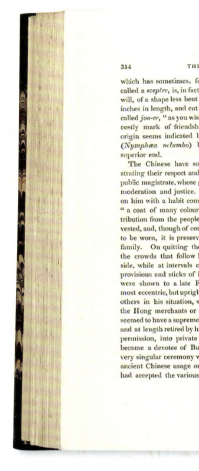

354 THE CHINESE.

which has sometimes, for want of a better name, been called a *sceptre*, is, in fact, an emblem of amity and good-will, of a shape less bent than the letter S, about eighteen inches in length, and cut from the *jade* or *yu* stone. It is called *joo-ee*, "as you wish," and is simply exchanged as a costly mark of friendship; but that it had a religious origin seems indicated by the sacred flower of the lotus (*Nymphæa nelumbo*) being generally carved on the superior end.

The Chinese have some singular modes of demon-strating their respect and regard on the departure of any public magistrate, whose government has been marked by moderation and justice. A deputation sometimes waits on him with a habit composed of every variety of colour, "a coat of many colours," as if made by a general con-tribution from the people. With this he is solemnly in-vested, and, though of course the garment is not intended to be worn, it is preserved as an honourable relic in the family. On quitting the district, he is accompanied by the crowds that follow his chair, or kneel by the way-side, while at intervals on the road are placed tables of provisions and sticks of incense burning. These honours were shown to a late Fooyuen of Canton, a man of a most eccentric, but upright character, who, unlike so many others in his situation, would never take anything from the Hong merchants or others under his authority. He seemed to have a supreme indifference for human grandeur, and at length retired by his own choice, and the Emperor's permission, into private life, from whence it is said he became a devotee of Budh. On his quitting Canton, a very singular ceremony was observed, in conformity with ancient Chinese usage on such rare occasions; when he had accepted the various demonstrations of homage and

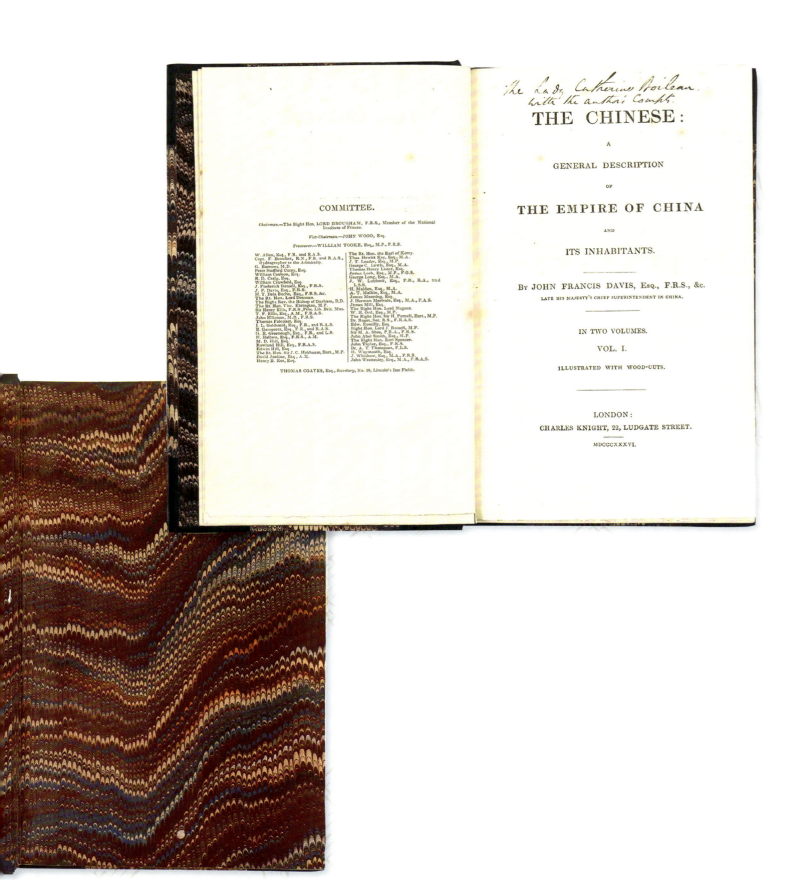

*The Lady Catherine Boileau,
with the author's Compts.*

THE CHINESE:

A

GENERAL DESCRIPTION

OF

THE EMPIRE OF CHINA

AND

ITS INHABITANTS.

BY JOHN FRANCIS DAVIS, Esq., F.R.S., &c.

LATE HIS MAJESTY'S CHIEF SUPERINTENDENT IN CHINA.

IN TWO VOLUMES.

VOL. I.

ILLUSTRATED WITH WOOD-CUTS.

LONDON:
CHARLES KNIGHT, 22, LUDGATE STREET.

MDCCCXXXVI.

1

Translation of the Chinese account of the Porcelain Tower at Nankin communicated by Sr. Tradescant Lay to Captain James Lig James. R.N. —

An Obelisk of three stories once composed the Site of the Porcelain Tower and was dedicated to Girk Wang the Fostering King (a name given to Buddha) this Obelisk underwent various repairs and decays ever changing its designation, up to the time of Gwen Shun, when it was destroyed by fire. In this state it remained till the 10th Year of Gyng lo when the present structure was raised as a token of Gratitude to the Empress and a record to Posterity, of the high veneration in which her character and virtues were held. It was 19 years building and was completed about 6 Years after the death of Gyng lo. —

The Architect who superintended the work set up and framed the Edifice in conformity with a magnificent Plan — his name was She-Lang-Hwang; it consisted of nine Stories and was adorned with Lwolé (a peculiar kind of porcelain stained with sundry colors.)

In a Paou Ta or Pagoda. (called an throne being the Shrine of some Buddhistic Deity) This Pagoda was erected to spread abroad the virtues of a former illustrious Princess it is exactly 32 reeds, 9. cubits, 2. inches and 9 tenths in height — the Spire is overlaid with shining Brass. which preserves its lustre without being liable to tarnish; upon this Spire are the heads of nine Cloud loving Dragons from its Summit 72 Bells (Ling) are suspended by 8 chains. Above and below are 8 angles from which 80 Bells are pendant; the entire number of Bells amounts to 152. On the outside of the nine Stories are lamps consisting of 140 bowls (Ex XXV. 31) Below in the 8 Sided temple which is in the heart of the Pagoda. there are 12 lamps

2

Lamp bowls of Lwolé or Porcelain — When all the lamps are lighted they require 64. kin of oil — these are destined to illuminate the world of good and evil men. and for ever avert the calamities incident to human life —

On the top of the Spire is a bronze pot having two mouths weighing 900 kin or catties — A heavenly pan computed to weigh 450. kin

On the East of the Pagoda is a road dedicated to Gu-ting-Nae-heung-Shin. or all the Sea born Deities — On the South the Garden of To-kwang-heung-kwo-foo, or the nine walk and wide stone house garden — On the West the Sae-ping bridge or bridge of Hospitality — On the North the Great River. —

The premises are in circuit 9. le and 13, paces in which are enclosed all the temples and positions — From the time of Gyng lo who rebuilt it it has been the flowing light of 100 ages and perpetuates a Gratitude ten thousand fold whence it is called the temple of Gratitude

The whole fabrick cost more than 2.405,264 taels; of the 9 iron balls which form the spire the largest is 6 reeds 3. cubits round the smallest 4 reeds 6. cubits round. — the height of the whole is 3600 kin. This spire serves to avert noxious influences it sheds a light in the night time which is one Pearl or bead (the Priest use rosaries and count with beads) It defends from water which is another bead — It defends from wind which is another bead — It defends from dust which is another bead a fourth — One Ingot of Gold weighing 40 taels, Tea one Picul, Silver 1000 Taels, Carbuncle one lump weighing 100 kin precious stones one lot

3

Happy many 100 Strings Yellow Silk two pieces. The book of Fortunes one copy. The book of Amita-fuh one copy. All these tend to control demoniacal Agencies; And the Royal book of the present Dynasty, not containing two laws on the same subject. —

The Chih-woo-Ling tablet states that in the fifth year of Hea King 5th Month and 15th day between the hours of 3 and 5 PM the God of Thunder driving some strange insects before him struck this tower and in a moment injured three sides of the nine stories

The Might of the God was Majestic and Terrible

The Religion (or law) of Buddh has nothing partial here it can do no harm — The Governor and Lieut. Governor addressed the Emperor and Obtained from him permission to repair the tower. the work was commenced on the sixth day of the Second month of the 7th Year Kea-King and was finished on the Second day of the Sixth month following

Within the Tower of Gratitude the Priests fear the Gods at all times ——

End of the Translation

4.

Ancient records speak of a mound of Earth surrounded by water outside the Seu Pader or all precious gate of Nankin

In the days of Tae Kang (A.D. 343) of the Tsin Dynasty there was an Abbot named Lew-sa-ho living in a small square Pagoda on this mound

Kien wan (A.D. 550) of the Tsin Dynasty changed the name Kuntoo and called it Chang kaw. he repaired the Agnets Wang Obelisk raising it to 3 stories that it might serve as a Pagoda.

Keenking of the Lang Dynasty (A.D. 650) liberally repaired the Buddhistic temple and called it Teenhee

Partoo of the Leung Dynasty (A.D. 960) altered its designation to Tse-gan-ging-ching or Obelisk of the rectitude of discriminating Mercy

In the time of demise of the Mongol Dynasty (A.D. 1333) It was destroyed by fire. —

Yung Lo of the Ming Dynasty (A.D. 1412) commenced the present edifice in the 10th Year 6th month 15th day at noon

It was finished in the 6th Year Heuenlih on the first day of the 8th month (A.D. 1431) it was 19 years building —

罗氏编号 1078

《中国帆船"耆英"号大观》
（其衣喊挨炯知 A description of the Chinese junk, "Keying"）

出　　版：伦敦，凯特利（Kellett），1848 年
载体形态：8 开，32 页 + 卷首 1 幅钢版凹印插画 +4 幅钢版凹印图版
装　　订：布面，内装有印刷纸面
版　　本：伦敦英文初版。

内　　容：

　　1846 年，英国商人在广东购买了一艘中式平底方帆船，以在《南京条约》上签字的清政府钦差大臣耆英的名字命名，经一年多航行，于 1848 年 3 月成为最早抵达欧洲的中式帆船。这些英国商人利用当时西方对中国的好奇，把带着大量中国工艺品和数名华人船员的"耆英"号当成流动陈列馆牟利。这册标价 6 便士的小册子，是供登船游客购买的纪念册，在五年多的展览期内，有数以十万计的欧洲游客登船参观。

　　这本小册子收录了一幅"希生广东老爷"的肖像，该老爷声称"清五品官员"，曾经跟随名为凯利特（Kellett）的英国船主乘坐"耆英"号商船远航英伦。小册子题名页背面贴有一张书票，上书"其衣喊挨炯知"和"希生"以及"Keying"和"Hesing"等毛笔字样。小册子正文介绍了船主凯利特（Kellett）除了教给希生一些英语口语，还教他用英文字母写自己的名字。书票上还盖有"曾瑞之印"。希生也许只是个别号，而曾瑞才是希生的本来姓名。书票纸张为金黄色斑汉纸或和纸。题名页上还有书主题签：韦尔德（C.R. Weld）。而韦尔德是《英国皇家学会史》的作者，正是他对首次进入伦敦东印度船坞的中式帆船表现出了极大的专业兴趣。

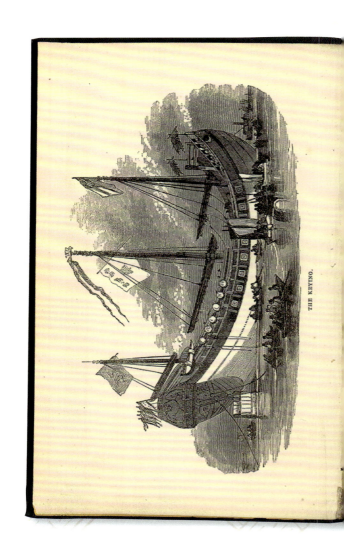

CHAPTER IV.

RISE AND PROGRESS OF THE CHINESE PEOPLE, CAUSES OF ITS UNITY AND GENERAL HOMOGENEITY, AND OF CERTAIN PECULIARITIES IN THE SOUTH-EASTERN CHINESE.

In order to understand aright the circumstances under which the politico-religious rebellion has come into existence and the people who originated it, we must devote a little time to a cursory view of the rise and progress of the Chinese nation as a whole; and then note some differences that, in the midst of the general and wonderful homogeneity, do nevertheless distinguish the South-Eastern Chinese from the rest of the nation.

The original seat of the Chinese people was the northern portion of Chih le, the province in which the present capital Peking happens to be situated.

How the first Chinese, the founders of the nation, came to be in that locality, is one of those questions connected with the origin and spread of the human race generally which can only receive a conjectural solution. All we do or can know positively is that the first portion of authentic Chinese history tells us that the Emperor Yaou, who reigned 4,200 years ago, had his capital at the now district city of Tsin chow, situated about 100 miles only to the south of the present capital Peking. From this most ancient location the people spread gradually westward and southward, thus steadily increasing its territory. The usual course of the process was, first colonization of the newer regions, and displacement from them of whatever aboriginal inhabitants were found; and

afterwards political incorporation with the older territory. At times however the process was reversed, and military conquest of the aboriginals preceded their displacement by an industrial occupation of their lands. Lastly I have to draw special attention to one other mode in which the Chinese have effected territorial extension, a mode which exemplifies in a striking manner the peculiarity, and the innate strength of Chinese civilization. The whole nation with its country, has been conquered by some adjacent barbarous people; has then, under cover of the political union thus effected, penetrated into, and partially colonized the original country of its conquerors; and ultimately has freed itself by force, and taken political possession of its new colonies after having previously effected a mental subjugation of its conquerors by dint of superior civilization. Something of this kind happened with the Khitan Tartars who had possession of the north of China Proper, after that with the Mongols who had the whole country, and it is well known to be the process in operation for the 200 years last past under the present rulers, Manchoos, whom the Chinese colonists are partially superseding in their own old country, Manchooria.

I have already noticed the distinction between China Proper and the Chinese Empire. Let the reader note now that the territorial distinction marked by these terms has existed *in fact* from the earliest periods of Chinese history. *China proper* means at all periods that portion of the east of the Asiatic continent which has been *possessed and permanently occupied by the Chinese people.* The Chinese Empire means at all periods besides China Proper, those large portions of the whole Asiatic continent occupied by Tartar-Nomads, or other non-Chinese peoples, but which have from time to time been under the sway of the Emperor of China, and more or less directly ruled by Chinese officers and armies. China Proper has at all periods been characterized by Chinese civilization; that is to say its population generally besides being physically of the same race, has always been governed in its domestic, its social, and (with

D 2

CHAPTER IV.

RISE AND PROGRESS OF THE CHINESE PEOPLE, CAUSES OF ITS UNITY AND GENERAL HOMOGENEITY, AND OF CERTAIN PECULIARITIES IN THE SOUTH-EASTERN CHINESE.

Original Seat of the People, and Modes of Progress, 34. China Proper, and Chinese Empire, 35. Cause of Unity and Homogeneity, 38. Meditations on the Great Pyramid, 39. The great Southern Watershed, 43. The South-Eastern Chinese, 44.

CHAPTER V.

M. HUC'S OPINIONS OF THE CHINESE.

L'Empire Chinois, 51. Chinese Catholics, 52. Foreign Missionaries, 53. M. Huc's Opportunities, 54. The Two British Embassies, 55. Opportunities of Foreigners at the Five Ports, 56. Errors of l'Empire Chinois, 59. Character of the Chinese, 63. Scandinavian Sea-King and Learned Chinese, 67. Chinese Character illustrated from Language, 68. Various Opinions contrasted, 72.

CHAPTER VI.

HUNG SEW TSEUEN, THE ORIGINATOR OF THE REBELLION, HIS EARLY BIOGRAPHY AND HIS ADOPTION OF CHRISTIANITY.

Hung sew tseuen's Parentage and Youth, 74. His Vision, 76. Christian Missionary Tracts, 79. Hung sew tseuen reads them, 80. Is converted, and believes he has a Mission, 81.

CHAPTER VII.

HUNG SEW TSEUEN'S ESTABLISHMENT OF A NEW SECT OF CHRISTIANS IN KWANG SE, AND CAUSES OF HIS SUCCESS.

His first Converts, and Departure for Kwang se, 84. Society of Godworshippers established, 85. Hung sew tseuen with Mr. Roberts at Canton, 87. Acknowledged Chief of Godworshippers in Kwang se, 88. Causes of Spread of Religious Movements, 89. Character of Kwang se Chinese, 91. Causes of their Conversion by Hung sew tseuen, 92. Dr. Gutzlaff's Chinese Testament, 94. Godworshippers destroy Idols, and are persecuted, 96.

CHAPTER VIII.

ORIGIN OF THE GROSSER FANATICISMS OF THE NEW SECT OF CHRISTIANS.

Alleged Descents of God into the World, 98. Proclamations respecting them, 99. Will of God communicated by Yang sew tsing, 102. Why accepted by Hung sew tseuen, 103.

CHAPTER IX.

RETROSPECTIVE ACCOUNT OF THE ESTABLISHMENT OF THE MANCHOO POWER IN CHINA.

Chinese Rebel overthrows Native Dynasty, 106. Chinese General invites the Aid of the Manchoos, 107. They establish themselves in Peking, 108. Their Second Emperor Kang he, 109. Suppresses a Rebellion, and conquers Formosa, 110.

CHAPTER X.

FORMATION OF CHINESE POLITICAL SOCIETIES AGAINST THE MANCHOO DOMINATION, AND ORIGIN OF CHINESE INSURRECTIONS AND REBELLIONS GENERALLY.

Secret Political Societies in South-Eastern China, 112. Origin of Chinese Insurrections, 113. Origin of Bandit Rebel Leaders, 117. Occidentals' Misconceptions on Chinese Robbers, Pirates, and Rebels, 118. Chinese Civilization, 120. Present Rebellions foreseen by Writer, 121.

CHAPTER XI.

CONVERSATIONS OF THE OLD EMPEROR TAOU KWANG WITH A HIGH MANDARIN RESPECTING BRITISH PROJECTS AND THE STATE OF SOUTHERN CHINA.

Imperial Administrative Levees, 123. Their Object, 124. How the Emperor's Conversations became known, 125. The Mandarin Pih kwei, 126. Has an Audience with the Emperor, 127. Emperor inquires about English Barbarians, 128; and their Troops at Hongkong, 129. Emperor promotes Pih kwei, and exhorts him to do his Duty, 130. Concludes the English Barbarians are mere Traders, 132. Describes his Inner Garments, 133. Speaks about Opium-smoking, 134. Inquires about the Future Conduct of English Barbarians, 135.

罗氏编号 **1224**

《额尔金出使中国日本记》2 卷
（ **Narrative of the Earl of Elgin's mission to China and Japan in the years 1857, 58, 59. 1−2** ）

作　　者：［英］俄理范（Laurence Oliphant, 1829−1888）

出　　版：爱丁堡和伦敦，布莱克伍德（William Blackwood），1859 年

载体形态：8 开，XIV+492；XII+496 页 +5 幅地图 +20 幅石印图版，大部分彩色 +50 幅木刻插图

装　　订：绿色全小牛皮面烫金。

版　　本：英文初版。

内　　容：

　　作者以私人秘书身份参加了第二次鸦片战争期间额尔金（James Bruce, 8th Earl of Elgin, 1811−1863）为首的英国使团。回国后写成此书，从独特的视角回顾了第二次鸦片战争期间的一系列重大事件。其中关于英法军队、外交官在中国的一系列军事与政治活动，包括长江口岸通商问题的协商，《天津条约》从商谈到签订的完整过程的记载，具有较高的文献参考价值。

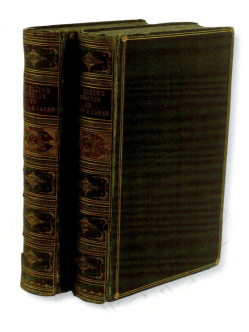

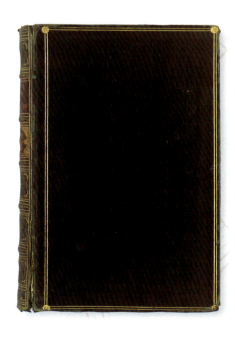

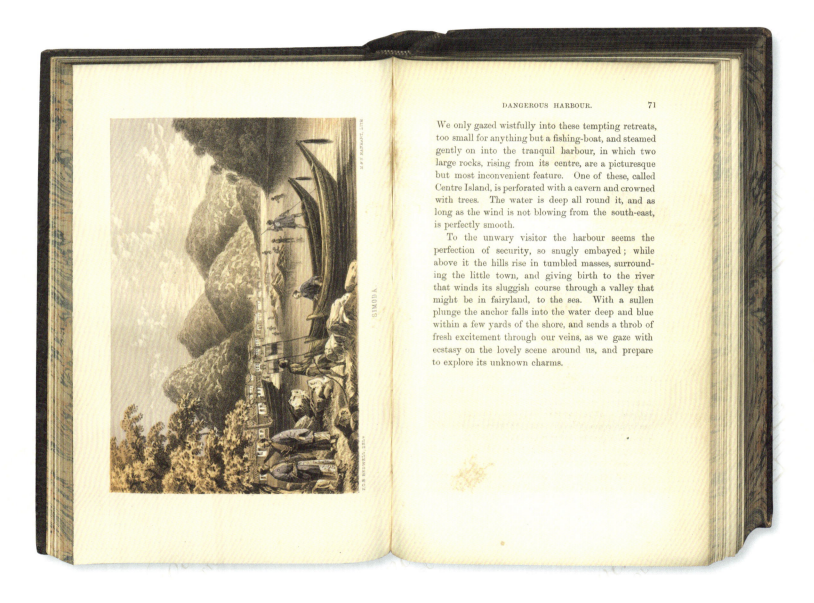

SIMODA.

We only gazed wistfully into these tempting retreats, too small for anything but a fishing-boat, and steamed gently on into the tranquil harbour, in which two large rocks, rising from its centre, are a picturesque but most inconvenient feature. One of these, called Centre Island, is perforated with a cavern and crowned with trees. The water is deep all round it, and as long as the wind is not blowing from the south-east, is perfectly smooth.

To the unwary visitor the harbour seems the perfection of security, so snugly embayed; while above it the hills rise in tumbled masses, surrounding the little town, and giving birth to the river that winds its sluggish course through a valley that might be in fairyland, to the sea. With a sullen plunge the anchor falls into the water deep and blue within a few yards of the shore, and sends a throb of fresh excitement through our veins, as we gaze with ecstasy on the lovely scene around us, and prepare to explore its unknown charms.

326 DENSE CROWDS.

wedged, not only down to the water's edge, but into it up to their waists, in order to gaze at their ease on the phenomenon before them. Thus an oblique plane of upturned faces and bare heads extended almost from the surface of the water to the eaves of the houses; and up to the last day of our residence the banks were always more or less crowded with spectators, watching the movements of the barbarians. A long straight reach extends from below the bridge of boats to the point of the junction of the river and the grand canal, which enters the Peiho at right angles from the southward, and here terminates its extended course of about 600 miles.

Directly facing us, as we steamed up this reach, past a line of our own gunboats, which were anchored in it, was a picturesque line of buildings, abreast of which the allied Admirals were moored. This fragile and somewhat fantastic construction suggested the notion of a summer palace. We were informed that as such it had, in fact, served the Emperor Kienlung, in honour of which happy event it had been invested by imperial patent with the title of "The Temple of Supreme Felicity," under which auspicious designation it was now about to serve as our abode.

We were soon clambering up the steep bank, finding some difficulty in freeing ourselves from the services which were officiously pressed upon us by the Chinamen who crowded it, and who, thrusting forth helping hands, seemed anxious to show us every mark of civility. We found, when we stood within

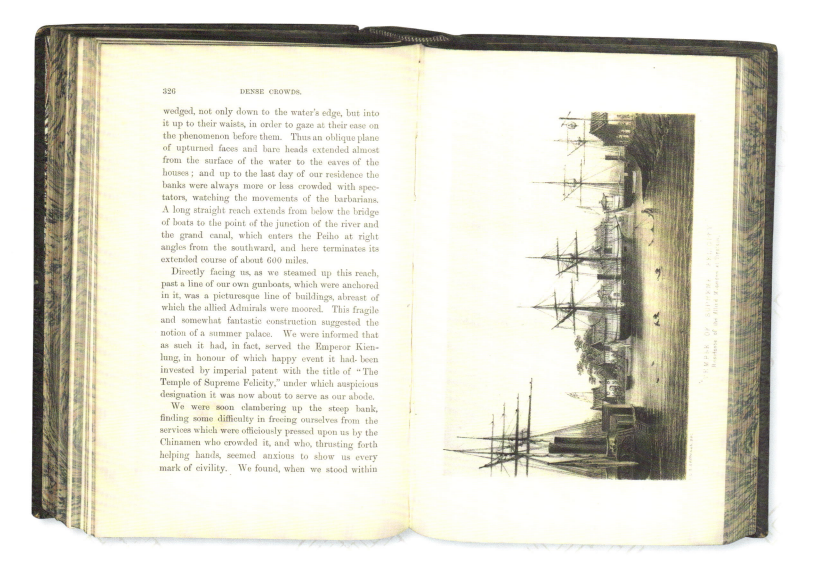

brought him into close and intimate contact with their officials; and he possessed their confidence to an extent probably never accorded to a European. As Lord Elgin had the highest opinion of this gentleman's capacity and judgment, it was most desirable that the Chinese should place him in the position relatively to themselves in which Lord Elgin most wished to see him. From this period Mr Lay was in daily communication with the Chinese Commissioners, and affairs were thus early put into a train which enabled them to be brought to a speedy and satisfactory conclusion.

The mission of Mr Lay, however, being somewhat of a confidential or non-official character, Lord Elgin kept up his official intercourse with the Commissioners by insisting that the Kwang-fang should be obtained without delay. In this application he was quite successful: the Kwang-fang was sent down from Pekin, and the much-vexed question of full powers set finally at rest.

Such was the nature and such the results of the first interview of Lord Elgin with the Imperial Commissioners. It did not last a quarter of an hour; nor did the Ambassador again visit the "Temple of the Oceanic Influences," or meet the Commissioners, till he went there finally to sign the treaty. At the ceremony above described, the Commissioners were dressed in the plain but handsome costume of the Chinese mandarin, the only mark denoting their high rank being the opaque red button and peacock's feather;

a tippet of rich maroon silk covered their shoulders and arms; and with the exception of one or two rings, their persons were devoid of all ornament. As is usual upon all occasions of ceremonial interviews, numbers of minor officials crowded the apartment, eagerly listening to the conversation, while four or five intelligent-looking secretaries took notes in writing of all that passed.

Kweiliang, First Imperial Commissioner.

The senior Commissioner, Kweiliang, was a venerable man, of placid and benevolent expression, with

罗氏编号 **1252**

《旅华十二年》
（Twelve years in China: the people, the rebels, and the Mandarins）

作　　者：［英］施嘉士（John Scarth，生卒年不详）

出　　版：爱丁堡，康斯特布尔（Thomas Constable），1860 年

载体形态：8 开，XX+328 页 +11 幅石印图版，8 幅部分上色

装　　订：半小牛皮面烫金

版　　本：英文版。

内　　容：

　　作者系英国商人，从商业角度出发，描述了当时中国的茶、丝、糖业的生产、贸易状况，并有相当篇幅是关于太平天国运动情况的记载。作者在书中指出清政府的腐败与苛政是导致太平天国运动的主因，并站在同情者的角度，为太平天国运动做了辩护，反映了当时一部分西方人士的观点。

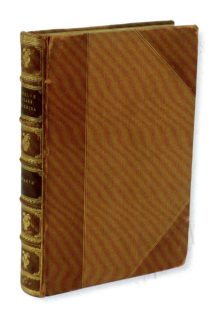

Rebels at Shanghai

CHAPTER XIX.

THE REBELS AT SHANGHAI.

Shanghai seized by a secret society—Docile character of the citizens—Tai-ping-wang acknowledged—Foreign property respected—A heroine—The siege operations—Singular details—A conchologist—Two marine deserters—Curious contrivances—Conspiracies in the city—Picturesque costumes—Rebels' penal code—Motley arms—Silk armour—Desire for rank—Bribery—The leaders described.

THERE is very little doubt, that had no insurrection troubled other parts of this celestial empire, Shanghai would have remained in peaceful quietude. The rebellion was both the cause and the excuse for the capture of the city. Many people deny the right of a political *status* to the men that held Shanghai against the government for eighteen months; as the narrative proceeds, we shall learn how far these people are correct.

It was taken on the 7th September 1853, by members of a secret society, with wide ramifications, and who, it was well known, aimed at the overthrow of the Tartar dynasty. The local government had no power to resist; indeed, the body-guard of the Taou-tai appears to have been in league with the captors. The Che-heen[1] was killed, an officer not likely to be favoured by the men who aided in his assassination, as, doubtless, not a few had felt the weight of his power. The people of Shanghai, a quiet peaceable race, had nothing whatever to do with the outbreak, the whole being planned and carried

[1] Equivalent to a mayor, but appointed by the Government.

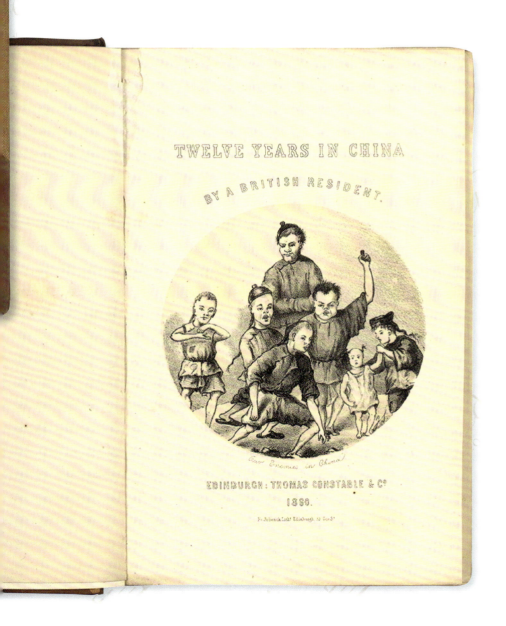

TWELVE YEARS IN CHINA

BY A BRITISH RESIDENT.

Our Enemies in China

EDINBURGH: THOMAS CONSTABLE & C°
1860.

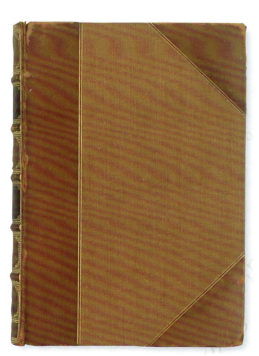

罗氏编号 1259

《中国经典卷二：孟子》

(The Chinese classics: with a translation, critical and exegetical notes, prolegomena, and copious indexes. In seven volumes. Vol. II., containing the works of Mencius)

编 译 者：［英］理雅各（James Legge, 1815－1897）

出　　版：香港，自印；伦敦，特鲁布纳（Trübner），1861 年

载体形态：8 开，VIII+128+498 页

装　　订：半小牛皮面

来　　源：简略题名页有书主题记

版　　本：英文版。

内　　容：

　　理雅各是英国近代最重要的汉学家之一，系统翻译了大量中国传统经典。本书是其 28 卷译作中的第二卷，除《孟子》一书的原文与译文外，还加入了大量的批注与解释。理雅各翻译中国传统经典，注重精研原著，并博采前人译本所长，力求所译有据，因此受到欧洲学界的一致好评。

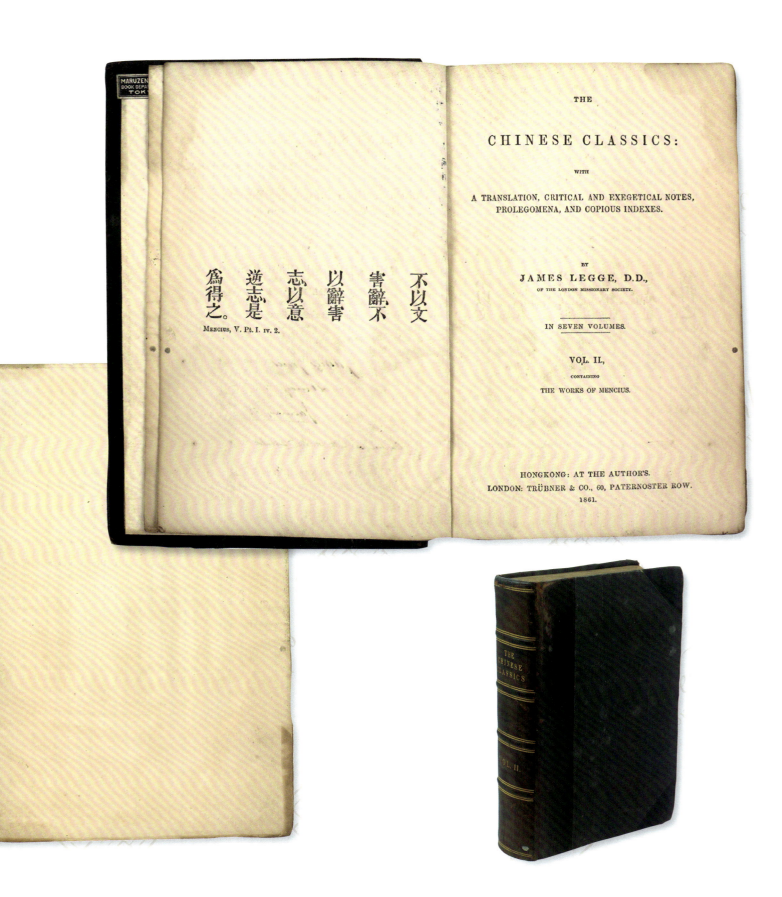

THE

CHINESE CLASSICS:

WITH

A TRANSLATION, CRITICAL AND EXEGETICAL NOTES,
PROLEGOMENA, AND COPIOUS INDEXES.

BY

JAMES LEGGE, D.D.,

OF THE LONDON MISSIONARY SOCIETY.

IN SEVEN VOLUMES.

VOL. II,

CONTAINING

THE WORKS OF MENCIUS.

HONGKONG: AT THE AUTHOR'S.
LONDON: TRÜBNER & CO., 60, PATERNOSTER ROW.
1861.

不以文害辭不以辭害志以意逆志是爲得之。

MENCIUS, V. Pt. I. iv. 2.

BOOK I.
KING HWUY OF LEANG. PART II.

樂也直好世俗之樂耳

曰寡人非能好先王之

以好樂有諸王變乎色

見於王曰王嘗語莊子

如孟子曰王之好樂甚

未有以對也曰好樂何

於王王語暴以好樂暴

莊暴見孟子曰暴見

梁惠王章句下

CHAPTER I. 1. Chwang Paou, seeing Mencius, said to him, "I had an audience of the king. His Majesty told me that he loved music, and I was not prepared with anything to reply to him. What do you pronounce about that love of music?" Mencius replied, "If the king's love of music were very great, the kingdom of Ts'e would be near to *a state of good government*."

2. Another day, *Mencius*, having an audience of the king, said, "Your Majesty, *I have heard*, told the officer Chwang, that you love music;—was it so?" The king changed colour, and said, "I am unable to love the music of the ancient sovereigns; I only love the music that suits the manners of the *present age*."

CH. 1. HOW THE LOVE OF MUSIC MAY BE MADE SUBSERVIENT TO GOOD GOVERNMENT, AND TO A PRINCE'S OWN ADVANCEMENT. The chapter is a good specimen of Mencius' manner,—how he slips from the point in hand to introduce his own notions, and would win princes over to benevolent government by their own vices. He was no stern moralist, and the Chinese have done well in refusing to rank him with Confucius. 1. Chwang Paou appears to have been a minister at the court of Ts'e. The 曰 preceding 好樂如何 is unnecessary. If we translate it, we must render—'He then said.' But the paraphrasts all neglect it. 'Ancient

至於此極也父子不見兄

曰吾王之好鼓樂夫何使我

篇之音舉疾首蹙頞而相告

於此百姓聞王鐘鼓之聲管

眾臣請爲王言樂今王鼓樂

樂與眾樂樂孰樂曰不若與

孰樂曰不若與人曰與少樂

得聞與曰獨樂樂與人樂樂

乎今之樂由古之樂也曰可

王之好樂甚則齊其庶幾

3. *Mencius* said, "If your Majesty's love of music were very great, Ts'e would be near to *a state of good government!* The music of the present day is just like the music of antiquity, *in regard to* effecting that."

4. *The king* said, "May I hear from you the proof of that?" *Mencius* asked, "Which is the more pleasant,—to enjoy music by yourself alone, or to enjoy it along with others?" "To enjoy it along with others," was the reply. "And which is the more pleasant,—to enjoy music along with a few, or to enjoy it along with many?" "To enjoy it along with many."

5. *Mencius* proceeded, "Your servant begs to explain *what I have said about* music to your Majesty.

6. "Now, your Majesty is having music here.—The people hear the noise of your bells and drums, and the notes of your fifes and pipes, and they all, with aching heads, knit their brows, and say to one another, 'That's how our king likes his music! But why does he reduce us to this extremity *of distress?*—Fathers and sons cannot

sovereigns,' i. e., Yaou, Shun, Yu, T'ang, Wǎn and Woo, is a better translation of 先王 than 'former kings.' 3. 由 猶. 4. 可得 聞 與, as in prec. ch. 獨樂樂—the second 樂 is *loh*, 'joy,' 'pleasure.' So, in the next clause, and after 孰. 5. 爲 (low. 3d

tone) 王, 'for the sake of your Majesty.' 6. 鼓樂—鼓 is a verb,—作. The ancient dict., the 說文, makes a difference between this, and the same word for 'drum,' saying this is formed from 支 named p'ǎh, while the other is formed from 支. The difference of form is

路也禮門也惟君子能由
欲其入而閉之門也
以不賢人之招招賢人而
欲見賢人而不以其道猶
庶人庶人豈敢往哉況乎
人死不敢往以士之招招
旌以大夫之招招虞人虞
庶人以旃士以旂大夫以
問招虞人何以曰以皮冠
焉取非其招不往也曰敢

may lose his head.' What was it *in the forester* that Confucius thus approved? He approved his not going *to the duke*, when summoned by the article which was not appropriate to him."

6. Chang said, "May I ask with what a forester should be summoned?" Mencius replied, "With a skin cap. A common man *should be summoned* with a plain banner; a scholar *who has taken office*, with one having dragons embroidered on it; and a great officer, with one having feathers suspended from the top of the staff.

7. "When the forester was summoned with the article appropriate to the summoning of a great officer, he would have died rather than presume to go. If a common man were summoned with the article appropriate to the summoning of a scholar, how could he presume to go? How much more may we expect this refusal to go, when a man of talents and virtue is summoned in a way which is inappropriate to his character!

8. "When a prince wishes to see a man of talents and virtue, and does not take the proper course *to get his wish*, it is as if he wished him to enter *his palace*, and shut the door against him. Now, right-

之云乎. 5. See III. Pt. II. i. 2. 6. The explanation of the various flags here is from Choo He, after the Chow Le. The Dict. may be consulted about them. 何以=何用. 7. A man of talents and virtue ought not to be called at all. The prince ought to go to *him*. 閉 之門.—this is another case of a verb followed by the pronoun and another objective;—lit., 'shut him the door.' 詩云—see the She-king, II. v. Ode IX. st. l. Julien condemns the translating 周道 'the way to Chow,' but that is the meaning of the terms in the ode; and, as the imperial highway, it is used to indicate figuratively the great way of righteousness. 厎—in the ode 砥, the upper tone. The ode is attributed to an officer of one of the eastern States, mourning over the

是路出入是門也詩云周
道如底其直如矢君子所
履小人所視萬章曰孔子
君命召不俟駕而行然則
孔子非與曰孔子當仕有
官職而以其官召之也。
[孟]孟子謂萬章曰一鄉之
善士斯友一鄉之善士一
國之善士斯友一國之善
士天下之善士斯友天下

ousness is the way, and propriety is the door, but it is only the superior man who can follow this way, and go out and in by this door. It is said in the Book of Poetry,

'The way to Chow is level like a whetstone,
And straight as an arrow.
The officers tread it,
And the lower people see it.'"

9. Wan Chang said, "When Confucius received the prince's message calling him, he went without waiting for his carriage. And so—did Confucius do wrong?" Mencius replied, "Confucius was in office, and had its appropriate duties. And moreover, he was summoned on the business of his office."

CHAPTER VIII. 1. Mencius said to Wan Chang, "The scholar whose virtue is most distinguished in a village shall make friends of all the virtuous scholars in the village. The scholar whose virtue is most distinguished throughout a State shall make friends of all the virtuous scholars of that State. The scholar whose virtue is most distinguished throughout the empire shall make friends of all the virtuous scholars of the empire.

oppressive and exhausting labours which were required from the people. The 'royal highway' presents itself to him, formerly crowded by officers hastening to and from the capital, and the people hurrying to their labours, but now travelled slowly and painfully along. 9. See Con. Ana. X. xiii. 4.

Ch. 8. THE REALIZATION OF THE GREATEST ADVANTAGES OF FRIENDSHIP, AND THAT IT IS DEPENDENT ON ONE'S-SELF. 1. 'The virtuous scholar of one village,—he shall make friends of the virtuous scholars of (that) one village': —the first 善 is in the superlative degree, and 友 is not only 'to be friends with,' but also 'to realize the uses of friendship.' The eminence attained by the individual attracts all the others to him, and he has thus the opportunity of learning from them, which no imitation be-

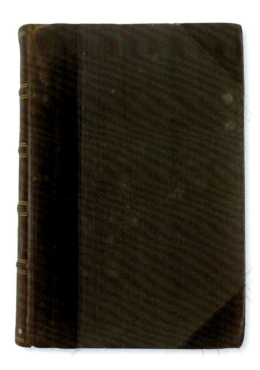

罗氏编号 **1297**

《认字新法　常字双千》
（The analytical reader. A short method for learning to read and write Chinese）

编　　者：［美］丁韪良（William Alexander Parsons Martin, 1827－1916）

出　　版： 上海，美华书馆，1863 年

载体形态： 24×16 厘米，IV+142 页

装　　订： 20 世纪红色半摩洛哥山羊皮面，书脊烫金，有数叶略微泛黄

版　　本： 英文初版。

内　　容：

　　编者系美国新教传教士，是著名的"中国通"。本书是他为汉语初学者编写的教材兼常用字字典。本书采用部首拆字的方法来记忆汉字，同时对于汉语常用字这一概念的运用也别具心裁。内容上突出实用性，在当时新教传教士编纂的众多以宣传教义为主要内容的识字教材中显得独树一帜，显示了编者对中国语言文字及中国社会的深刻认识与理解。

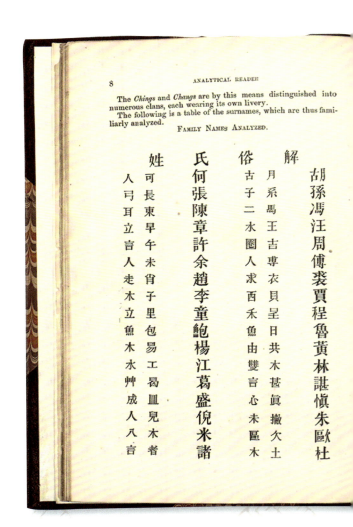

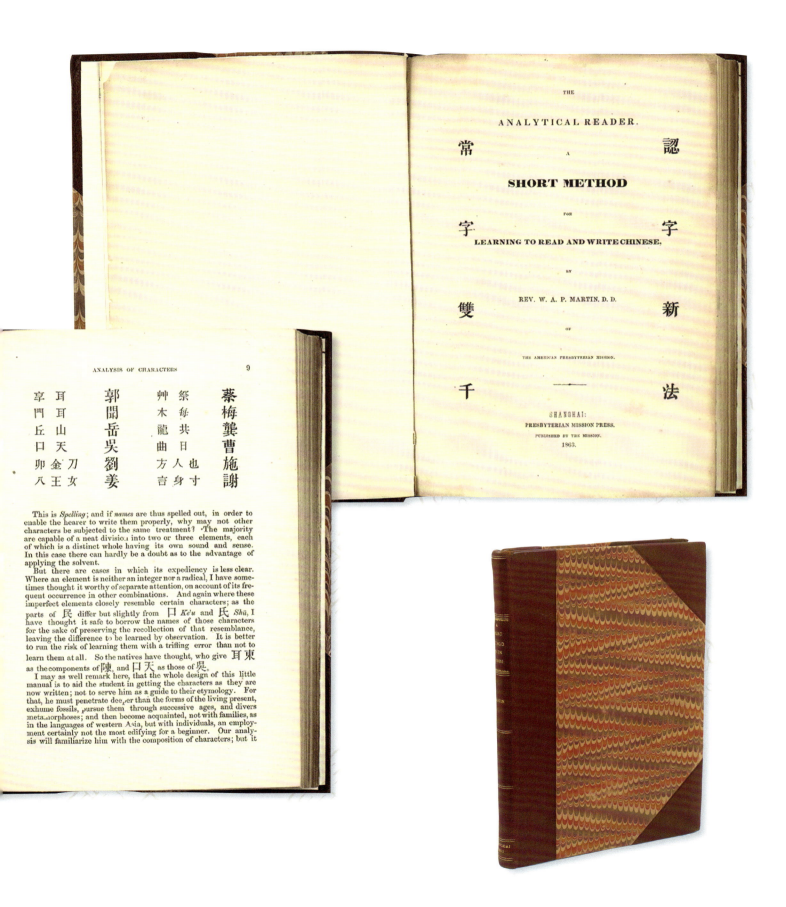

常字雙千編韻字新法一名認

第一章論古始

造物
未生民來　前有上帝　惟一眞神　無聖能比

遂亦和土　將為靈矣　命處賜基　千百皆與

六日力作　先闢天地　萬物多焉　既希且異

呼万考同口音圖

其禁令而自取罪戾哉

右第一節記上主造物之多所以備人之用也人奈何犯

告云可食　或當見耳　聞言摩拿　得罪因此

凡所求者　毋不立予　然欲善惡　勿聽手取

復使宜家　女兮往事　謂之曰夫　爾我如自

罗氏编号 1351

《太平天国亲历记》2 卷

（太平天國 Ti-ping tien-kwoh；the history of the Ti-ping revolution, including a narrative of the author's personal adventures. 1−2）

作　　者：［英］吟俐（Augustus Frederick Lindley, 1840−1873）

出　　版：伦敦，戴（Day），1866 年

载体形态：25.8×16.5 厘米，XX+424；VIII+428−844 页 + 卷首 1 幅石印插画 +10 幅着色石印图版 +8 幅套色石印图版 +2 幅轮廓着色地图 +9 幅木刻插图

装　　订：出版社深紫色布面烫金

来　　源：兰辛（Gerrit L. Lansing）的藏书票

版　　本：英文初版。

内　　容：

　　本书是为数不多的外国人站在太平天国角度写成的著作。由于作者在太平天国控制地区活动了近四年，尽管书中内容有不少值得推敲，甚至明显不实之处，但作为反映太平天国运动在军事、政治、民事、宗教信仰等方面情况的一手文献，特别是其中关于英国对华政策的内容，弥足珍贵。

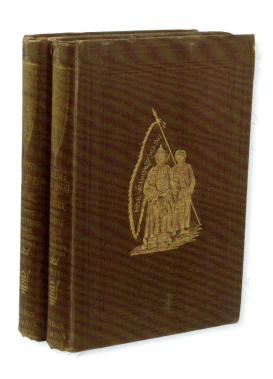

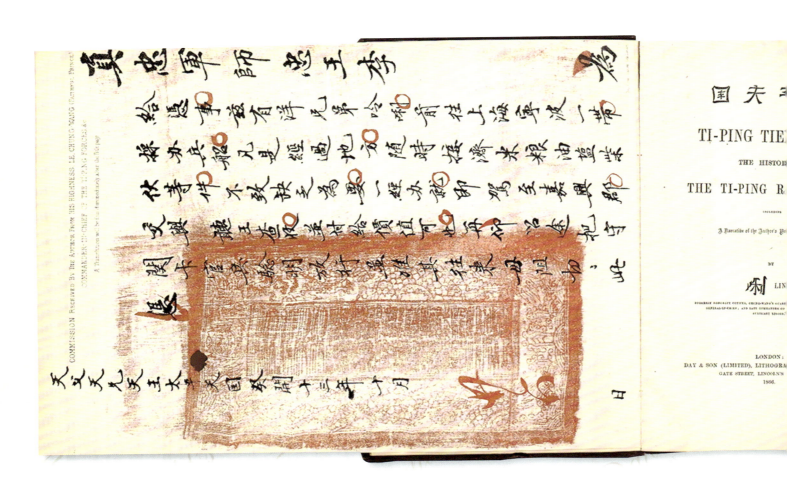

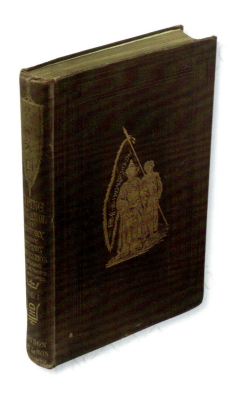

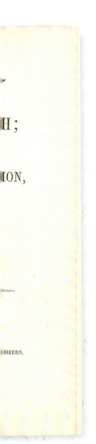

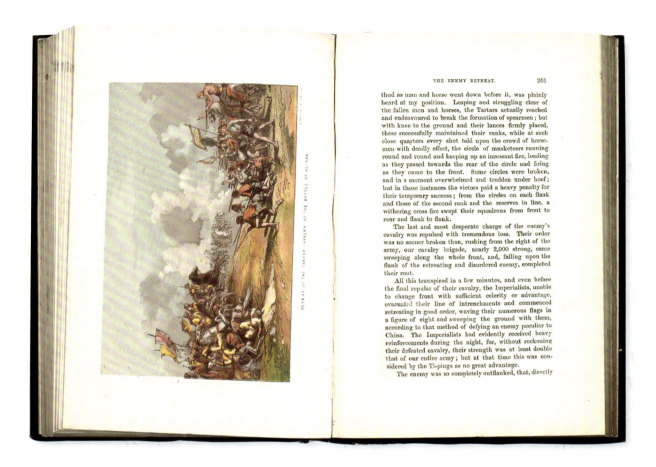

THE ENEMY RETREAT. 261

thud as man and horse went down before it, was plainly heard at my position. Leaping and struggling clear of the fallen men and horses, the Tartars actually reached and endeavoured to break the formation of spearmen; but with knee to the ground and their lances firmly placed, these successfully maintained their ranks, while at such close quarters every shot told upon the crowd of horsemen with deadly effect, the circle of musketeers running round and round and keeping up an incessant fire, loading as they passed towards the rear of the circle and firing as they came to the front. Some circles were broken, and in a moment overwhelmed and trodden under hoof; but in those instances the victors paid a heavy penalty for their temporary success; from the circles on each flank and those of the second rank and the reserves in line, a withering cross fire swept their squadrons from front to rear and flank to flank.

The last and most desperate charge of the enemy's cavalry was repulsed with tremendous loss. Their order was no sooner broken than, rushing from the right of the army, our cavalry brigade, nearly 2,000 strong, came sweeping along the whole front, and, falling upon the flank of the retreating and disordered enemy, completed their rout.

All this transpired in a few minutes, and even before the final repulse of their cavalry, the Imperialists, unable to change front with sufficient celerity or advantage, evacuated their line of intrenchments and commenced retreating in good order, waving their numerous flags in a figure of eight and sweeping the ground with them, according to that method of defying an enemy peculiar to China. The Imperialists had evidently received heavy reinforcements during the night, for, without reckoning their defeated cavalry, their strength was at least double that of our entire army; but at that time this was considered by the Ti-pings as no great advantage.

The enemy was so completely outflanked, that, directly

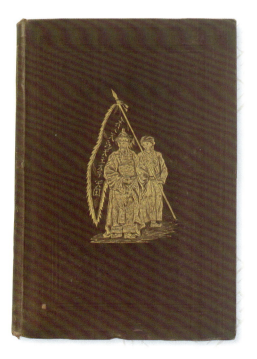

罗氏编号 1372

《中国文献纪略》

（Notes on Chinese literature: with introductory remarks on the progressive advancement of the art; and a list of translations from the Chinese, into various European languages）

作　　者：［英］伟烈亚力（Alexander Wylie, 1815－1887）
出　　版：上海，美华书馆，1867 年
载体形态：4 开，IV+VIII+XXVIII+260 页
装　　订：出版社 1/4 布面
版　　本：英文初版，1901 年再版。

内　　容：

　　作者系英国传教士、著名汉学家，致力于东西文化交流工作，在华近 30 年，成绩斐然。同时他还致力于中国古典文献的收藏，其私藏二万余册中文藏书现为牛津大学图书馆馆藏的重要组成部分。《中国文献纪略》一书在汉学史上具有重要意义，其中介绍了二千多部文学、数学、医学和科学技术等方面的中国古典文献，长期被西方汉学研究者奉为中国古典文献目录方面的圭臬。

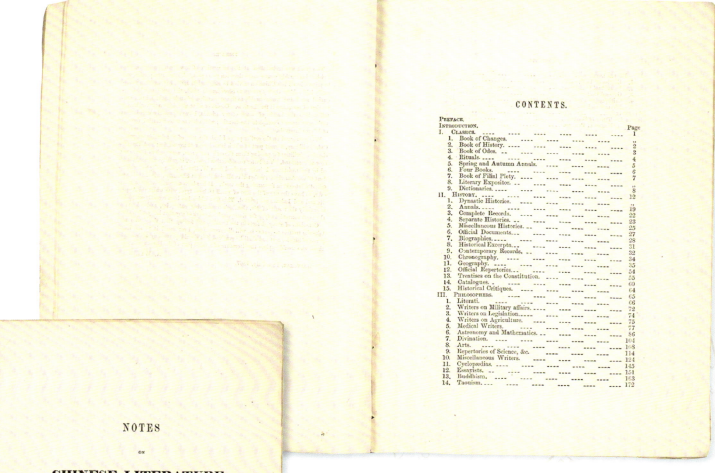

CONTENTS.

PREFACE.
INTRODUCTION.   Page
I.   CLASSICS.   1
  1. Book of Changes.   2
  2. Book of History. ....   "
  3. Book of Odes.   3
  4. Rituals.   4
  5. Spring and Autumn Annals.   5
  6. Four Books.   6
  7. Book of Filial Piety.   7
  8. Literary Expositor. ....   "
  9. Dictionaries.   8
II. HISTORY.   12
  1. Dynastic Histories. ....   "
  2. Annals.   19
  3. Complete Records.   22
  4. Separate Histories.   23
  5. Miscellaneous Histories.   25
  6. Official Documents.   27
  7. Biographies.   28
  8. Historical Excerpta.   31
  9. Contemporary Records.   32
  10. Chronography.   34
  11. Geography.   35
  12. Official Repertories.   54
  13. Treatises on the Constitution.   55
  14. Catalogues.   60
  15. Historical Critiques.   64
III. PHILOSOPHERS.   65
  1. Literati.   66
  2. Writers on Military affairs.   72
  3. Writers on Legislation.   74
  4. Writers on Agriculture.   75
  5. Medical Writers.   77
  6. Astronomy and Mathematics.   86
  7. Divination.   104
  8. Arts.   108
  9. Repertories of Science, &c.   114
  10. Miscellaneous Writers.   124
  11. Cyclopædias.   145
  12. Essayists.   151
  13. Buddhism.   163
  14. Taouism.   172

NOTES

ON

CHINESE LITERATURE:

WITH

INTRODUCTORY REMARKS

ON THE

PROGRESSIVE ADVANCEMENT OF THE ART;

AND A

LIST OF TRANSLATIONS FROM THE CHINESE,
INTO VARIOUS EUROPEAN LANGUAGES.

BY

A. WYLIE,

Agent of the British and Foreign Bible Society in China.

SHANGHAE:
AMERICAN PRESBYTERIAN MISSION PRESS.
LONDON:
TRÜBNER & Co. 60, PATERNOSTER ROW.
1867.

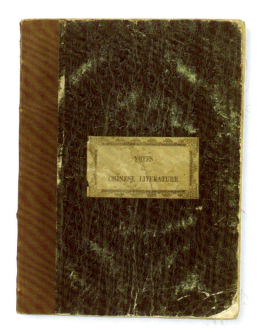

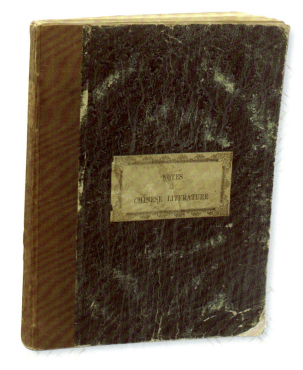

罗氏编号 **1395**

《最古老与最新奇的帝国：中国和美国》
（ **The oldest and the newest empire: China and the United States** ）

作　　者：［美］施惠廉（William Speer, 1822－1904）

出　　版：哈特福德，斯克兰顿（S. S. Scranton），1870 年

载体形态：8 开，672 页 +39 幅图版

装　　订：出版社浮饰布面

版　　本：英文初版，同年辛辛那提英文增订版。

内　　容：

　　作者系美国传教士，早年在广东地区担任医药传教士，返美后在加利福尼亚的华工社区中活动。本书第一部分介绍了包括科举制在内的中国政治、经济、社会、文化情况，同时与当时的西方文明作了对比。第二部分则主要讨论在美华工以及华人移民问题，也是本书的重点所在。作者在当时美国国内排华声浪渐起的背景下，基于自己的实际经历，给予了华人劳工和移民群体相当高的正面评价，肯定了华人劳工和移民群体在美国西部开发中所起的巨大作用，驳斥了当时排华声浪中的各种不实之词。

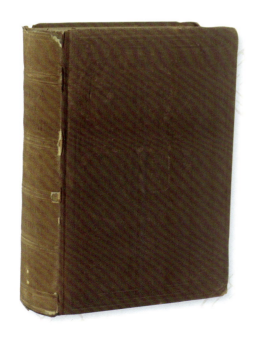

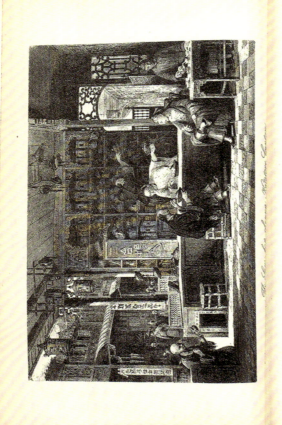

THE OLDEST

AND

THE NEWEST EMPIRE:

CHINA AND THE UNITED STATES.

BY

WILLIAM SPEER, D.D.,

CORRESPONDING SECRETARY OF THE PRESBYTERIAN BOARD OF EDUCATION.
FORMERLY MISSIONARY IN CHINA AND TO THE CHINESE IN CALIFORNIA.

Who does not see that henceforth every year, European commerce, European politics, European thoughts and European activity, although actually gaining greater force, and European connections, although actually becoming more intimate, will nevertheless ultimately sink in importance; while the Pacific ocean, its shores, its islands, and the vast regions beyond, will become the chief theatre of events in the world's great hereafter?

WILLIAM H. SEWARD.

HARTFORD, CONN.:
PUBLISHED BY S. S. SCRANTON AND COMPANY.
SAN FRANCISCO, CAL.: H. H. BANCROFT & CO.
1870.

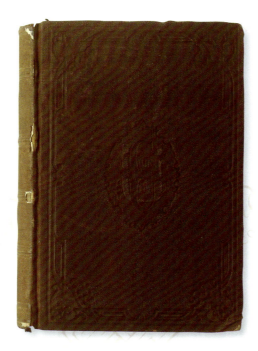

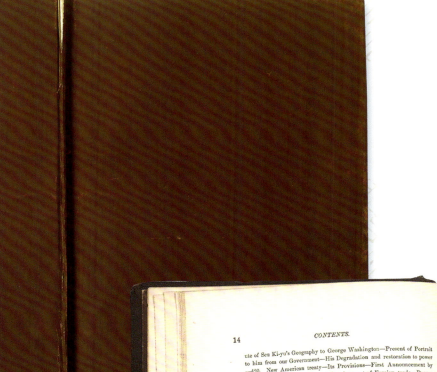

14   *CONTENTS.*

ute of Seu Ki-yu's Geography to George Washington—Present of Portrait to him from our Government—His Degradation and restoration to power —420. New American treaty—Its Provisions—First Announcement by the Atlantic Cable—426. Recent Development of Foreign trade—Danger of Alienation of Chinese territory—427. Honorable career of Mr. Burlingame—Origin of Mission to Western Powers—429. Recent treaty with China, its Effects—Honors to the Embassy—431. Treaty with England, Presentation to Queen—Address of Lord Stanley—433. Treaties with other European Powers—Probable Effects—435.

CHAPTER XV.
ANCIENT CONNECTIONS WITH THIS CONTINENT.

Variety of Races found on this Continent—Civilization of Aztecs, Toltecs, Peruvians, etc.—438. Question of their Origin—438. Asiatic Source—Dates of their Arrival—438. Evidence from Agencies of Nature—Great Ocean Currents, Pacific Gulf Stream—Courses of Winds, Monsoons—Typhoons—439. Evidence from Recent Wrecks on our coast—Japanese and Chinese junks, Remains on this Continent and the neighboring Islands—442. Spread of the Malay family among Pacific islands—444. Evidence from Legends among Asiatic nations, Tartars, Japanese, etc.—445. Translation from Chinese Encyclopædia, on *Fu-sang*—Interesting Discussions as to Application—Opinions of eminent Scholars—446. Corroborations from Aztec Customs, etc.—Letters of Cortez—Oriental character of Aztec life and institutions—Answer to objections—Aztecs certainly Buddhists—Other Legends—449. Evidence from Resemblances of Modern American Languages and Customs to Asiatic—454. Tribes on either side of Behring's straits—Resemblances of Tchuktchis, Malemutes, Esquimaux, etc.—455. Athapascas and Apaches—456. Customs and Legends in Peru, Oriental and Buddhist—457. Remains of Wonderful Military Roads, described by Humboldt—459. Future of Peru and Mexico—461.

CHAPTER XVI.
CHINESE IMMIGRATION.

Ancient Separation of Old and New Hemispheres—Anglo-Saxon Occupation of New—Tuition of African Race—Advent of Asiatic—462. Emigrations of Chinese Races in former Ages—463. To other Asiatic Regions—Chinese in Indian Archipelago—Pleasing picture of Chinese Life in Borneo—In Java—464. Reasons for opposition to Intercourse—468. Commencement of Immigration here—Early Usefulness—470. Interest in them, subsequent Opposition—471. All from Province of Canton—472. No Coolies in California—What are Coolies?—No Caste in China—473. Motives and Means of Emigration—478. Hindû Coolies in Guiana—479. Chinese in Cuba—In Peru and Chincha Islands—Terrible Crimes of Coolie trade—479

CONTENTS.   15

Prohibitions of by various Nations—English, French and American Conventions with Chinese Government—483. Validity of Contracts for Labor —485. Extent of future Immigration—Causes of Increase in the Past—486. Number of Chinese in California—487. Their Dispersion over other States, Territories and Countries—488. Influence of Varieties of Population of different Provinces on future Immigration—489. They must be treated as Freemen—Laws necessary for Emigrant Ships—490. Fidelity to Contracts—491. Families should be brought—Our Duty—492.

CHAPTER XVII.
CHINESE LABOR.

Elements which make Chinese Labor peculiar—493. Its Characteristics—Industry of the People—Exhibitions of this in China—Illustrations to foreigners—494. Economy—Utilization of Materials—Regard for Utensils, Time, etc.—Wages—496. Intelligence—General Information—Cheerfulness and Patience in Work—497. Variety of Employments—Early Occupations in this Country—499. Faults of Chinese—500. Difference in Individuals—Practical Difficulties in Employing Chinese—502. Fields for Application of Chinese Labor—Characteristic of Servants—502. Usefulness in Agriculture—Value in California—503. Cultivation of Cotton—Original Seats of it in Asia—Cotton Regions of China—Peculiar Adaptation of Pacific Coast to Cotton—504. British Plans for Cotton Culture in Indian Archipelago—Superiority of our Advantages—506. Manufacture of Silk, its great Value—Extraordinary Advantages of Pacific coast—Chinese Labor an important item—509. Silk at recent Agricultural Fair—Japanese Colony—Comparison of Japanese and Chinese—510. Variety of Moths which produce Silk, a provision for various climates—512. English Experiments in India—Varieties in China and America—English Silk Supply Association—513. Manufacture of Silk in the United States, Extent, Results, Prospects—517. Other Chinese Textile Plants—520. Introduction of Tea—Success of British in Assam—Tea Plant in Java, Brazil and our Southern States—521. Rice—Sugar—Fruits—Pea-nuts—Value of Bamboo—523. Capacity of Chinese as Common Laborers—Workmen in factories—Miners—524. Employment on Public Works—Our Debt to them in construction of Pacific Railroad—Immense Field for their employment—525. Value as Consumers of American products—527. Favorable Testimonials from various classes of Americans—528.

CHAPTER XVIII.
POPULAR GOVERNMENT IN CHINA.

Objectionable Sources of Information as to Chinese institutions—Roman Priests, British Opium Traders—531. Juster Estimate needed—Resemblance to

They sometimes become somewhat merry at the table, and some even intoxicated. But while drunken men of every other nation may be seen reeling, swearing, behaving indecently, in the streets of the cities and towns of California, a drunken Chinese is never seen.

Their own poor are provided for out of the funds of the companies and by subscriptions among those who have the means. They manage to bear what is a heavy burden. And many a sick man has been sent back to China in the same way. I have heard of cases of sick Americans and white foreigners in the mines to whose relief the Chinese had contributed handsomely.

In their native land the Chinese are accustomed to give money freely to religious and benevolent objects. The structure of society there, the denseness of population, the number of the poor, and the distinct Buddhist promises of reward to the benevolent and specifications of punishment upon the cruel, the selfish and the avaricious, have a powerful effect in stimulating acts of charity and liberality. An immeasurable amount of poverty and suffering meets the eye of the foreigner in China. But yet those who have the means dispense money with much generosity. Our missionaries, particularly during the scenes of famine, sickness and general distress which have accompanied the recent wars and rebellions, have often witnessed the most liberal efforts made to feed the hungry with rice and other food, to supply clothing to the destitute, and to provide medicines for the sick and coffins for the dead. In some cases charitable Chinese gentlemen, who were not Christians, seeing the benevolent labors of missionaries, have voluntarily put considerable sums of money into their

hands, to be used in connection with them. At Canton there are large native hospitals for aged persons, for lepers and for foundling children. Within a few doors of my house was a warehouse where coffins were gratuitously furnished to the poor. We often saw bridges or other conveniences erected by persons of fortune for the accommodation of the public, and tea given gratuitously on the street to the thirsty coolies and laboring men.

This summary view of the moral aspect of the Chinese immigration to this country suffices to show of what strange and diverse elements heathen morality is composed. It is like the conglomerate rock in which fragments of what is solid and beautiful are imbedded in a soft and worthless mass, from which they easily fall out; the whole of which crumbles under the assaults of the winds and rains and is unfit for the walls of a house. It is hard to convey to a Christian mind the idea of how so much knowledge of what is right can be mixed with so much uncertainty and perplexity; so much of effort to do right with such want of correct principles and motives in it; so much of beneficence to the suffering with so much of selfishness; such a sense of the evil and destructive nature of sin with such helplessness in resisting its temptations; such flashes of light to show the narrow path of life and the rewards and penalties of the future world, with such indifference to follow their guidance and willful turning to ways of their own choice. It is our encouragement to know that in this mass there are elements which, when pulverized and wet and moulded, and subjected to the power of fire, will come out in forms which will be valuable and enduring.

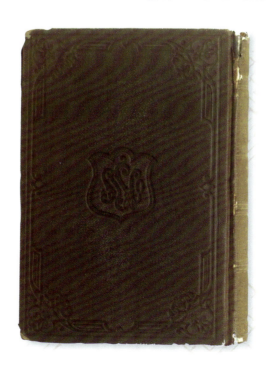

罗氏编号 **1410**

《中药的贡献与中国自然史》
（ Contributions towards the materia medica & natural history of China. For the use of medical missionaries & native medical students ）

作　　者：［英］施维善（Frederick Porter Smith，［1833–1881］）

出　　版：上海，美华书馆，1871 年

载体形态：8 开，VIII+240 页

装　　订：红色半羊皮面

版　　本：英文初版。

内　　容：

　　作者系英国医药传教士，在汉口开设了第一家西式医院。他在中国生活期间，学习了《本草纲目》等中国传统药典、医书以及之前欧洲出版的中国植物学著作，随后写成了本书。这是西方学者所写的第一本关于中国本土药材的书籍。在本书中作者开列了各种中医使用的药材，对这些药材的形态、药用价值等做了详细的介绍，供在华的西医参考使用。同时书中关于中国植物、矿物的信息，也在相关学科领域具有一定的学术价值。

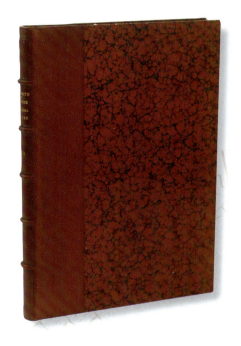

seeds are sour, and somewhat acid, staining the saliva of a deep saffron yellow. These fruits are only used externally, the pulp being applied to swellings and injuries. They are more commonly used by dyers, the colouring principle, called Crocine, resembling the polychroite of saffron. The flowers are very oppressively fragrant, and are supposed to be used in flavouring tea. A Gardenia grandiflora is spoken of by LOUREIRO as a native of Cochin China. This is the 越桃 (*Yueh-t'au*) of the Chinese and is merely a variety of Gardenia Radicans.

GARLIC.—蒜 (*Suan*).—See Allium sativum.

GARNET.—紅砂 (*Hung-sha*).—This is a mineral substance described by HANBURY as a "coarse, reddish-brown stone, which, when examined by a lens, is seen to consist of transparent, angular fragments, mostly of a pale, pinkish hue, mixed with some of a yellowish-brown, or more rarely greenish-black. S. Gr. 3.848." GUIBOURT sets it down as aluminous, and akin to garnet. A substance sold under this name in the Hankow drug-shops, and said to be capable of removing opacities of the cornea consisted of cinnabar. Garnets, or Jacinths, are found in the Lu-shan, a range of mountains in Kiangsi, not far from Kiukiang. See Grenatite.

GELATINE.—魚膠 (*Yü-kiau*), (膘膠) (*P'iau-kiau*).—See Isinglass.

GENDARUSSA.—秦艽 (*T'sin-k'iu*).—The drug sold under the name is brought from Liau chau in Shansi, and from places in Honan. It is in the form of dried, twisted, wrinkled, brown roots, varying a good deal in size. These roots, doubtfully refered to the Justicia Gendarussa of botanists, have a very bitter taste. They are boiled with milk, and given in rheumatism, dysuria, fever, jaundice and in carbuncle. Diphoretic and diuretic properties belong to this root, without doubt.

GENTIAN.—龍膽草 (*Lung-tan-t'sau*).—This "dragon's gall plant" is probably the Gentiana asclepiadea of botanists, with other species. The Chinese term is applied to any intensely bitter plant, but there is no need for any confusion between this plant and the *Hwang-lien*, the Justicia of systematic writers. The long, reddish-brown, numerous rootlets sold in the shops as *Lung-tan-t'sau*, are attached to a short, twisted, rhizome, which is seen on section to be much closer, and more of a brown colour then the European gentian-root. The taste is agreeably bitter. It is brought from Hing-ngan fu in Shensi, and is prescribed in much the same cases as the Gendarussa. It is believed to be useful in nocturnal sweats, hematuria and in ophthalmia. All bitter medicines are set down by Chinese physicians as eminently antiphlogistic and anti-rheumatic in their healing qualities.

GIN.—荷蘭酒 (*Ho-lan-tsiu*).—This "Dutch spirit" is scarcely known to the Chinese. The Pekingese make a spirit much stronger, but something like gin. It is flavored with some sort of berries which give it a pleasant flavour, and a greenish colour. It is made in Hupeh by northern people, and is called 碧緑酒 (*Pih-luh-tsiu*).

GINGER.—乾薑 (*Kan-kiang*), 白薑 (*Peh-kiang*).—The Chinese ginger grows in Hupeh and Kiangsi to a large extent, but is eaten largely in the green state as a condiment and corrective. It has a very fragrant smell, but is too sticky to make a very excellent preserve. Ginger sweetmeat (糖薑) is largely exported from the south of China. Dry ginger is not easily made from the Chinese root, as the skin does not so easily separate by maceration.

103

It is met with in flat pieces of an inch in length, much shrivelled and wrinkled. The taste is much inferior to that of the West Indian and other gingers. Stimulant, diaphoretic, stomachic, carminative, tussic, rubefacient and vulnerary properties are commonly refered to this drug, which is largely used in regular and domestic practice. Ginger is applied to the forehead and temples in headache, to the gums in toothache, and to the bites of animals. It is said to have some good effect in opthalmia, and in epiphora, when applied as a wash.

GINGKO.—銀杏 (*Yin-hang*), 白果 (*Peh-kuo*).—Gingko, or Jingko, is a Japanese name formed from *Yin-kuo* ("silver fruit,") the seeds of the Salisburia adiantifolia, a Taxaceous (Yew) tree of great beauty. It has been introduced into Europe for some years, and its yellow, fine, plum-like fruits sometimes ripen in warmer latitudes of the Continent. They are resinous, bitterish, and astringent. The "white fruit," or *Peh-kuo* of the shops are the nutlike, oval, pointed seeds, from three quarters to an inch long, keeled lengthwise on two sides, and having a whitish brown, smooth, hard shell. The kernel consists of two yellow, mealy cotyledons, covered with a beautiful, thin, reddish membrane. The Chinese consume these nuts at weddings, the shell being dyed red. They have a fishy taste, and are supposed to benefit asthma, coughs, irritability of the bladder, blenorrhoea and uterine fluxes. They are said to be peptic and anthelmintic, and are similarly used by the Japanese to promote digestion. They appear to cause peculiar symptoms of intoxication, and occasionally to destroy life. They are sometimes used to wash clothes, and are digested in wine, or oil, to make a kind of detergent cosmetic. The pulp contains a peculiar, crystallizable, fatty principle, called by chemists Gingkoic acid. The wood of the tree is made into seals, which are used by quacks as charms in the treatment of diseases. Those brought from Lin-kiang fu in Kiangsi, and from Siuen-ching hien in Ngan-hwui, are esteemed to be the best. They are not much used here at the present time.

GINSENG.—人參 (*Jin-san*), 黃參 (*Hwang-san*), 神草 (*Shin-ts'au*).—This far-famed drug is the root of an Araliaceous plant determined by MEYER to be a distinct species, the Panax Ginseng. The American Ginseng (洋參) is the product of Panax quinquefolium, and is largely used in Central China. There is an Indian species, described by Dr. WALLICH as a native of Nepal, and refered by him to a Panax Pseudo-ginseng. The latter closely resembles the Chinese root. This drug is the cinchona of China, and is brought from Fung-tien fu in Shingking, and from Tsun-hwa chau in Pehchihli. 遼參 (*Liau-san*), brought from Liau chau in Shansi is said to be a Ginseng. Formerly two classes of this drug were sold, the 關東人參 (*Kwan-tung-jin-san*) from Manchuria, now represented by that coming from Shingking, and the 關西人參 (*Kwan-si-jin-san*), which came from 上黨 (*Shang-tang*), in Shansi, answering to the Lu-ngan fu of the present day. The latter class of drug, although the name is still retained, is represented by species of Campanula and Adenophora, called 黨參 (*Tang-san*), used in the place of the real Ginseng. The plant is probably cultivated in Corea or Pehchihli to satisfy the great demand for it, the Shingking drug being almost entirely an imperial monopoly. Corean Ginseng (高麗參) ranks next after the Manchurian supply, and in fact constitutes the only available drug in the hands of traders. This is, however, often adulterated with Japanese Ginseng, which is

CONTRIBUTIONS

TOWARDS THE

MATERIA MEDICA & NATURAL HISTORY

OF CHINA.

FOR THE USE OF

MEDICAL MISSIONARIES & NATIVE MEDICAL STUDENTS.

BY

FREDERICK PORTER SMITH, M.B., LONDON,

Medical Missionary in Central China.

SHANGHAI:
AMERICAN PRESBYTERIAN MISSION PRESS.
LONDON:
TRÜBNER & CO., 60 PATERNOSTER ROW.
1871.

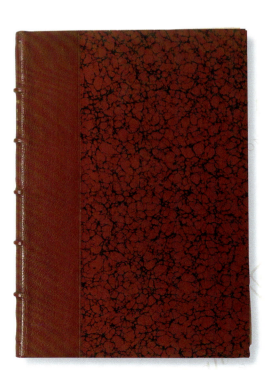

罗氏编号 1414

《英华萃林韵府》2 卷
（A vocabulary and hand-book of the Chinese language romanized in the Mandarin dialect. 1－2）

编　　者：［美］卢公明（Justus Doolittle, 1824－1880）

出　　版：福州，隆顺洋行，1872 年

载体形态：4 开，II+VIII+548+II；II+VIII+696 页

装　　订：半小牛皮面，磨损，首卷书脊缺损

来　　源：书主题记：阿其荪（G.Acheson），及日期：1899 年

版　　本：英文初版。

内　　容：

　　卢公明系美国传教士，在华二十余年，主要活动于福州地区，从事文化、教育事业。其代表作为《中国人的社会生活》（Social Life of the Chinese），内容涵盖政治、经济、习俗、宗教等多方面，反映了他对清末福州社会状况的深入观察。《英华萃林韵府》虽是词典的体例，但编者旨在"提供读者一些最适用的英文词汇在中文中的对应表述"，因此还收录了大量常用中文短语以及历史、语言、民俗、律例等相关资料，使其更像一部小型的百科全书。

英 華 萃 林 韻 府

A

VOCABULARY AND HAND-BOOK

OF THE

CHINESE LANGUAGE,

ROMANIZED IN THE MANDARIN DIALECT.

IN TWO VOLUMES COMPRISED IN THREE PARTS.

BY REV. JUSTUS DOOLITTLE,

AUTHOR OF "SOCIAL LIFE OF THE CHINESE."

VOL. I: PART I.

FOOCHOW:
ROZARIO, MARCAL, AND COMPANY.
London: Trubner & Co.   New York: Anson D. F. Randolph & Co.   San Francisco: A. L. Bancroft & Co.
1872.

---

chin i, 嚥 'to, 嗞 i.
Salivary glands, 生水核 shĕng shui 'ho.
Sallow or pale, 黃食 'huang shih, 面黃面黑 mien 'huang ĕrh 'hei, 青黃 'ching 'huang. 面若黃金紙 mien jé 'huang chin chih; and swarthy, 面體熏黑 mien 'ti li 'hei.
Sally or rush out, to 突戰 'tu chan; forth, 撞出 chuang 'chu, 奕出 i 'chu.
Salmon, 鉤吐魚 kou 'tu yü.
Salt, 鹽 yen, 鹽 yen, 滷 lu; fine 細鹽 hsi yen; they have put in too much 鹽放多了 yen fang to liao; commissioner, 鹽運司 yen yün ssü; pond, 鹽池 yen 'chih; well, 鹽井 yen ching; boiler, 灶 戶 tsao 'hu; water, 鹹水 hsien shui; fish, 鹹魚 hsien yü; marsh, 鹽田 yen 'tien; eat 食鹽 shih yen; cellar, 鹽窖 yen chung; coarse 粗鹽 'tsu yen; can it again become 還能成鹽嗎 'huan nĕng 'chĕng yen ma.
Salt, to 下鹽 hsia yen, 落鹽 lo yĕn, 醃 yĕn; unable to 醃不起 yen pu 'chi; not thoroughly to 醃不透 yen pu 'tou.
Salted already, 下了鹽 hsia liao yen, 加過鹽 chia kuo yen; turnips, 大頭菜 ta 'tou 'tsai; duck eggs, 鹹鵝蛋 hsien ya tan.
Saltless, 無鹹的 wei hsien ti.
Saltpetre, 硝 hsiao; foreign 洋硝 yang hsiao; and sulphur, 硝磺 hsiao 'huang; works, 硝廠 hsiao 'chang.
Salts, epsom 朴硝 'po hsiao; glauber's 玄明粉 hsien ming fĕn; purying 芒硝 mang hsino
Salty or saltish, this water is 這個水鹹的 chè ko shui hsien ti; it is exceedingly 鹹鹹的 kou hsien ti; taste, 鹹味 hsien wei.
Salubrious or healthy, 平和 'ping 'huo, 淳和 'chun 'huo, 土氣和平 'tu 'chi 'huo 'ping, 水土好 shui 'tu 'hao.
Salutation or compliments, 奉參 fĕng 'chūan, 拱揖 kung i, 恭喜 kung hsi, 請安之語 'ching an chih yü.
Salute with cannon, a 號砲 'hao 'pao, 敬砲 ching 'pao; to fire 散號砲 fang 'hao 'pao, 放砲 fang 'pao 'ching 'hao.

Salute or greet, to 請安 'ching an, 拜拜 pai pai, 行禮 hsing li; in Chinese fashion, 拱 kung; and part, 拱別 kung pieh; with folded hands, 拱手 kung shou.
Salvation or redemption, 救人之事 chiu jĕn chih shih, 救贖之事 chiu shu chih shih; of souls, 靈魂之救 ling 'hun chih chiu.
Salve or plaster, a 膏藥 kao yao, 藥膏 yao kao, 膏藥料 kao yao liao.
Samarcaud, 撒馬兒罕 sa-ma-ĕrh-'han.
Same or alike, 同 'tung, 無二 wu ĕrh, 一也 i yeh; as a lake, 和湖相同 'huo 'hu hsiang 'tung; mind, 一心一意 i hsin i i; very far from the 大不相同 ta pu hsiang 'tung; as one's father and mother, 和父母一樣 'huo fu mu i yang; expression may be used, 都說得 tu shuo tĕ; as before, 依舊 i chiu, 仍舊 jĕng jan, 如故 ju ku; as before. The way is still the 還是那麼樣 'huan shih na mo yang; it is all quite the 都是一個樣 tu shih i ko yang; as pattern, 照樣 chao yang, 依辦 i pan, 依樣 i yang; as I, 和我一樣 'ho wo i yang; color. Precisely the 與漆色無二 yü 'chi sè wu ĕrh; species, 同類 'tung lei; these two are the 這兩個相同 chè liang ko hsiang 'tung; all the 皆然 chieh jan; age, 同年 'tung nien.
Sample or muster, 貨樣 'huo yang, 樣子 yang tzŭ, 辦頭 pan 'tou; sell by 依辦賣 i pan mai; buy by 依辦買 i pan mai; like the 照辦子 chao pan tzŭ; same as 照辦 chao pan, 對辦 tui pan; unlike the 不對辦 pu tui pan, 不照樣 pu chao yang; to answer for a 作樣子 tso yang tzŭ; of cloth, 布樣子 pu yang tzŭ.
Samshu, (distilled and fomented Chinese liquors,) 酒 chiu, 三燒 san shao, 黃酒 'huang chiu; made from pears, 黃梨酒 shuo li chiu; one jar of 一提燒酒 yi 'chĕng shao chiu.
Sancian, Island of 三洲塔 san chou 'tang.
Sanctify or consecrate, to 崇敬之 shĕng ching chih, 使為靈善 shih wei shĕng shan, 作聖 tso shĕng, 成聖 'chĕng shĕng.
Sanctification, 潔淨之事 chieh ching chih shih, 潔淨 chĕng ching.
Sanction or assent, to 允 yün, 定倒 ting li, 定規.

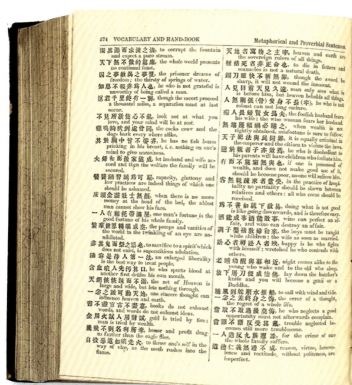

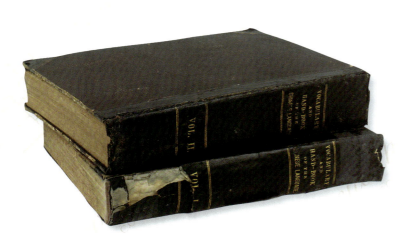

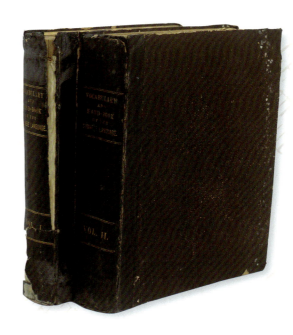

罗氏编号 989–1007, 1019–32, 1058–66, 1081–83, 1094–98, 1106–11, 1118–21, 1126–30, 1140–43, 1147–53, 1158–77, 1186–88, 1199–1213, 1217–23, 1233–51, 1254–58, 1266–80, 1287–94, 1302–14, 1316–30, 1336–47, 1355–69, 1373–81, 1418–35, 1441–49, 1452–67, 1470–80, 1545

《香港殖民地法令集》5 卷
（Hong Kong colonial ordinance 1844–68 & 1873–76）

作　　者：［香港立法局］（Hong Kong Legislative Council）

出　　版：香港，［香港立法局］，1844–1876 年

载体形态：对开，184 页；221 页；452 页；74 页。23.5×15.5 厘米，322 页

装　　订：黑色半小牛皮面，书脊红标印字烫金

来　　源：英国上议院，有"上议院图书馆处理"印章。

内　　容：

　　罗氏藏书中有不少档案、官方报告类的收藏，其中以这套香港殖民地法令集最有特色。这套法令集收录了 1844 年至 1876 年间香港当局颁布的各色法令近 300 种，涵盖了刑事、民事、诉讼条例、监狱管理、行政机构规章等各领域，如实反映了港英当局逐步将英国司法体系移植到香港的过程，也是了解殖民统治初期港英当局如何管理香港的重要历史文献。

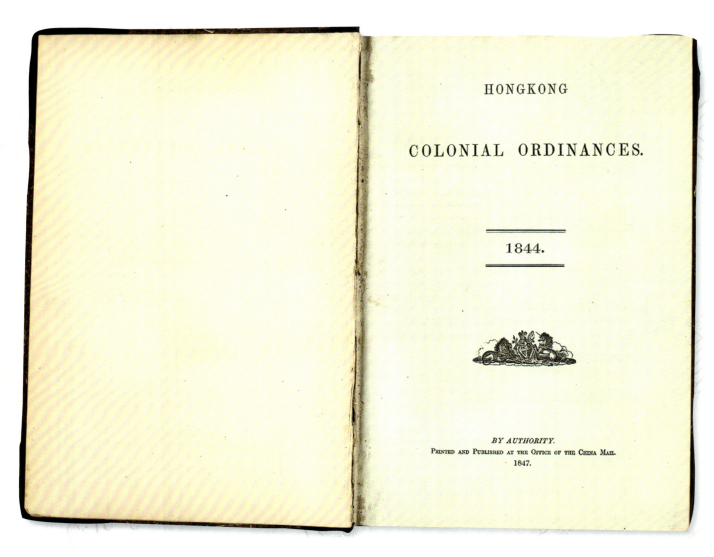

HONGKONG
COLONIAL ORDINANCES.

1844.

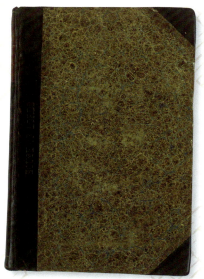

BY AUTHORITY.
PRINTED AND PUBLISHED AT THE OFFICE OF THE CHINA MAIL.
1847.

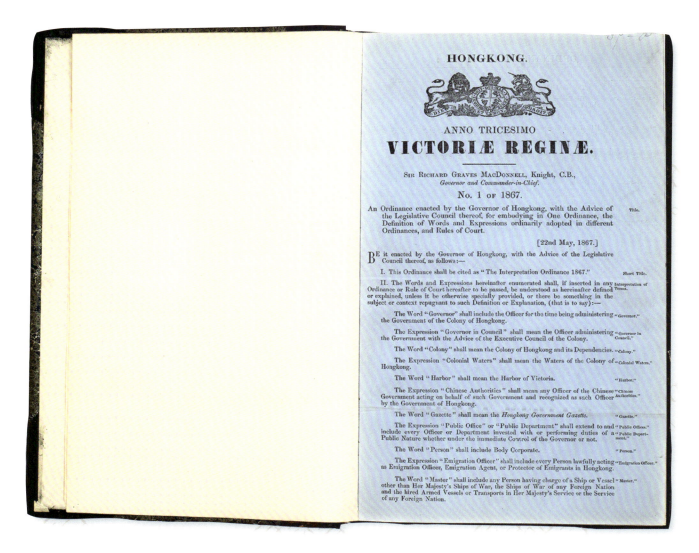

HONGKONG.

ANNO TRICESIMO
VICTORIÆ REGINÆ.

Sir Richard Graves MacDonnell, Knight, C.B.,
Governor and Commander-in-Chief.

No. 1 of 1867.

An Ordinance enacted by the Governor of Hongkong, with the Advice of the Legislative Council thereof, for embodying in One Ordinance, the Definition of Words and Expressions ordinarily adopted in different Ordinances, and Rules of Court. — Title.

[22nd May, 1867.]

BE it enacted by the Governor of Hongkong, with the Advice of the Legislative Council thereof, as follows:—

I. This Ordinance shall be cited as "The Interpretation Ordinance 1867." — Short Title.

II. The Words and Expressions hereinafter enumerated shall, if inserted in any Ordinance or Rule of Court hereafter to be passed, be understood as hereinafter defined or explained, unless it be otherwise specially provided, or there be something in the subject or context repugnant to such Definition or Explanation, (that is to say):— — Interpretation of Terms.

The Word "Governor" shall include the Officer for the time being administering the Government of the Colony of Hongkong. — "Governor."

The Expression "Governor in Council" shall mean the Officer administering the Government with the Advice of the Executive Council of the Colony. — "Governor in Council."

The Word "Colony" shall mean the Colony of Hongkong and its Dependencies. — "Colony."

The Expression "Colonial Waters" shall mean the Waters of the Colony of Hongkong. — "Colonial Waters."

The Word "Harbor" shall mean the Harbor of Victoria. — "Harbor."

The Expression "Chinese Authorities" shall mean any Officer of the Chinese Government acting on behalf of such Government and recognized as such Officer by the Government of Hongkong. — "Chinese Authorities."

The Word "Gazette" shall mean the *Hongkong Government Gazette.* — "Gazette."

The Expression "Public Office" or "Public Department" shall extend to and include every Officer or Department invested with or performing duties of a Public Nature whether under the immediate Control of the Governor or not. — "Public Office." "Public Department."

The Word "Person" shall include Body Corporate. — "Person."

The Expression "Emigration Officer" shall include every Person lawfully acting as Emigration Officer, Emigration Agent, or Protector of Emigrants in Hongkong. — "Emigration Officer."

The Word "Master" shall include any Person having charge of a Ship or Vessel other than Her Majesty's Ships of War, the Ships of War of any Foreign Nation and the hired Armed Vessels or Transports in Her Majesty's Service or the Service of any Foreign Nation. — "Master."

罗氏捐赠图书编号 4095

《清代图书馆发展史》
（ The development of Chinese libraries under the Ch'ing Dynasty, 1644－1911 ）

作　　者：谭卓垣

出　　版：上海：商务印书馆（ The Commercial Press, Ltd. ），1935 年

载体形态：23×15.5 厘米，IX+107 页

内　　容：

　　本书是我国近代图书馆学家谭卓垣的代表作，是他在美国芝加哥大学的博士论文，1935 年由商务印书馆以英文原文出版，20 世纪 80 年代有中文译本，将题名改为《清代藏书楼发展史》。书中对清代宫廷和私家藏书的状况作了梳理和介绍，并以西方图书馆学的理论方法对我国古代藏书观念与实践的利弊得失作了批判性的分析。谭卓垣是我国最早的几位图书馆学博士之一，本书发行之初即得到主流媒体《大公报》的高度评价，在今天依然是一部有价值的图书馆史专著。

　　罗氏藏书中理所当然地有许多与中国相关的资料，藏书史之类的专著更是在他的专业范围之内。其中有不少是在国内反而不太受关注、不太容易见到的图书资料，像这一册英文的清代图书馆主题专著也是一例。

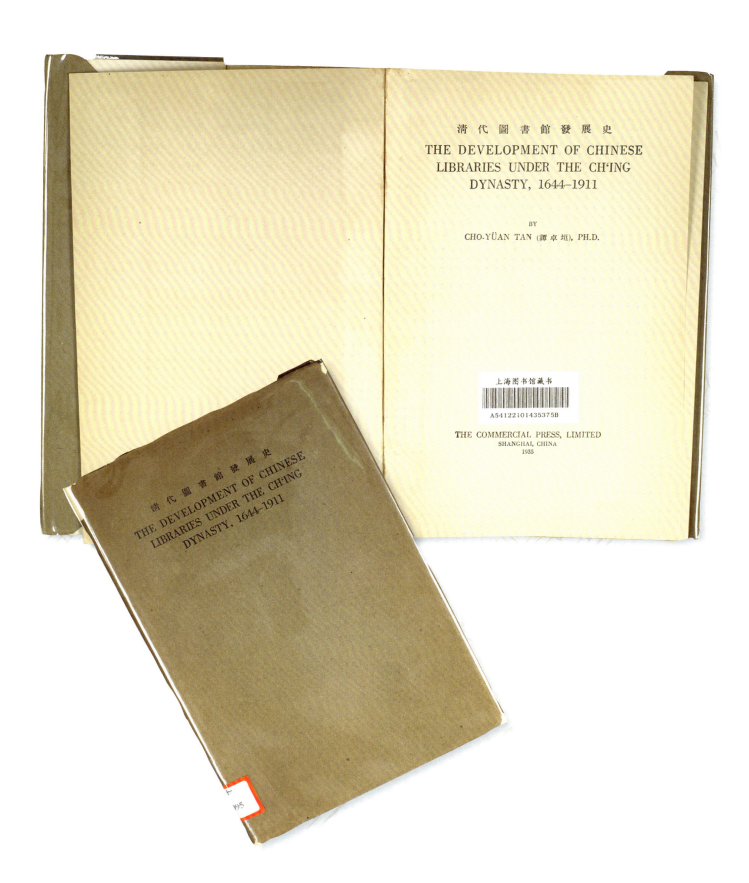

Various theories have been suggested to describe the purpose of such a monumental piece of work. Perhaps the most direct motive was, as the emperor stated in one of his decrees,[1] to preserve literature. He foresaw that if no special attempt was made to collect both modern and ancient literature, some of it would in all probability be lost. In order to fulfill this purpose, he carried his book campaign on such a vast extent that hardly any book would escape him. One author says[2] that the underlying purpose of the appointment of the Ssu Ku commission was to find an excuse for destroying all anti-dynastic works, and there is evidence that Chien Lung did burn a tremendous number of books[3] in connection with this compilation. Another hints that Chien Lung's idea in setting up the Ssu Ku Chuan Shu was to shift the attention of Chinese scholars from political activities to scholastic careers. In other words, he wanted to free the Manchu dynasty from Chinese antagonism. There was also a moral motive in this undertaking as expressed, though vaguely, by the emperor himself.[4]

The reason why I collect books for this 'Four-treasure Library' is not so much to win myself a good name for preserving literature, but rather as the philosopher Chang has said, 'to institute the fundamental principles of the universe, to establish the truth for the people, to pass on the teachings of past sages and to bring peace to the everlasting generations.'

There may be some truth in each of the reasons given above, but careful examination of the fact indicates that personal glorification was probably a principal motive of Chien Lung. When the compilation of the Ssu Ku Chuan Shu was in process,

[1] Descriptive Catalogue, op. cit., p. 2.
[2] S. Meng, Ch'ing Chao Chuan Chi, Preface.
[3] See page 41.
[4] Chien Lung, Record of the Wên Yuan Pavilion, in Library Science Quarterly, I, 153.

the emperor feared his life might not last long enough to see its completion and thus in the year 1773 he ordered Wang Chi Hua (王際華), Yu Min Chung (于敏中) and others to make two manuscript copies of the more important portions of the whole collection, called the Ssu Ku Chuan Shu Wei Yao (四庫全書薈要), the Essential Selection of the 'Four-treasure Library.' The first copy was finished in 1779 in 11,266 volumes and a second one was completed the following year. This unnecessary duplication suggests that Chien Lung wanted to have his name connected with the largest literary work ever produced, for he required that every volume should bear his own seal. This was merely one of the many examples of Chien Lung's aspiration for personal glorification.

It should be remembered, however, that the direct cause of the compilation of the Ssu Ku Chuan Shu was some new discoveries in the great encyclopædia, Yung Lo Ta Tien.[1] The idea was supposedly originated by Chu Yun,[1] a literary chancellor of Anhwei province, who memorialized the throne calling to the attention of the emperor the fact that there were many invaluable works in that collection totally unknown to the literary world. He further proposed that a commission be appointed to make special investigations and recommendations. After some opposition, the project was ultimately adopted. But then the scope of the work was extended to a much larger field than originally proposed. In the year 1773, the Ssu Ku Commission was instituted and the compilation of the 'Four-treasure Library' launched.

The Commission consisted of 361 officials of various ranks,[2] chiefly specialists in every field of learning. Although the

[1] According to Liang Chi Chao, the discovery was made by Chuan Tsu wang (全祖望), and Lee Mu Tang (李穆堂), but in Chun Ping Shih Yeh Cheng, Lee Meng Fu says that this idea was originated by Hsu Chien Hsieh (徐乾學).
[2] In an unpublished thesis of W. T. Yen, called Ssu Ku Chuan Shu . . . and Its Influence upon Chinese Culture, he gives a detailed statement concerning the personnel, distribution of offices, and the function of each in page 18-21.

罗氏捐赠图书编号 6242

《国际象棋习题的乐趣》
（The enjoyment of chess problems）

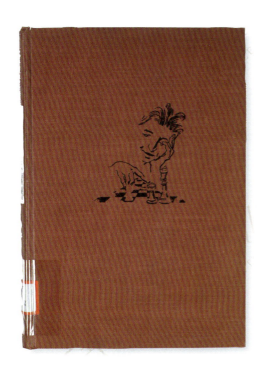

作　　者：〔美〕肯尼斯·S·霍华德（Kenneth S.Howard, 1882−1972）

出　　版：费城：戴维·麦凯公司（Davic McKay Company），1943 年

载体形态：21×14 厘米，IX+222 页

版　　本：初版。

内　　容：

　　本书是一册国际象棋习题集，包含各种类型的习题共 200 题。作者霍华德与美国国际象棋名家弗兰克·马歇尔同时代，是历史悠久的马歇尔国际象棋俱乐部的创始人之一，也是著名的国际象棋习题创作者，出版过多部习题类的著作，本书在 20 世纪 60 年代仍有再版。

　　罗闻达先生的藏书中有不少国际象棋相关的图书，而且有很多是习题，这类实用型的图书通常不会是以收藏为目的购置的，虽然无法据此推断先生的棋力，但先生有手谈的雅好应该是没有疑问的。

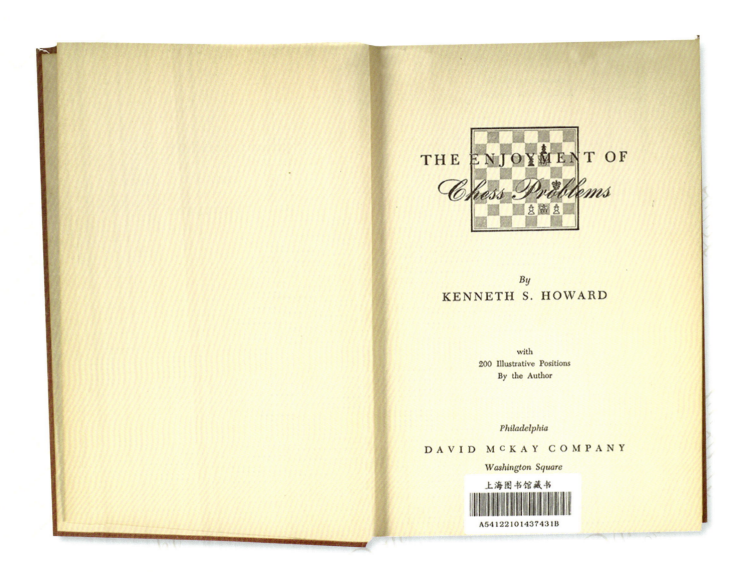

THE ENJOYMENT OF
Chess Problems

By
KENNETH S. HOWARD

with
200 Illustrative Positions
By the Author

Philadelphia
DAVID McKAY COMPANY
Washington Square

罗氏捐赠图书编号 **2374**

《十八世纪印本书籍爱好者指南》
（ Guide de l'amateur de livres à gravures du XVIIIe siècle ）

作　　者：［法］亨利·科恩（Henri Cohen, 1806－1880）

出　　版：日内瓦，Biblipthèque des Érudits, 1951

载体形态：25×17 厘米；XXVI 页＋卷首 1 幅插画＋正文与索引 1247 页

装　　订：四分之一皮封面，书脊有烫金花纹及书名，书口金色染印，内有原平装封面。

版　　本：1912 年巴黎 Librairie a Rouquette 版，1951 年日内瓦 Biblipthèque des Érudits 版。

内　　容：

　　本书是专门介绍 18 世纪法国出版的印本书籍目录，由 Seymour de Ricci 修订。1912 年第六版的 1951 年重印版，分为上下两卷。罗闻达先生将原本平装的书籍进行了重新装订，使得此版本成为独具特色的重装本。

　　18 世纪的法国正值第一帝国时期，同时浪漫主义兴起，社会急剧变化，这一时期出版书籍的内容与旧法国古典主义时代产生了较大的变化，正是基于这一背景，作者将目录的范围选定在了这一时期的插画本上。全书以 A－Z 的编排方式，汇集整理这一时期的插图书籍，对每种书籍的版本进行了详尽的描述，收录的书籍十分全面，是研究这一时期法国出版、社会文化、历史的重要参考书目。

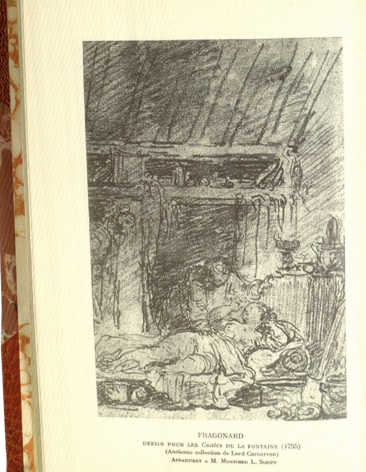

FRAGONARD
DESSIN POUR LES *Contes* DE LA FONTAINE (1795)
(Ancienne collection de Lord Carnarvon)
APPARTIENT A M. MORTIMER L. SCHIFF

HENRI COHEN

GUIDE DE L'AMATEUR

DE

LIVRES A GRAVURES

DU XVIIIe SIÈCLE

SIXIÈME ÉDITION
REVUE, CORRIGÉE ET CONSIDÉRABLEMENT AUGMENTÉE
PAR
SEYMOUR DE RICCI

PREMIÈRE PARTIE

PARIS
LIBRAIRIE A. ROUQUETTE
18, Rue La Fayette, 18
—
1912

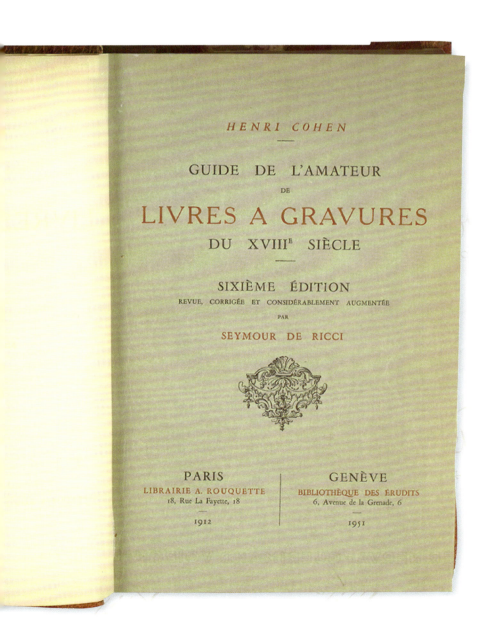

HENRI COHEN

GUIDE DE L'AMATEUR

DE

LIVRES A GRAVURES

DU XVIIIᵉ SIÈCLE

SIXIÈME ÉDITION

REVUE, CORRIGÉE ET CONSIDÉRABLEMENT AUGMENTÉE

PAR

SEYMOUR DE RICCI

PARIS
LIBRAIRIE A. ROUQUETTE
18, Rue La Fayette, 18
1912

GENÈVE
BIBLIOTHÈQUE DES ÉRUDITS
6, Avenue de la Grenade, 6
1951

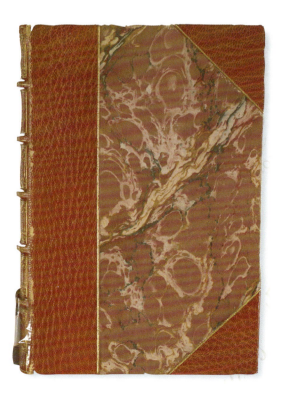

罗氏捐赠图书编号 **4037**

《羽管键琴与击弦古钢琴》
（ **The harpsichord and clavichord: an introductory study** ）

作　　者：［英］雷蒙·拉塞尔（Raymond Russell, 1922 – 1964）
出　　版： 伦敦：费伯（Faber）和费伯（Faber），1959 年
载体形态： 25.5×19 厘米，208 页 +108 幅图
版　　本： 初版。

内　　容：

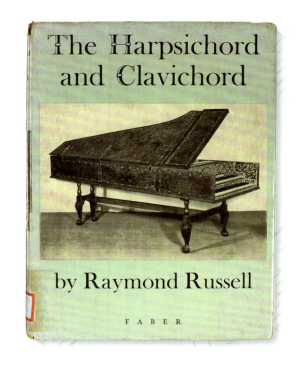

　　作者是一位英国的键盘乐器研究与收藏家。本书内容是作者通过走访欧洲各国的收藏机构，对古代乐器实物进行考察而完成的，介绍了现代钢琴的前身"羽管键琴"和"击弦古钢琴"以及其他类似的古代键盘乐器。书中以国别为线索，介绍了自 16 世纪至 19 世纪的各种类型、各种风格的古代键盘乐器，包含工艺方面和音乐方面技术规格的比较详细的描述。书后附有索引和 103 幅实物拍摄的图片及说明。

　　罗闻达先生出身于一个艺术家家庭，学生时代在乌普萨拉大学攻读哲学与音乐。他的藏书中包括了大型的音乐工具书、古代音乐作品的总谱、现代音乐研究论著等等，显然超出普通音乐爱好者通常涉足的领域，可见其在音乐方面的兴趣并没有因为转行成为目录学家而止步。这一册书中还发现夹有四份另一本图书的残页，这些残页来自 1741 年出版的作者为尼尔斯·布雷林（Nils Brelin）的瑞典语图书，同样是关于古代键盘乐器的。

CHAPTER EIGHT

SCANDINAVIA, CENTRAL AND EASTERN EUROPE, SPANISH PENINSULA

The instruments coming from the groups of countries listed above are treated briefly in this chapter for three reasons. (1) In some cases the instrument making in a country was on so small a scale, and so few instruments have survived, that it is impossible to produce a detailed study of work which was, in fact, of little general musical importance. (2) In the case of Eastern Europe it has proved difficult to obtain direct access to such material as is preserved there. (3) The Spanish Peninsula, as so often, is the exception. Important problems of musical performance are inseparable from the instruments made in that part of Europe, but the amount of detailed information available at present is inadequate for more than the most superficial report.

SCANDINAVIA

We have already seen that German harpsichords and clavichords, chiefly of eighteenth century Hamburg manufacture, were imported into Scandinavia. In addition, during the early eighteenth century, native instrument making took root in these countries. In 1739 Niels Brelin, at one time the pastor of Volstadt, near Carlstadt, published in the Stockholm *Vetenskaps Akademiens Handlingar* an account of his new plan for a harpsichord, which contained a special design of jack, and a set of sympathetic strings. In 1741 Brelin described, through the same medium, a clavicytherium with eight variations of tone, controlled by pedals. This suggests a general interest in, and experience of, instrument making; and from that time Baltic makers appear regularly.

The Nordiska Museum in Stockholm has a clavichord of 1742, compass C – d³, by Philip Jacob Specken, as well as a two manual harpsichord by this maker, with a five octave FF compass, and dated 1737. Pehr Lundborg of Stockholm has left three clavichords dated between 1787 and 1796, now in the Nordiska and Musikhistoriska Museums; all have a compass FF – a³, and the earliest example has octave strings in the bass. The latter Museum also has an organ and clavichord combined, a most unusual combination, made by Lundborg in 1772.

Lundborg's pupil, Mathias Peter Kraft, was Court instrument maker at Stockholm in 1780; there is a rectangular pianoforte by Kraft in the Göteborg Museum, dated 1802, and

112

a five and a half octave clavichord, FF – c⁴, dated 1806, in the Nordiska Museum. Pehr Lindholm, of Stockholm (1742–1813) made numbers of clavichords of compass FF – c⁴, some with octave strings in the bass, and there are examples in The Historical Museum, Abo, Finland, in Copenhagen and elsewhere, made between 1776 and 1803. By the latter year Lindholm had taken into partnership H. J. Söderström, his son-in-law, who was maker of a clavichord dated 1816 which is now in the Nordiska Museum. This clavichord, also, has the five and a half octave compass which was becoming common in the early nineteenth century.

Harpsichord makers are further represented by Gottlieb Rosenau of Stockholm, who made a double manual harpsichord of 1786, with two unisons and an octave, and five octave FF compass, now in the Claudius collection in Copenhagen (plate 96). Johan Broman made a clavichord of 1756, and a five octave double manual harpsichord of 1750, which are in the Nordiska Museum. This harpsichord is unusual in that, while only an eight foot instrument as regards pitch, its length is twelve feet. There were other Swedish instrument makers working both in this period and also into the nineteenth century; they are mostly represented today by one or two clavichords each (plates 97 and 98).

Among Danish clavichord makers is M. Christensen of Copenhagen, by whom there is a clavichord dated 1759 in the National History Museum at Frederiksborg. In 1777 Johan Jesper Jørgensen of Odense made a clavichord, compass FF – f³, which is in the Musik-historisk Museum, Copenhagen. H. P. Moller, an eighteenth century maker of clavichords and pianofortes in Copenhagen, was also a musical inventor; he founded the present day firm of Hornung and Moller, which, apart from pianoforte making, has revived the manufacture of harpsichords and clavichords. Moritz Georg Moshack also of Copenhagen, is represented by a clavichord, FF – f³, in the Norsk Folk Museum in Oslo.

A clavichord of four and a half octaves, C – f³, is preserved in the Oslo Folk Museum; it was made at Moss (Norway), and it is signed *H. Jansen, Hoc fecit, Moss, 1757.*

CENTRAL AND EASTERN EUROPE

Turning towards Central Europe, we find a considerable amount of work going on in Poland. Michael de Pilzna of Rzeszow worked in the fifteenth and sixteenth centuries as a clavichord maker in Cracow, and was followed in the latter century by Krzysztof Kiejcher. The seventeenth century saw Martin who worked in Cracow about 1609, Bernard Przeworski who died there in 1620, and Kasper Hauk. All these men are recorded by the National Museum, Poznan, as harpsichord, clavichord and spinet makers. This museum contains an anonymous eighteenth century harpsichord with two manuals, one of which has been fitted with hammer action; the maker's inscription is now partly illegible, but the instrument is believed to be of German or Polish origin. There is also a clavichord by Johann Christof Maywaldt of Weigandsthal, built in 1729, compass C – e³. A clavichord by Maywaldt dated 1729, possibly the same instrument, is or was in the Schlesisches Museum, Breslau.[1] Christian Gottlob Mazlowski of Poznan was at work in the early nineteenth century.

(1) Valdrighi.

113

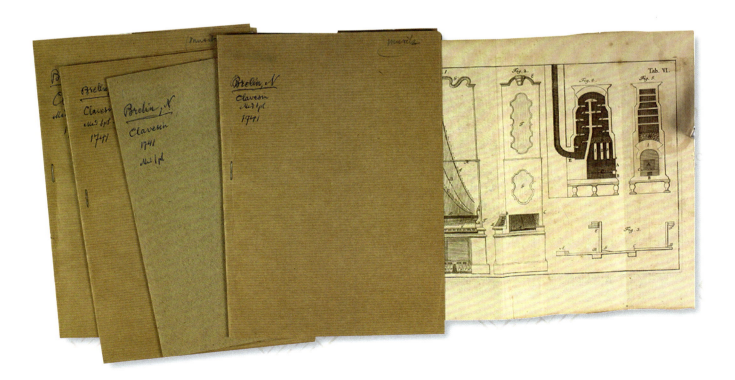

罗氏捐赠图书编号 **1680**

《佛国记》

（A record of buddhistic kingdoms: being an account by the Chinese monk Fa-Hien of his travels in India and Ceylon (A.D. 399－414) in search of the buddhist books of discipline）

作　　者：［英］理雅各（James Legge, 1815－1897）

出　　版：纽约，Pargon Book Reprint Corp.，Dover Publications, Inc.，1965

载体形态：23×12.5 厘米；XI 页＋卷首 1 幅木板画插画＋英文正文 123 页＋中文正文 54 页

装　　订：平装

来　　源：有罗信（Staffan Rosén）签名及藏书票（包罗万象合一知行／忠信笃敬远大前程）

版　　本：1886 年 Clarendon Press 版，1965 年 Paragon Book Reprint Corp.、Dover Publications 版。

内　　容：

　　东晋僧人法显（334-420）是第一位有记载到达印度的中国人，在游历印度、斯里兰卡等国家后，法显回国写成《佛国记》（又名《法显传》《历游天竺记》等）。该书记载了法显游历中亚、南亚各国的经历，在宗教与地理领域有丰富的内容，在海内外广泛流传。最早的西文译本是 1836 年巴黎出版的汉学家雷慕沙所译法语本。英文译本最早可追溯到 1848 年莱德利（J.W. Laidly）在浸礼会内部印行的版本。其后 1869 年伦敦出版了比尔（Samuel Beal）英译本。但汉学家翟理斯（Herbert Allen Giles）批评此译本较为粗糙，1869 年翟氏也在伦敦出版了自己所译的版本。

　　理雅各是英国伦敦会传教士，在华长达三十年，在此期间潜心研究中国典籍，在香港居住期间，与王韬合作翻译出版了《中国经典》《东方圣书》等书，将《论语》《中庸》《道德经》等著作介绍到欧洲。《佛国记》是理雅各回到英国，就任牛津大学汉学教授期间所翻译的作品。在翻译的过程中，理雅各主要参考了《中国佛教手册》（Handbook for the Student of Chinese Buddhism）、《东方僧院》（Eastern Monachism）等西方广为流传的佛教著作。在翻译的手法上主要采用了直译的方式，并配合大量脚注来解释原文重要字词和疑难句，具有极强的学术性，因此使得此版本成为《佛国记》英译本中最为通行的本子，此后多次再版。

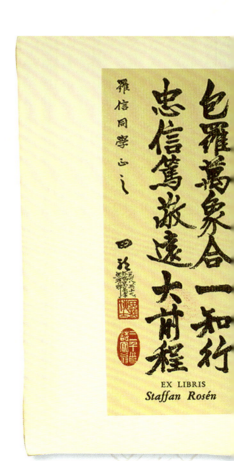

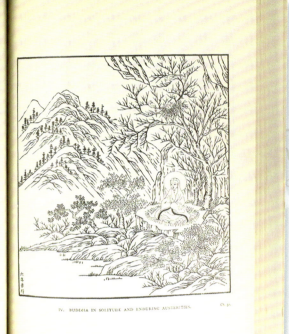

88   *THE TRAVELS OF FÂ-HIEN.*

the rocks, into which the Bodhisattva entered, and sat cross-legged with his face to the west. (As he did so,) he said to himself, 'If I am to attain to perfect wisdom (and become Buddha), let there be a supernatural attestation of it.' On the wall of the rock there appeared immediately the shadow of a Buddha, rather more than three feet in length, which is still bright at the present day. At this moment heaven and earth were greatly moved, and devas in the air spoke plainly, 'This is not the place where any Buddha of the past, or he that is to come, has attained, or will attain, to perfect Wisdom. Less than half a yojana from this to the south-west will bring you to the patra[1] tree, where all past Buddhas have attained, and all to come must attain, to perfect Wisdom.' When they had spoken these words, they immediately led the way forwards to the place, singing as they did so. As they thus went away, the Bodhisattva arose and walked (after them). At a distance of thirty paces from the tree, a deva gave him the grass of lucky omen[2], which he received and went on. After (he had proceeded) fifteen paces, 500 green birds came flying towards him, went round him thrice, and disappeared. The Bodhisattva went forward to the patra tree, placed the kuśa grass at the foot of it, and sat down with his face to the east. Then king Mâra sent three beautiful young ladies, who came from the north, to tempt him, while he himself came from the south to do the same. The Bodhisattva put his toes down on the ground, and the demon soldiers retired and dispersed, and the three young ladies were changed into old (grand-) mothers[3].

At the place mentioned above of the six years' painful austerities, and at all these other places, men subsequently reared topes and set up images, which all exist at the present day.

Where Buddha, after attaining to perfect wisdom, for seven days contemplated the tree, and experienced the joy of vimukti[4]; where, under

[1] Called 'the tree of leaves,' and 'the tree of reflection;' a palm tree, the borassus flabellifera, described as a tree which never loses its leaves. It is often confounded with the pippala. E. H., p. 92.
[2] The kuśa grass, mentioned in a previous note.
[3] See the account of this contest with Mâra in M. B., pp. 171-179, and 'Buddhist Birth Stories,' pp. 96-101.
[4] See note 2, p. 38.

IV. BUDDHA IN SOLITUDE AND ENDURING AUSTERITIES.

A RECORD OF
BUDDHISTIC KINGDOMS

BEING AN ACCOUNT BY THE CHINESE
MONK FÂ-HIEN OF HIS TRAVELS IN INDIA
AND CEYLON (A.D. 399-414) IN SEARCH OF
THE BUDDHIST BOOKS OF DISCIPLINE

Translated and annotated
with a Corean recension of the Chinese text

by

JAMES LEGGE

PARAGON BOOK REPRINT CORP., NEW YORK
DOVER PUBLICATIONS, INC., NEW YORK

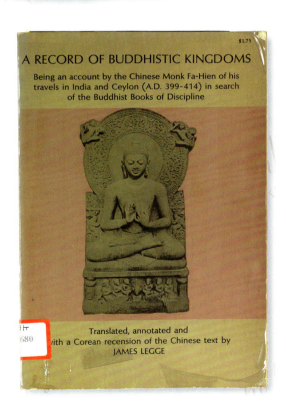

A RECORD OF BUDDHISTIC KINGDOMS

Being an account by the Chinese Monk Fa-Hien of his travels in India and Ceylon (A.D. 399-414) in search of the Buddhist Books of Discipline

Translated, annotated and with a Corean recension of the Chinese text by
JAMES LEGGE

罗氏捐赠图书编号 6487-6488

《普朗克、爱因斯坦、玻尔和索末菲的量子理论》
（The quantum theory of Planck, Einstein, Bohr and Sommerfeld）

作　　者：［美］贾格迪什·梅赫拉（Jagdish Mehra, 1931-2008），

　　　　　　［德］赫尔穆特·雷兴贝格（Helmut Rechenberg, 1937-2016）

出　　版：纽约，海德堡，柏林：施普林格（Springer-Verlag），1982 年

载体形态：24.5×17 厘米，XLVII+372 页；VI+［373］-878 页

内　　容：

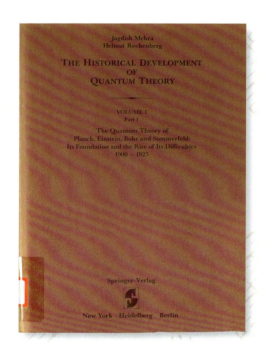

　　本书是印度裔美籍物理学家贾格迪什·梅赫拉撰写的介绍量子理论的专著《量子理论发展史》（The historical development of quantum theory）的第一卷，共上下两册，主要描述了量子理论的形成和早期发展历程。这部书是一部庞大的现代物理学专业书，共六卷九册，出版时间跨度也很大，第一至第四卷出版于 1982 年，第五卷出版于 1987 年，第六卷出版于 2001 年。罗氏藏书中现有这套书的前四卷。

　　量子理论专著出现在一位藏书家和目录学家的书架上似乎有一些突兀，但在罗氏捐赠的藏书中我们还能看到爱因斯坦、普朗克、玻尔等人的传记之类，现代物理学很可能也是有着哲学背景的罗闻达先生感兴趣的领域之一。这些与他的专业无关的藏书，或许可以从一定程度上揭示他日常的阅读范围，让人们更深入地了解藏书家的学识和修养。

constants. By carrying through the variational calculation, Bose obtained the solution

$$p_r^s = B_s \exp\left(-\frac{rh\nu_s}{\beta}\right), \quad r = 0, 1, 2, \ldots \qquad (300)$$

with

$$B_s = A_s\left[1 - \exp\left(-\frac{h\nu_s}{\beta}\right)\right], \quad s = 0, 1, 2, \ldots. \qquad (300a)$$

where β denoted a temperature-dependent constant. Upon substituting the expression for p_r^s into the equation for the total energy ($E = \sum_{r,s} r p_r^s h\nu_s$), he arrived at the result

$$E = \sum_r \frac{8\pi\nu_r^2}{c^3} V \frac{h\nu_r}{\exp(h\nu_r/\beta) - 1}. \qquad (301)$$

Since, because of the entropy–temperature relation, $\partial S/\partial E = 1/T$, the quantity β assumed the value kT, Eq. (301) represented indeed the energy density distribution of blackbody radiation, i.e., $E/V = \sum_r \rho_r$, with ρ_r satisfying Planck's law.

The basic method, developed by Bose in his derivation of Planck's law outlined above, was a consistent use of the division of the quantum-theoretical phase space of the light-quanta in cells of volume h^3. Such a method had been suggested earlier for material particles or molecules by Otto Sackur (1911) and especially by Max Planck (1915b, c). However, none of Bose's predecessors had given the simple solution obtained by the physicist from Dacca, which implied the two simple steps: first, to evaluate the number of cells in phase space as the number representing the possible sites of the quantum-theoretical objects under investigation; second, to determine the probability of a given distribution by counting the number of realizations of this distribution among the possible sites. Thus Bose completed a long line of arguments, which Planck had started nearly twenty years earlier with his quantum-theoretical treatment of the phase space of resonators (Planck, 1906). One may ask, therefore, why Planck had not arrived at Bose's conclusion himself. The decisive reason must be seen in Planck's goal, expressed from the very beginning of his theory of blackbody radiation: he had considered this radiation as emerging from the interaction between resonators and electromagnetic radiation and had never thought of it as a kind of free radiation. Bose, a quarter of a century later, adopted Einstein's point of view by treating ensembles of free light-quanta. He recognized that light-quanta could be considered as relativistic massless particles (see Eq. (296)). In agreement with Planck's procedure, however, he assumed that light-quanta were indistinguishable; that is, in computing the thermodynamic probability (or the entropy via Boltzmann's relation), only the occupation numbers of the cells played a role, not

the fact which individual light-quantum was in which specific cell.[870] Bose's derivation, therefore, signified the final link in a chain of arguments begun by Planck and continued by Debye.

Einstein acknowledged the receipt of Bose's paper on the derivation of Planck's law in a handwritten postcard to Bose, in which he stated 'that he regarded the paper as an important contribution and that he will have it published' (Bose, Conversations, quoted in Mehra, 1975b, p. 130). The postcard was of great help to Bose, who had applied earlier that year for a two-year leave to study abroad, but by June he had not received a definite reply. As Bose recalled:

As soon as they [the Senate Council] showed it to [D. J.] Hartog [the Vice-Chancellor] it solved all problems. As a student Hartog had spent some time at the University of Paris and he understood something of what such an experience could do for a young man. That little thing [Einstein's postcard] gave me a sort of passport to the study leave. They gave me leave for two years and rather generous terms. I received a good stipend. They also gave a separation allowance for the family, otherwise I would not have been able to go abroad at all. Also return fares and additional travel allowance. That was very generous. Then I also got a visa from the German Consulate just by showing them Einstein's card. They did not require me to pay the fee for the visa! (Bose, Conversations, quoted in Mehra, 1975b, p. 130)

In early September 1924 Bose sailed from Bombay to Europe. After some stops for sightseeing on the way, he arrived around mid-October in Paris, his first station. A year later he went to Berlin.[871]

Two and a half months before leaving India—and before he received Einstein's postcard— Bose sent a second paper to Einstein dealing with the problem of thermal equilibrium between radiation and matter. In the accompanying letter he wrote: 'I have ventured to send you the type-written paper in English; it being beyond me to express myself in German (which will be intelligible to you). I shall be glad if its publication in *Zeitschrift für Physik* or any other German journal can be managed. I myself know not how to manage it. In any case, I shall be grateful if you express any opinion on the papers, and send it to me at the above address' (Bose to Einstein, 15 June 1924). Einstein did not answer Bose immediately, but he translated Bose's paper again and submitted it to *Zeitschrift für Physik*; it was received on 7 July 1924 and published in September 1924 under

---

[870] That in Planck's evaluation of the probability of blackbody radiation the energy quanta of radiation were not indistinguishable in the sense of the classical description had already been noted by Ehrenfest and Kamerlingh Onnes (1914).

[871] Bose had not gone to Berlin straight away from Dacca because he felt that his knowledge of German was not good enough. In Paris he was introduced to Paul Langevin and became a member of a circle of Bengali students. He tried to find a place in Madame Curie's laboratory to learn modern experimental techniques, but Madame Curie advised him first to learn French well. Bose then found a place in Maurice de Broglie's private laboratory, where—guided by Alexandre Dauvillier—he acquired some knowledge of X-ray spectroscopy and crystallography.

《奥洛夫·鲁德贝克〈鸟书〉》

（ Olof Rudbeck's book of birds: a facsimile of the original watercolours 【 c.1693-1710 】 of Olof Rudbeck the Younger in the Leufsta Collection in Uppsala University Library ）

作　　者：［瑞典］罗闻达（Björn Löwendahl）编辑，
　　　　　　Stockholm Coeckelberghs 上色

出　　版：斯德哥尔摩，Björn & Bröjesson，1986

载体形态：2 册，44.5×26 厘米；第一册正文 99 页＋图 6 页，第二册
　　　　　　165 页插图

装　　订：金色印花布面函套，布面精装两册。

内　　容：

　　该书记录了瑞典著名博物学家奥洛夫·鲁德贝克观测到的不同品种鸟类的绘图。据考证，这些画完成于 1693-1710 年之间，1739 年起被保存在瑞典乌普萨拉市附近的 Leufsta 区，期间鲜有学者关注。直至 1985 年地区政府将这批画作移交给乌普萨拉大学图书馆，才重新进入学界的视野。著名生物学家林奈（Carl von Linné）1728 年在乌普萨拉大学学习医学与自然史期间，受到奥洛夫的影响，参加了多种鸟类学讲座，奥洛夫的鸟类学研究成为林奈物种分类（即林奈种）的来源之一。

　　本书瑞典语第一版出版于 1985 年，同年出版了德语版。英文版是由罗闻达编辑，多位生物学家指导而成。内容包括了奥洛夫的生平、自然史研究、鸟类学相关著作评注、图片索引等内容，是罗闻达作为出版业者的代表作品之一。

罗氏捐赠图书编号 2070

《古琴》
（Qin）

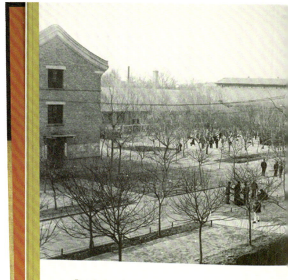

作　　者：［瑞典］林西莉（Cecilia Lindqvist, 1932-　　）
出　　版：斯德哥尔摩：阿尔贝特·邦尼尔斯（Albert Bonniers），2006 年
载体形态：29.5×19 厘米，272 页，附 CD

内　　容：

　　本书是一部对中国古琴文化的综合介绍，用瑞典语撰述，曾获瑞典奥古斯特文学奖。作者林西莉是 20 世纪 60 年代在北京大学留学的瑞典留学生，从王迪先生学琴，并有幸接触过查阜西、管平湖等老一辈琴人。这段经历使她成为热忱的中国文化爱好者、研究者和传播者。书中图文并茂地介绍了琴的历史、形制、规格、技法，也论及琴曲的内涵、琴文化的延伸等音乐以外的东西，不但涵盖了传统琴学的主要内容，也通过对亲身经历的描述，展示了我国自 20 世纪 60 年代到 21 世纪初的社会面貌的发展变迁，有明确的帮助西方人深入了解中国文化的用意。本书附一张 CD，是作者本人演奏的录音，其中包括《广陵散》（节选）、《碣石调幽兰》等难度较高的曲目，可见作者的专业功底。

　　罗闻达先生长年从事中国相关的文献书目研究，与国内许多学者和机构结下了深厚的友谊，而他的这一册藏书也是中瑞两国人民友谊的美好见证，颇有纪念意义。同时，本书装帧设计十分精致，在罗氏诸多高品质的藏书中也十分显眼。

Södra delen av Pekings
universitet med studentbostäder
och samlingslokaler.

Mitt studentpass för 1962.
Kontrollen av alla som skulle
in på universitetsområdet var
rigorös. Alla måste ha pass.

universitetet Harvard, mitt i en berömd trädgård med anor
från Mingdynastin (1368–1644), arrangerad på klassiskt vis
som en daoistisk dröm om paradiset. Här fanns ett högt konst-
gjort berg med underliga klippor och cypresser, slingrande
vattendrag som mynnade ut i sjöar med lotus, paviljonger med
svängda tak, kamelryggsbroar, täta bambulundar – inne i en av
dem bodde den internationellt kände filosofen Feng Youlan –
och ett vattentorn utformat som en kinesisk pagod. Bostäderna
för studenter och lärare i den delen av campus såg ut som klas-
siska tempelbyggnader eller som nätta villor i kinesiserande
stil. Kontrasten till kasernerna i den nybyggda södra, råa delen
kunde inte ha varit större.

Den enkla maten portionerades
ut till studenterna i emaljerade
matskålar.

Till minnet av min lärare Wang Di (1929–2005)
enastående qinspelare och hängiven forskare

GULLA LINDQVIST

Qin

ALBERT BONNIERS FÖRLAG

En berättelse om det kinesiska instrumentet qin
och dess betydelse i den bildade klassens liv,
om musiken, dikterna, människorna och alla
föreställningar förbundna med qin – inte minst hur
man skall leva sitt liv – och något om vad jag upplevde
när jag hamnade djupt inne i detta.

罗氏捐赠图书编号 2563

《多国家与文化书籍选目》
（A selection of books on various countries and cultures）

作　　者：［瑞典］罗闻达（Björn Löwendahl）

出　　版：Hua Hin，Ban Suksamran，2007

载体形态：30×19 厘米；卷首 1 幅插画 + 正文 100 页

内　　容：

　　本书是罗闻达先生在泰国编辑出版的贩书目录，包含 236 种书籍，语种多为英语、法语、意大利语等，也有丹麦语、瑞典语等。罗氏将书籍按国家与文明进行板块分类，其中包括：泰国；越南、老挝、缅甸；马来群岛；中国；朝鲜；日本；西伯利亚与蒙古；缅甸；印度、尼泊尔；波斯；南俄罗斯与外高加索；东地中海国家（阿拉伯半岛与土耳其）；俄罗斯与波罗的海国家；斯堪地纳维亚、冰岛、法罗群岛和格林兰岛；中欧与西欧；非洲；西印度群岛与南美。从此书可以看出罗氏所藏书籍所涉及领域的广泛性，东西方文明都有所涉及，除了历史类书籍之外，还有科学、工艺美术、植物学等内容。

23. MONEY, JAMES WILLIAM BAYLEY: Java; or, How to manage a colony. Showing a practical solution of the questions now affecting British India. 1-2.

London, Hurst and Blackett, 1861. 8vo. XVI + 332; + VIII + 316 pp. + 5 tables (2 folding).

Publisher's cloth, pp. 10-11 in volume one browned.

First edition.   £300

BATAVIA IMPRINT

24. RADERMACHER, JAKOB CORNELIS MATTHAEUS: Naamlyst der Planten, die gevonden worden op het eiland Java. Met de beschryving van eenige nieuwe geslagten en soorten. 1-3.

Batavia, gedrukt in d'E: Compagnies Boek-drukkery, by Egbert Heemen (vols. 1-2) & Pieter van Geemen (vol. 3). 1780-82. 4to. 60; + II + 68 + 88 + 81-88 + 40; + IV + 84 (of 102) + 42 + II + 70 pp.

Original marbled boards, leaves E1 & E2 (pp. 33-36) in vol. 3 in duplicate.

Extremely rare, but three complete copies at least survive: one in the Royal Library, The Hague, one in the University Library at Leiden, and one in the British Library. There is also an incomplete copy in the Hunt Library and another in Helsinki, according to Stafleu.

A founder member of the Bataviaasch Genootschap der Konsten en Wetenschappen, Radermacher's writings epitomise the advanced scientific work pursued by distinguished servants of the Dutch East India Company (VOC). An authority on the possessions of the VOC, Radermacher wrote extensively on the town of Batavia and the islands of Borneo and Sumatra. In the present work, he concentrates on the extraordinary botanic riches of the island of Java. A pioneering work of geographical botany, the *Naamlyst der planten* opened the way for the commercial exploitation of Java and its many useful plants.

Pritzel 7392. John Landwehr, VOC, 615. Stafleu & Cowan 8501.   £7000

THE NEW TESTAMENT IN DAYAK

25. Surat brasi Djandji Taheta tuhan dan djuru-salamat ikei Jesus Kristus.

Njelo, Rambangan hong Lewu Kapstad, tan ah Afrika, awi Pike dan Philip, 1846. 8vo. IV + 458 pp.

Dark blue cloth, red label on spine.

First edition of the New Testament in the Land Dayak dialect, spoken in the inlands of Borneo. It was translated by Johann-Friedrich Becker and August Hardeland, missionaries of the Rhenish Missionary Society, which had established a station at Palopetak, South Borneo in 1835. The book was printed at Capetown in 1846, under the supervision of Hardeland; copies reached Borneo in 1848, and the whole edition (1500 copies) was exhausted by 1854.

Darlow & Moule 1459.   £600

26. TAVARES DE VELLEZ GUERREIRO, JOAÔ: Jornada, que Antonio de Albuquerque Coelho, Governador, e Capitaõ General de cidade do nome de Deos de Macao na China, fez de Goa atè chegar á dita cidade no anno de 1718. Dividida em duas partes.

Lisboa Occidental, na Officina da Musica, 1732. 8vo. XVI + 428 pp. Text printed within woodcut frame throughout.

Contemporary limp vellum.

This work, originally published at Macao in 1718 (Boxer, 11), contains an account of the voyage of the Governor of Macao from Goa to Macao, made in the year 1718, and recounts visits to various places in India, the Malay Peninsula, Indo-China, and China. The second part (pp. 187-422) relates to Albuquerque's stay at Johore (October 1717 to April, 1718), where he became involved in the coup d'état of the Sumatran adventurer Raja Kechil, which affected the Miningkabau conquest of the most powerful Malay kingdom of the day. The author was Albuquerque's chief-of-staff, and wrote this narrative soon after the Governor's arrival in Macao, May 1718.

Not in Cordier.   £1350

THUNBERG, CARL PETER: *See item 55.*

27. WALBAUM, CHISTIAN FRIEDRICH: Ausführliche und merckwürdige Historie der Ost-Indischen Insel Gross-Java und aller übrigen Holländischen Colonien in Ost-Indien.

Leipzig & Jena, bey Johann Christoph Crökern, 1754. 8vo. XVI + 480 pp. Engraved vignette on title.

Contemporary marbled boards, new label on spine.

First edition of an early German description of Java compiled from printed narratives of Ernst Christoph Barchewitz, Johann von der Behr, Johann Jacob Mercklein, and other VOC employees, and from other printed sources.

Landwehr, VOC, 491.   £1950

CHINA

28. A complete view of the Chinese Empire. Exhibited in a geographical description of that country, a dissertation on its antiquity, and a genuine and copious account of Earl Macartney's embassy from the King of Great Britain to the Emperor of China.

London, printed and published by G. Cawthorn, 1798. 8vo. VI + LXXII + 224 + 275-456 pp. + 1 engraved portrait. Pp. 225-274 omitted in pagination.

Contemporary mottled calf, spine attractively decorated in gilt in compartments, black label, rubbed.

Cordier, BS, 4, col. 2391.   £450

Löwendahl *Rare Books*

14   15

A SELECTION OF BOOKS
ON VARIOUS COUNTRIES
AND CULTURES

HUA HIN

MMVII

Löwendahl
RARE BOOKS

A SELECTION OF BOOKS
ON VARIOUS COUNTRIES
AND CULTURES

HUA HIN

MMVII

罗氏捐赠图书编号 3473

《中国历史新手册》
（Chinese history: a new manual）

作　　者：〔英〕魏根深（Endymion Wilkinson）

出　　版：剑桥（马萨诸塞州）、伦敦，Harvard University Asia Center，2012

载体形态：25×17 厘米；XXVI 页 + 卷首 1 幅插画 + 正文与索引 1247 页

来　　源：内封前页有魏根深赠罗闻达题签，内夹作者向罗闻达寄送徐家汇藏书楼主题明信片。

内　　容：

　　作者魏根深（Endymion Wilkinson）是英国学者、外交家，曾任欧盟驻华大使，后在美国哈佛大学任教授。作者自 20 世纪 60 年代开始研究中国历史文化，手册的雏形出版于 1973 年，经过长时间的修订增补，于 1998 年出版第一版《中国历史手册》，并于 2000 年再版，此后作者继续潜心修改增订，历时十二年，终于在 2012 年出版了第三版，修订达百万字，书名也因之改为《中国历史新手册》。魏氏凭借此书享誉西方汉学界，2014 年此书获得了欧洲汉学儒莲奖（Stanislas Julien Prize）。2015 年此书出版了第四版，增加了新时期的研究成果。

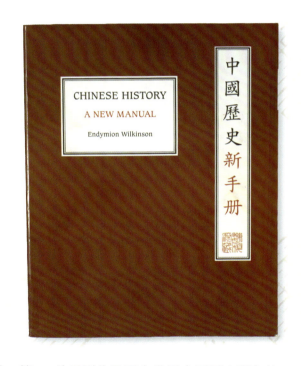

　　此书涵盖了从上古时期到 21 世纪研究中国历史、文化、社会、经济、教育的文献，对这些文献的刊刻、保存、流转与传播的情况进行了较为完整的归纳与介绍。全书由 14 个单元共计 76 章组成。第 1-9 单元内容包括语言、人文、地理、政治与教育、信仰、文学艺术、农业与饮食、科学技术、商业、史学史；第 10-13 单元以断代的方式梳理中国历史研究的一次文献与二次文献；第 14 单元则收录了全世界中国历史研究的文献书目、数据库等。美国宾州大学教授梅维恒（Victor H.Mair）在书后题词中称该手册为"钻研中国历史文化的学者不可或缺的参考指南"。

CHINESE HISTORY
A NEW MANUAL

for Björn
Bibliophile, rare book
collector, author, and publisher
in the China field Sans
pareil,   *With Best Wishes,*

Endymion
December 17, 2012

Harvard-Yenching Institute Monograph Series 84

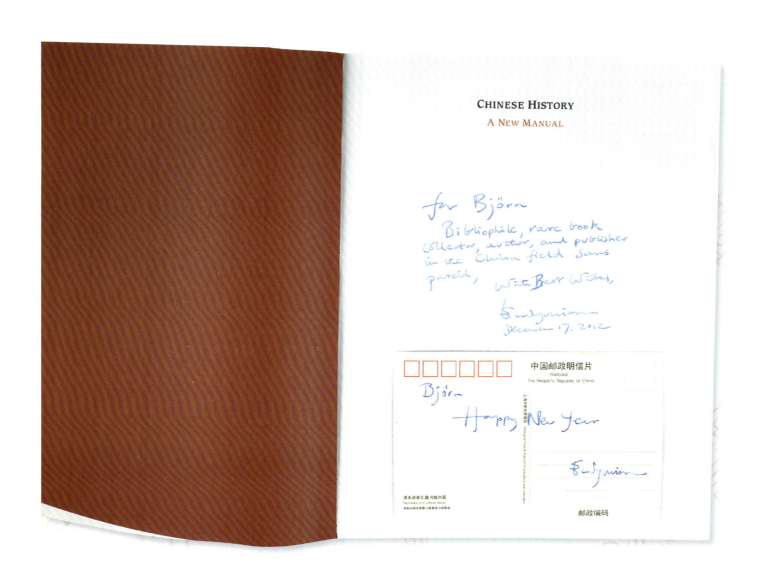

书香犹在忆故人

——与瑞典著名藏书家罗闻达先生交往的点滴回忆

韩 琦

今年 8 月我在韩国访问，刚刚送走顺便来访的家人，就在 23 日接到罗闻达先生（Björn Löwendahl，1941.9.2-2013.8.24）从泰国来电，告知赴韩一切行程均已安排妥当，约定 27 日在首尔见面。正在我憧憬再次会面之时，不料次日即接到其女的来信，告知他突然去世的消息。他爽朗的笑声犹在耳边回响，然而一夜之间竟天人永隔。在奎章阁，我发现自己已无法静下心来认真读书，与罗闻达先生因书结缘之后的一些小事时时浮上心头。

我与罗闻达先生在 2005 年 11 月相识。记得当时因参观嘉德拍卖会预展，去和老朋友艾思仁、冯德堡见面。他们相邀中午一起聚餐，那日却是素昧平生的罗先生做东，并由此认识其夫人和子女。初次见面，不仅他慈眉善目、彬彬有礼的样子给我留下了深刻印象，而且听高大硕壮的罗先生不无幽默地介绍其瑞典名字 Björn 本意是"熊"，一桌人忍俊不禁。

那日在饭桌上其实令我最为兴奋的是见到他个人收藏的西文中国书目的手稿。即便惊鸿一瞥，已觉收藏之富，惊喜无限。当时我心里感叹：在近 20 年的时间内便能收罗规模如此齐全，如果没有渊博的学识，对西方版本学、书籍史和中西关系史的深入了解和坚持不懈的努力，是绝无可能的。两人谈话十分投机，他还兴奋地提到新购的比利时耶稣会士卫方济的天文学著作。此书在西方也已十分稀见，喜欢满世界看书的我也只在巴黎天文台见过，不禁大加赞叹。虽是首次见面，谈话开心之余，他竟然约我为他的目录写一导言。尽管令我受宠若惊，但是席间多场面之语，我并未十分当真。但事实证明我错了，罗先生一向是言出必行之人。

时隔半年的 2006 年 5 月，我们再次在北京见面，他很认真地重提写序之事：邀我趁 8 月赴德国开会之便顺访瑞典，到他家看书，以便下笔。这次斯德哥尔摩之行着实让我大饱眼福：除了看书之外，我还访问了乌普萨拉，一则因为那里有瑞典植物学家林奈的故居，二是乌普萨拉大学保存了一些 17、18 世纪流传到那里的耶稣会士的中文著作，包括南怀仁的《坤舆全图》。冯德堡先生亲自驾车，三人同行，还一起参观了大学古老的解剖学剧场。一起在林奈故居合影的珍贵照片，已成为不可再得的纪念。

2006 年 8 月 25 日作者与罗闻达先生在林奈故居前合影。

罗先生认真、心细，对事情从来一丝不苟。自第一次会面直至书目出版，他每到北京，总是将目录的修改稿给我，让我提意见，并请我帮助做了外国人汉名索引。2008 年，《从西文印本书籍看中西关系、中国观、文化影响和汉学发展》正式出版，皇皇两巨册，包罗了从 1477 年至 1877 年之间的一千余种西人有关中国的著作。在此序中，我给他取了汉名"罗闻达"，寓意有二：一是此名和他的姓的发音十分相近；二是和他的秉性十分贴合，博学多闻，开朗达观，豁达大度。

罗先生的书目出版后，获得了国际学术界的广泛赞誉，多家图书馆想购买此藏书。2008 年，当徐文堪先生得知之后，特意来电，要我将目录寄给他一阅。他随后马上写了报告，商请上海社会科学院购买。后来报告转到上海图书馆，中间经过许多曲折，最后在吴建中馆长的大力支持下，又由我从中协调，罗先生和上海图书馆达成了购买的协议，藏书在 2010 年落户上海图书馆徐家汇藏书楼。罗先生为此感到十分快慰。

罗先生是一个不知疲倦的人。他在编完目录之后，仍常常往返于伦敦、香港的书展，每有所获，都十分兴奋地打电话告诉我。2012 年，他出版了书目补编，与前编相同，补编主要收录了 19 世纪 70 年代之前约 400 年间出版的欧洲有关中国及其周边国家的著作，内容涉及宗教、历史、风俗、科技、地理等多方面内容。补编收录的范围，和前编可互为补充，包括 280 余种（编号 1552-1838）印本书籍，其中有三部摇篮本，最珍贵的是普林尼的《自然史》（1473）。来华传教士的著作仍占多数，如利玛窦著作的法文本，卫匡国《鞑靼战纪》的拉丁文本、法文本、英文本，安文思《中国新史》（1688）英文本，以及法国国王路易十四派遣来华的"国王数学家"的著作，包括塔夏的《暹罗行纪》（1686）、白晋的插图本《中国现状》（1697）、李明的《中国近事报道》英文本（1697），还有卫方济的《中国经典》（1711），启蒙运动思想家伏尔泰、狄德罗、魁奈有关中国的论著，《赵氏孤儿》的英文本（1759）等。此外，19 世纪法国、德国、英国早期汉学家（如阿伯儿、儒莲、理雅各、艾约瑟等）的著作，马克思有关中国论述的报刊文章，以及欧洲 18、19 世纪学术刊物上有关中国的论述都有收录。除了印本之外，还包括五部重要手稿，如康熙年间随教廷特使多罗来华访问的 Illarione Sala 的手稿，对研究中西"礼仪之争"有重要的学术价值，十分珍贵。记述 1805-1806 年俄国使节来华访问的 Rochus van Suchtelen 的法文手稿，对研究嘉庆年间清廷和俄国的外交关系有重要学术价值。此外，收藏中还包括一些稀见的铜版画，如康熙时代宫廷画家意大利传教士马国贤的《避暑山庄三十六景图》中的八幅铜版画，这些画均保存在欧洲和中国台湾，中国大陆至今没有收藏；还有 17 世纪末法国印刷的有关中国的人物铜版画（如孔子、老子、利玛窦、徐光启、顺治、康熙、汤若望、南京教徒沈福宗等），是欧洲人最早认识中国的图像资料，即使在欧洲也十分稀见。收藏中还有一幅 1755 年到达欧洲（葡萄牙、英国）的广东人林奇官的像，以及 1793 年到达伦敦的香山人林亚九的像，都十分珍贵。

罗先生对西方书籍的版本十分专精，了然于心。2011 年 9 月 6 日，我们一起在上海见面，共同参观了徐家汇藏书楼，再次和这批书见面时，他显得十分兴奋。他还给我专门讲解了比利时耶稣会士安多《数学概要》一书的纸张问题，指出书名页的用纸和别的纸的帘纹不同，说明书名页是后来的书商为了推销库存的书而加以重新印刷，改印了新的年份。这纠正了我以前的错误观念，即认为安多的书自从1685年首次出版后，到1729年还再次出版，说明其影响持久。这一经历让我第一次体会到西方书籍版本的复杂性。他不仅是一位藏书家，也是一位学者。他总是虚怀若谷，好学不倦。他写了一些文章，谈论早期汉学在欧洲的转变。他觉得欧洲人对中国有一个十分复杂的认识过程，要做

2013年3月7日摄于云南丽江，显示了其可爱的"老顽童"样子。

深入细致的研究，才能有完整的认识。但他十分害羞，总觉得文章还有完善的余地。虽然我力劝他发表，但他始终没有应允。

罗先生对待目录编纂工作的态度也值得钦佩。一有疑问，会马上查阅书刊和工具书，或多方写信求教。对书中出现的任何一丝信息，他都要仔细考证，在目录中加以注明。2011年6月，当我在瑞典他的家中看到一本法文本研究西安景教碑的著作上面有"李少白"签名，我马上意识到这位中国人可能就是19世纪中叶在巴黎东方语言学校教授汉语的中国老师，当即面告罗先生，在我的提示下，他马上求购了巴黎东方语言学校校史一书，并把这个信息加进目录补编中。他精于考订，对书籍中出现的版本信息，都有细致入微的描述。因此，他的解题目录完全可作为重要的学术工具书。

罗先生一直觉得，好的书应有好的藏处；而他编纂目录所需的参考书，也应该和藏书收藏在一起，这样才能方便学者利用。故而在这些书出售之后，他就拟好了遗嘱，请我修改中文版，在他过世后将参考书悉数捐赠给上海图书馆。

尽管我们每次见面谈论的话题都离不开书，但是见面次数多了之后，罗先生也时常聊一些学界的掌故和他个人的轶事。他出身于一个艺术家家庭，其父

颇具歌剧歌手的天分，但后来成为摄影师。大学时，罗先生进入乌普萨拉大学学习哲学和音乐，本来着意专研德国哲学家维特根斯坦，后来因与导师们争执而放弃论文，但对哲学的兴趣使他转向目录学的研究。他开起了书店，并出版目录，在当时还颇有名气。他对科学、哲学和美学的历史均有造诣，对自然史也有特殊的品味，对瑞典人在这方面的贡献多有了解。20 世纪 80 年代，他就对早期的游记和林奈经由东印度公司船只派到中国的博物学家的著作感兴趣，但使他真正转向对中国的兴趣，是美国历史学家孟德卫教授《神奇的土地》（1985）一书，此后他致力于西方学者有关中国书籍的收藏，奠定了他在藏书方面的最大成就。

罗先生也是会生活之人，常驻泰国，并时时出游，往返伦敦、香港和北京、上海之间。安排旅程也是极其干净利落，效率极高。每到北京，他常会和我联系，请我到一家云南餐馆吃饭，他十分嗜辣，席间常常念叨着想去云南一游。今年 3 月初，我正好也要到云南考察，于是邀他一起游大理、丽江，还到虎跳峡、玉龙雪山，他玩得十分开心。他喜欢喝酒，每逢吃饭，都要点上好的葡萄酒；有时饭后，他还即兴跳舞，有孩子般的天真，完全忘却了自己已是 70 余岁的老人。我从来没有听他谈过身体的任何不适，只是个子高，关节有些不好，走路多了，需要休息。然而没想到这么健康快活的人却走得这么突然。

2013 年 3 月 8 日摄于云南虎跳峡。

罗先生在补编的序中曾这样写道："我很幸运有这样一份职业，从事它的本身就是一种奖赏。很少有人在活着的时候就已经永生，但我们都憧憬着某种永不完结的生命：我希望能够出版内容更广的第二个补编，也许在我八十岁甚至九十岁的时候。如果不幸我不能完成，那么我希望能够有人愿意继续这项探险。"

我也衷心希望能有人继续罗

先生的事业，广结书缘。更希望他的遗愿得以实现，罗氏藏书补编也能落户上海，和前编合为一体，成为全璧。而对于我来说，失去这样一位书中挚友固然是件憾事，但每当我想到去上海图书馆的时候，可以再次触摸罗氏藏书，翻阅罗先生生前用过的参考书，就如同与老朋友再会一次一般。尽管我是彻彻底底的无神论者，但是我相信在那一刻，罗先生一定会在那里开心地爽朗大笑。

原载 2013 年 11 月 4 日《文汇报》

"罗氏藏书"入藏记

黄显功

2010 年 11 月 26 日上午，瑞典"罗氏藏书"从外高桥海关保税仓库运抵上海图书馆历史文献中心。这个"罗氏藏书入藏日"是上海图书馆藏书史上值得铭记的重要的时刻。我有幸躬逢其盛，亲历此事的全过程，"罗氏藏书"入藏上图的曲折经历一直萦绕在脑海中，久久难忘。

上海图书馆的外文文献收藏，以 1949 年为界，之前的外文图书报刊，收藏于徐家汇藏书楼，并对外服务；1949 年以后出版的外文书报刊，在淮海中路新馆提供服务。藏于徐家汇藏书楼的外文文献来源多途，最受关注的部分是徐家汇藏书楼的旧藏，以汉学特色闻名中外。1956 年之后，除并入其他几处藏书机构的文献外，还曾入藏了巴金等人捐赠的外文图书，但历年购买的外文图书与报刊数量有限。2003 年徐家汇藏书楼修缮完成重新开放后，外文汉学文献的补充成为本馆文献采编的日常工作，不时有所增益。直到 2008 年，因一部汉学研究文献目录的出版，徐家汇藏书楼的文献资源建设迎来了一个重要的发展契机。

——

2008 年，瑞典藏书家、汉学家兼书商的罗闻达在瑞典出版了《从西文印本书籍（1477-1877）看中西关系、中国观、文化影响和汉学发展》。此书甫一问世，即受到国际学术界的重视和图书馆的关注。罗闻达的全名是比尔·乐文道尔（Björn Löwendahl），罗闻达是与乐文道尔音近的中文名字。他出生于 1941 年，大学主修数学，也学过音乐、历史和绘画。25 岁那年，他萌发了开古书店的念头。1965 年，他以 6000 克朗起步，在乌普撒拉大学附近创办了一家书店。他每两周去一趟斯德哥尔摩的古书拍卖会，从中学到了许多古书知识，入了古书经营的门道。在搜集了一批古书后，他 1971 年去了日本，把书卖给了图书馆。此行使罗闻达认识到必须有系统地建立自己的古书世界，形成自己的藏书特色。于是，他回到瑞典后，开始有系统地搜集著名植物学家林奈的著作和瑞典诺贝尔文学奖获得者的初版书。林奈的书在日本卖出了好价钱，瑞典女作家拉格洛夫的《骑鹅旅行记》初版书，在 2000 年也被他卖到了 7500 英镑。他游走于各大收藏机构之间，销售、交换了无数的珍籍，取得了不错的经营业绩。

但罗闻达更关注西方早期与中国相关联的书籍，一个原因是他在经营古书的过程中了解到，中国在历史上的影响比日本、印度还要大；另一原因是这些书的价格相对较便宜。于是，他几十年来乐此不疲，变成了一种特殊的爱好，由此也形成了他的收藏特色，谱写了他的书林故事。作为书商，他有一个不寻常之处是并不单纯地急于贩卖手头的书籍。虽然他认为每一本书阅读后就该脱手，没有一本不能卖的书，书籍就是应该流通的。但他对于辛勤搜寻得来的西方早期汉学书籍却是边读边做笔记，以做学问的方式进行一本本考证，编辑自己的专藏目录。在西方汉学界编写专题目录是一项学术研究工作。19 世纪 60 年代曾在上海亚洲学会北华分会（亚洲文会）任名誉馆员的法国学者高迪爱（1849-1925）曾编辑出版了五大卷《西人汉学书目》，成为中西关系史研究特别是西方人讨论中国问题的权威目录。罗闻达的目录补充了高迪爱所失收的珍稀图书，而且在编排上具有自己的特色。他将所收图书按印刷和出版年代的顺序排列，以此反映中国知识在欧洲的传播过程，也体现了某一时期欧洲汉学的发展脉络。如 1500 年前有 3 种书，1501-1600 年间有 36 种，1601-1700 年间有 230 种，1701-1800 年间有 442 种，1801-1877 年间有 840 种。罗闻达在目录中还广泛参考各种公私藏书，著录了较详细的版本信息。2008 年《从西文印本书籍（1477-1877）看中西关系、中国观、文化影响和汉学发展》正式出版，随即受到国际学术界和图书馆的关注。罗闻达在完成这一工作后，十分期望让这些书回到华文世界。

二

我国学术界了解到这一消息后，高度重视，积极行动。上海社会科学院图书馆研究员徐文堪、陈克艰在 2008 年上半年从在瑞典工作的一位美国友人处获得罗闻达所编书目的出版消息后，即联系到为该书撰写序言的中国科学院自然科学史研究所研究员韩琦先生，从其处借到这部书目进行了研究。他们本希望由上海社会科学院购买此批图书，经与上海社科院图书馆吴刚馆长商量研究，在 9 月 18 日转向上海图书馆发出了收购建议书。时任上海社会科学院副院长熊月之在建议书上手书："购买此书，有大益于学术研究、丰富馆藏，更有利于提升上海乃至中国重视文化建设的形象，有利于中西文化交流。特此附笔吁请。"

这两位学者在建议书中提出的推荐理由是：

一、这一批藏书本身具有很高的学术、资料和版本价值。从语种来看，使用的语言有拉丁语、英语、法语、德语、西班牙语、葡萄牙语、意大利语、俄语、瑞典语等十多种；从内容来看，涉及中国和周边国家的历史、宗教、风俗、地理、科学技术、语言文字等诸多方面，特别是对西方来华传教士的重要著作搜罗齐全，并有多种刊本，实属难得；从版本来看，多珍稀善本，其中有些书籍为上述高迪爱书目所失收，属世界孤本，而且绝大部分书籍是我国的重要图书馆如中国国家图书馆、上海图书馆、北京大学图书馆、中国科学院图书馆没有入藏的。

二、购买这批书籍将对我国的相关学术研究起到很大的推动和促进作用。近年来国内对中外关系史和国外汉学的研究日益活跃，正呈现方兴未艾之势。但不少研究机构和研究者都苦于看不到西文原著，如果我们将这一特藏引入，并通过数字化等手段使之广为流通，必将大大有功于学术界，受到国内外学者的热烈欢迎。上海市人民政府有关部门委托上海社科院每两年组织召开国际性的"中国学论坛"，至今已举办了三届。如果上海购买收藏这批书籍，将是本市乃至全国海外中国学研究的重要的基础建设。

三、在我国成功举办奥运会和即将在上海举办世博会之际，收购这批书籍将产生良好的国际影响。众所周知，1924 年成立的日本著名的东洋文库（Tokyo Bunko），是以英国记者莫理循（GF.Morrison，1862-1920）私人收藏的有关东方各国的西文书籍为其藏书基础的。这批书原在北京，但因当时中国积弱积贫、国力不振，无法筹款购买，于 1917 年被日本三菱财团的岩崎久弥购入，国人至今引以为憾。而在当今中国正和平发展的新形势下，如果通过友好商谈，以公平合理的价格将海外中国学特藏引进，并以合适的方式向公众介绍

和展示，无疑将对提升中国形象，促进中外文化交流和合作起到有益的作用。

徐文堪与陈克艰很期待地认为，如能将书目所载书籍整体购入，将是"中国学术界和文化界的一大盛事，这是可以预期的"。

我们是在接到上海社会科学院转来的函件后，首次获知了罗闻达目录出版与转让图书的信息。对于来自上海社会科学院的建议，上海图书馆领导高度重视，多次专题研究，并指示历史文献中心组织专家论证和核查书目中的图书。我们邀请了复旦大学教授周振鹤、李天纲，他们审读了书目后，分别在10月24日、26日向本馆郑重提出了整体购买的收藏咨询意见，徐家汇藏书楼组织人员将书目与馆藏进行了核对，于10月7号向业务处上报了核查情况汇报。罗闻达书目中前100种图书仅有8种重复，前200种有27种重复，前310种书籍中有38种重复……越是早期的图书重复率越低；同时指出，重复的图书也属于珍本之列，其版本价值仍然很高，值得收藏。于是我起草了"关于购买瑞典罗闻达所藏欧洲汉学文献的请示"上报图书馆，正式启动了"罗氏藏书"的引进工作。

三

徐文堪先生是一位热心的推荐者，自始就主动为上图传递有关方面的信息，并提供建议，积极促进"罗氏藏书"的引进工作。2008年9月23日，他给上海图书馆吴建中馆长寄来韩琦收到的瑞典冯德堡的信和书目中的部分书影，9月24日，又写信给吴建中，告知了罗闻达的好友冯德堡的个人情况和11月3日将来沪参加会议并介绍这批藏书的消息，因此，他建议图书馆与之接触一次。这个会议是复旦大学举行的"跨越空间的文化"学术研讨会，因为对这批藏书的兴趣和瑞典斯德哥尔摩大学罗多弼教授的建议，周振鹤教授邀请了罗闻达来沪参加此次会议。原以为因签证问题罗闻达可能无法到沪，但最终他还是得以成行，到复旦大学作了题为《后中世纪时代关于中国的西方著名文献——包括对中国书籍的译介》的报告，成为会议上唯一既无博士学位也无教授头衔的报告人。会议期间，周振鹤与他具体地商谈了正准备转让的这批图书及价格问题，建议罗闻达在原报价的基础上打八折。

11 月 3 日，罗闻达与合伙人冯德堡应约来到上海图书馆，副馆长周德明与我、王仁芳一起在中宾室接待了他。周馆长介绍了上海图书馆的文献收藏特色与影响力，表达了我们对这批藏书的收购意向，并坦率地表示，在现今全球经济不景气的形势下，筹集资金困难，希望他们在转让价格上友情考虑。虽然这是供需双方首次见面，但彼此都有深入推进的意愿，那次会谈并没有明确转让的价格。对于冯德堡先生我早有耳闻，他是英国伦敦著名的"寒山堂"书店的创始人，在图书交易方面具有丰富的经历，是西方著名的中国古籍与版画收藏家，创办了以收藏、研究与普及中国木刻版画为宗旨的欧洲木版基金会，与中国许多版画家有交往，那天在图书馆会谈结束后，我为他调出了几部他要看的古版画书。冯德堡在中国文化界的名声大大高于罗闻达，我特地从台湾《故宫月刊》上复印了《我多么想成为冯德堡的收藏》一文，加深了对他的了解。

11 月 11 日，冯德堡发来电子邮件，同意将整体转让的价格从 400 万英镑降到 390 万英镑。这是转让方首次调整的报价，成为我们之后继续讨论价格的新起点。

上海图书馆根据新情况，多次研究引进方案，在上海市古籍保护中心成立仪式的间隙，吴建中与周德明向参加活动的上海市委宣传部陈东副部长作了口头汇报。之后馆领导指示业务处吴建明处长和我联系中国图书进出口上海公司（以下简称中图公司），请该公司代理图书进口的一切手续，接着向上海市委宣传部作了书面请示汇报，请求予以支持。

四

2009 年是"罗氏藏书"引进过程中波澜起伏、又在彼此不断沟通中增进互信的重要阶段。一月份，中图公司研究决定全力协助我们购买"罗氏藏书"。1 月 22 日，我向周馆长汇报了中图公司的决定和令人感动的消息，若上海图书馆支付书款发生经费困难时，将由他们先行垫付，并不惜贷款为之。次日，周馆长即电邮吴馆长等人，建议出具本馆委托中图公司代理此事的书面证明，以明确其与外方对接商务流程，上海图书馆组成吴建明、黄显功等人的工作组全程参与，此项布置得到了吴馆长的同意，中图公司随后与罗闻达进行了直接的联系。

2月11日，中图公司总经理助理陈峰给我发来电邮，告知瑞典方面已来反馈。我随即向周馆长、吴建明报告，外方在等我们出招了，本馆随即又多次对如何报价进行了研究。

2月22日，徐文堪给吴馆长来信，转述了与韩琦通话的情况，罗闻达从泰国与韩琦电话中提及了上海图书馆"正通过一家中介机构与其商谈购书之事"。徐文堪很关注我们商谈进展，并热情地表示如需韩琦"从旁做些推动和帮助的工作，他当亦很乐意"。吴馆长接信后指示我今后直接与徐先生联系，向他介绍情况，必要时请韩琦协助沟通。

2月28号，徐文堪在给我的来信中写道："与您通过电话后，我与韩琦兄通电话，托他就我们所谈之事与罗闻达联系一下，他表示同意，并在当天给他（罗闻达）发了邮件。今天韩兄给我打电话说罗的夫人刚给他复信，告以罗已去巴黎，与贵馆的商谈至本月底，其他未多说，也未提及是否会延期，但他证实了现在确实另有一个买家（具体是谁没说）。"之前我与徐先生联系时只告诉了办公室的电话，而28日恰是星期六，他未能及时找到我，所以写信告诉了我们最新出现的情况。

与此同时，中图公司与外方进行了多次商务洽谈，23日陈峰在给我电邮中通知了进展，冯德堡要求中图公司在2月底完成转让的最后协议文本。这个要求显然是操之过急了。因此，馆领导决定，一方面向市委宣传部汇报，一方面请中图公司向外方明确表示完成协议在"月底是不可能的"。

3月11日，中图公司陈峰来信证实"外方说已经和另外一家"正在洽谈转让之事。经过中图公司的反复说明，外方同意再等一段时间。对此，我们已经预料到书目出版后的社会反响，出现有收藏此批藏书意愿的机构不可避免，而卖家选择买家也是商界常态，我们对此既要泰然处之，同时应继续努力。我从3月26号徐文堪给我来信中传递的"昨天韩琦先生又从北京打来电话"中得到了证实。在信中，徐先生向我推荐了一本团结出版社的最新图书——杨植峰著《帝国的残影——西洋涉华珍籍收藏》，"书中提及一些当下国际市场价格，虽然收的不多，但可能略有参考价值，可与罗藏目录对照看看"。接信后，我马上请书店为我买到了此书，其中的内容有助于增进对"罗氏藏书"的了解。

　　3月19日，上海图书馆得到市委宣传部的明确指示后，迅速部署了一系列工作，吴建明在之前与市委宣传部、市财政局征询的基础上，在经费筹集、报价方面制定了操作方案，经馆领导形成了共识后，即通过中图公司传递了信息。3月30日，陈峰在电邮中发来了准备给外方的信稿，在转让费处留空，等待我们的决定。上海图书馆在面对多家竞争谈判的情况下，再次阐明了本馆收藏西学文献的特点与优势，在前一段沟通的基础上，报出了离岸价320万英镑的新价格。在之后与外方的往返洽谈中，本馆与中图公司始终锁定这个价格不加价。虽然中间又出现了日本的意向买家，但我们坚信，有决心、有担当、有能力、有优势这四项条件其他竞争者并不同时具备。5月4日，上海图书馆举行行政例会，在听取了我的汇报后，决定选派人员亲赴瑞典藏书现场考察，当面落实谈判的内容，再次明确由周德明副馆长牵头负责"罗氏藏书"的引进工作。

　　进入2009年5月，中图公司作为本次图书交易的中介，以专业的商务沟通能力和规范的国际贸易规则，与外方进行了深入的联络，与外方取得互信，中图公司为此起草了意向书，以稳定图书持有者，为正式签订合同创造基础。同时中图公司还对如何利用财政、海关方面的优惠政策向图书馆提出了实施建议。

　　为了进一步落实"罗氏藏书"的引进，经上级领导同意，上海图书馆吴建明、王仁芳，中国图书进出口上海公司刘志华副总经理、刘怡茜四人组团，于11月8日至13日赴瑞典。11月9日上午，代表团应约前往罗闻达的寓所和存放图书的银行，对1700年前出版的全部藏书和1800年前的部分图书与书目进行了逐本核对，并对这些图书的封面、书脊和书名页分别拍摄了照片，随后与罗闻达就图书的进出口和付款交接等细节进行了沟通协商。吴建明针对他们请律师起草的合同文本表达了四个方面的意见：一是我馆有兴趣收藏这批图书，大半年来我们一直在积极向政府申报项目，安排落实经费，可以反映出我们的诚意；二是图书的验收交接地必须在上海；三是图书到达上海并经验收以后付款；四是双方在图书的交易过程中一旦发生问题，可以友好协商，如果协商不成，应在第三国进行仲裁，如新加坡，而不应在瑞典。对于第三点，刘志华进行了详细的解释。在到达地接收图书后付款是国家的财务规定，大宗款项向境外支付，必须提交合同、图书进口报关单和进口图书增值税的支付发票。对此说明他们表示不能接受，要求必须在收到定金（是所有款项，而不是部分）后才能发货，也可以由中方派人去瑞典点数装箱，甚至睡在书的旁边，前提是收到货款。在罗闻达的寓所，中外双方都坚持自己的底线，局面一度僵持。最后，外方建议中方找一个拍卖公司为第三方，由他们先行垫款，图书到达上海或北京点收确认后，再与拍卖公司结算，按此运作费用要增加 25%，但我们没有超额的经费，此方案不可取。鉴于双方的意见差距太大，中方表示回国后在一个月内给予回复。

对此我请示周馆长，不妨找韩琦出面斡旋，获准后，我即赴北京。我与韩琦并无交往，只是 2008 年我在首都图书馆主持"图书馆藏书文化与藏书票研讨会"时，在参加者名单中见到过他的名字，因此我请首都图书馆的马文大代我联络邀见。那天正值北京德宝拍卖公司在首都图书馆举行古文献秋季拍卖预展，傍晚抵达图书馆后，陈坚副馆长热情地邀请了看展的故宫翁连溪、藏书家韦力、美国的中国古籍专家艾思仁等一起晚餐。艾思仁是韩琦与罗闻达相识的引荐人，我趁他们在桌上观赏我送韩琦的《说笺》与新刻笺纸时，与韩琦在一旁悄悄地进行了交谈，请他向罗闻达、冯德堡说明国内公藏机构采购文献的规定，以及履行合同的解决方案，希望外方多与上海方面沟通，不要固执己见而导致功亏一篑。

由于韩琦是罗闻达在中国最信任的朋友，我们相信"民间外交"会发挥出积极的作用，果然瑞典方面的态度有所好转。于是，吴建中馆长给冯德堡发信，亲自作了解释：

"根据中国的规定，本馆作为图书收藏单位，不能办理图书的进口事务，我已委托中国图书进出口上海公司办理一切贸易程序，该公司就此将提供具体的操作方案与您讨论。我们购买本批图书是有诚意的，我建议给彼此再多一点时间，共同寻找一个在不违反中国法律规定情况下的可行性方案。

本周四，本馆将会召开一个专家咨询会，您的朋友韩琦博士、周振鹤教授将会出席，我将会与我的同事和专家们为此共同努力，希望得到您的支持与谅解。"

12 月 10 日下午，我在上海图书馆善本室主持召开了"西洋古籍珍本汉学图书（罗闻达藏书）专家咨询会"，邀请了周振鹤，李天纲等专家。刘志华、王仁芳介绍了赴瑞典考察的情况，用投影播放了藏书照片，王仁芳讲解了部分重要图书。本次会议形成的咨询报告，更加坚定了上海图书馆克服困难采购本批图书的信心与使命感。此举同时向瑞典方面表达了我们引进的态度，以增强他们的耐心。

五

我们各方都希望在 2010 年完成"罗氏藏书"的转让，在积极联系的过程中，彼此的谅解得到了进一步加强。在 2010 年春节长假后，吴建中收到了罗闻达的两封邮件，在回信中，吴建中再次强调了我们收藏的心愿和操作程序，并发出欢迎罗闻达与冯德堡一起到沪移交图书的邀请。我们的坦率与诚意，以及韩琦的努力，使罗闻达、冯德堡最终接受了我们的方案。双方花了几个月对合同的条款进行了一一修订、翻译，逐步达成了共识。

为了便于结算，在中图公司的建议下，罗闻达在香港注册了一家公司。之后，双方就交易的所有细节做了周密的讨论与安排，如对外方的运输方式、图书包装、清单形式等均提出了要求；在上海，一系列的进口审批、图书报审、免税申请、保险等均在有条不紊的紧张进行中，每一位参与者都犹如"助产士"一般满怀期待地等候着一个"婴儿"诞生。

10 月 25 日，英文版合同定稿，签署。

10 月 25 日，图书从瑞典起运。

11 月 5 日，上海图书馆王仁芳等人前往外高桥保税仓库，与罗闻达验书。

11 月 9 日，中图公司付款。

11 月 14 日，对方确认收到书款，图书清关。

11 月 26 日，图书出关送往上海图书馆。

2010 年 10 月 30 日，在上海图书馆贵宾厅，我再次见到了瑞典藏书家罗闻达先生。他与在场的上海图书馆领导和专家一样，满面春风，笑意盈盈，彼此十分愉快地交谈着。今天将在此举行"瑞典中国学罗氏专藏转让协议文本交换仪式"。为此，我特意为他准备了一份礼物，我策划的《书影掇英——覆刻上海图书馆藏宋本书影十种》，由上海图书馆党委书记穆端正先生持赠与他。我向他表示，为了纪念此次图书转让，我愿意请中国的优秀版画家为他制作一款藏书票，罗闻达欣然同意。转让仪式签字时，我站在罗闻达身后，只见他掏出钢笔在合同文本上两次没有写出字迹，我马上递上自己携带的水笔给他。仪式

2010 年 10 月 30 日在上海图书馆举行
"瑞典中国学罗氏专藏转让协议文本交换仪式"

结束后，我收回水笔对同事说："这支笔也有收藏价值了，它书写了一页中西图书交流的历史。"在 10 月 30 日协议签订之后的午餐中，罗闻达先生欣喜地表示，这批书就像是他的女儿，今天终于找到了他放心的婆家，了却了多年来的心愿。以后当他思念的时候，就可以来看看了。此番话坦露了一个藏书家兼书商对"爱女"的真情心迹。

11 月 6 日，上海图书馆吴建中馆长在世界中国学大会上宣布这一消息时，引起了学术界和媒体的强烈反响，深受好评。

在"罗氏藏书"抵沪日益临近之际，历史文献中心拟定了典藏、编目、服务的工作方案。对于如何称呼罗闻达的这批藏书，在以往的两年中，我们有各种不同的表述。于是，我专门起草了"关于罗闻达藏书专称的建议"，将对东洋文库"莫理循藏书"、香港大学"马礼逊特藏"等专题馆藏的调研，和与韩琦通话讨论的情况作了汇报，对这批藏书的专称倾向于以人来命名，简称为"罗氏

藏书",得到了吴建中的认可,此后成为来自于罗闻达的所有文献的专称。

11月26日中午,"罗氏藏书"从外高桥海关保税仓库正式运抵上海图书馆。我与同事一起将这批图书卸下卡车,开箱验收。这天被定为"罗氏藏书入藏日"。在这个特别值得纪念的日子里,上海图书馆、中图公司的领导和部分媒体记者在贵宾室喜气洋洋地迎接"罗氏藏书",当我们揭开了"西洋女郎"的红盖头时,我们充满了惊喜。我们终于见到了这批西方早期汉学文献专藏。12月20日至26日,在上海图书馆目录大厅举行了《汉学遗珍——上海图书馆藏"罗氏藏书"要籍展》,共选出15-19世纪出版物20种公开亮相,同时作为上海图书馆新馆开馆14周年的纪念。20日下午,上海图书馆举行了报告会,韩琦主讲《欧洲人眼中的中国科学——"罗氏藏书"及其价值》,我介绍了《现代活字印刷图书的早期历史:摇篮本——兼谈中国所藏摇篮本》。

首批"罗氏藏书"入藏后,罗闻达多次来沪探望"女儿"。我请他提出藏书票的设计要求。2012年8月29日在上海图书馆第一展厅参观《天工开物——徐龙宝版画展》时,他对徐龙宝的木口木刻花卉作品很欣赏,向我提出能否参照设计成他的藏书票?我当即请陪同参观的徐龙宝教授帮忙,他欣然应允。11月14日,罗闻达再次来沪,授权上海中西书局翻译出版《从西文印本书籍(1477-1877)看中西关系、中国观、文化影响和汉学发展》。签约后,我们在宾馆大堂咖啡厅见面,我送上了50张原作藏书票。他见到后非常高兴,当

2012年11月14日罗闻达先生
签赠作者的藏书票。

场用钢笔签名赠我一张留作纪念。事后得知,他向多位朋友签赠了这张满意的藏书票。

六

罗闻达作为书商和藏书家，一直没有停止珍稀图书的搜寻，同时，以汉学家的执着追求，继续着西方汉学文献的研究，不断增补《从西文印本书籍（1477-1877）看中西关系、中国观、文化影响和汉学发展》续编。这部书开创了国际汉学书目编制的新体例，从单纯的书目转为兼有学术评论的著述方法，成为国际汉学文献学的新里程碑。2012 年 3 月 12 日，他在给我的来信中告知了续编的近况，并寄来一小箱尚未定稿的打印件，书目编号为 1552 至 1838，共 287 种，其中有三部摇篮本、五部手稿，还有著名科学家林奈的签名本，以及一些铜版画。我明白他的愿望是此书目中的书也能归属上海图书馆收藏。虽然我们十分期望如此，但支付近千万元的经费并非易事，何况首批"罗氏藏书"的书款需几年才能分摊平衡。我们曾提出拆分选购的方案，罗闻达希望是整体，与书目正编图书合璧。当时国内正有几家机构在与之商洽中，我们谈判没有进展。当罗闻达在 2013 年 8 月 24 日意外去世后，我们失去了继续讨论的机会，如今手持罗闻达签赠的《从西文印本书籍（1477-1877）看中西关系、中国观、文化影响和汉学发展》续编，我心中感到难以言状的痛惜和遗憾。

但可敬的罗闻达先生在生前做出的一个令我们意想不到的决定，让上海图书馆受惠无穷。他在 2011 年 10 月 30 日拟好的遗嘱中，明确了将自己存放在泰国住所中的学术参考书全部作为遗产捐赠给上海图书馆。本馆国际交流处在完成了一系列法律程序后，在罗闻达家属的配合下，上海图书馆取得了图书的所有权。中图公司再次代理了图书进口的一切手续，同时还承担了从罗闻达住所清点、制单、装箱到储运离岸等本不属于图书进口业务范围的工作。

2016 年 5 月 31 日，在徐家汇藏书楼设立上海图书馆中西文化交流研究资料中心举行揭牌仪式时，上海图书馆吴建中馆长与中国图书进出口上海公司陈峰副总经理，举行了"罗氏藏书"捐赠部分的首批交接入藏仪式。罗闻达遗赠全部图书五千余本至 2017 年上半年分两批入藏徐家汇藏书楼。

"罗氏藏书"落户上海、入藏上海图书馆，前后历时十年，不论从当时还是在当今或未来，其价值与意义均值得我们回顾与思考。首先，此举是中国购买西方珍本专题图书规模最大的一项收藏，不仅丰富了上海图书馆的西方汉学文献专题收藏，而且还提升了上海图书馆在国际汉学领域的地位，彰显了国际大都市上海的文化软实力，成为上海图书馆在 2000 年从美国收购"翁氏藏书"之后的又一次重大收藏举措，是中国图书馆与学术界的盛事，体现了上海图书馆对文献资源建设的高度重视和"积淀文化，致力于卓越的知识服务"的使命意识。

其二、"罗氏藏书"的引进所透视的历史维度与时代节点，正是中西文化交流和西方历史发展的特殊阶段。这是欧洲人从 15 世纪发现"远东"，到 19 世纪后期"汉学"形成，认识中国的 400 年，也是西方工业文明迅速发展的 400 年，是哥伦布地理大发现（1492 年）后，新航路开通，西方列强争霸世界，兴起"中国热"的时期。2010 年恰逢利玛窦逝世 400 年纪念和世界文化交流的盛会——上海世博会举行，我们从"罗氏藏书"丰厚的书页中，可以深切地感受到中西历史相互激荡的风云变幻。所以，"罗氏藏书"在 2010 年落户上海就具有特殊的历史意义。

其三、"罗氏藏书"包括了欧洲学者 400 年间研究中国的重要著作。特别是将西方来华传教士的重要著作搜罗齐备，版本多样，尤具特色，有些还是世界孤本。为中国学者研究中西文化交流，认识文明互鉴，从历史上阐述建设人类文明共同体，促进当代中外交往与对话，提供了丰富的资源，令人从中获得深刻的启示。

其四、在"罗氏藏书"中还有两本特别珍贵的"摇篮本"。一本是 1477 年在意大利威尼斯出版的拉丁文《世界各地》、一本是 1480 年在意大利米兰出版的意大利文《曼德维尔游记》。这两种图书的入藏不仅改写了上海图书馆文献收藏中没有"摇篮本"的历史，同时是新中国建国后公藏机构首次购买的摇篮本，具有图书馆藏书史的标志性。

在 2020 年的《文明互鉴：上海图书馆徐家汇藏书楼珍稀文献展》上，"罗氏藏书"精品再次亮相。我们特邀著名篆刻家刻了一方"罗氏藏书"印章，以此作为入藏的纪念，钤印在我们的记忆中。

2020 年 12 月

图书在版编目（CIP）数据

罗氏藏书 / 黄显功主编.—上海：上海古籍出版社，2021.5
ISBN 978-7-5325-9820-5

Ⅰ.①罗… Ⅱ.①黄… Ⅲ.①私人藏书—图书目录—瑞典—
现代 Ⅳ.①Z845.32

中国版本图书馆CIP数据核字（2020）第238198号

篆　　刻　　刘葆国
责任编辑　　余鸣鸿
装帧设计　　严克勤
技术编辑　　隗婷婷

罗氏藏书

吴建明　黄显功　王仁芳　主编

上海古籍出版社出版发行

（上海瑞金二路272号　邮政编码 200020）

（1）网址：www.guji.com.cn

（2）E－mail：guji1@guji.com.cn

（3）易文网网址：www.ewen.co

上海界龙艺术印刷有限公司印制

开本 787×1092　1/8　印张 30.5　插页 4　字数 300,000

2021年5月第1版　2021年5月第1次印刷

ISBN 978-7-5325-9820-5

Z.460　定价：580.00元

如有质量问题，请与承印公司联系